Edited by Chris Longley

Foreword *WA Devereux*
Introduction

Published as part of the BBC Adult Literacy Project: the television programmes designed for adult non-readers first broadcast in October 1975 and the radio series Teaching Adults to Read for tutors, first broadcast on Radio 3 on Tuesdays at 7.00 pm from 28 October to 16 December 1975 and rebroadcast on Radio 3 on Tuesdays at 7.00 pm from 25 May to 13 July 1976.

Published to accompany a series of programmes prepared in consultation with the BBC Further Education Advisory Council.

© The Authors and the British Broadcasting Corporation 1975.
First published 1975. Published by the British Broadcasting Corporation, 35 Marylebone High Street, London W1M 4AA.
This book is set in 9pt 'Monophoto' Times New Roman. Printed in England by Jolly & Barber Ltd, Rugby. ISBN 0 563 10949 1

Foreword and Introduction

This book has been written to complement the BBC Radio series on training tutors for adult literacy work. For the BBC, as a representative of the mass media and the spoken word, to embark on a 3-year television and radio Adult Literacy Project to help those adults who have reading and writing difficulties, is in the best traditions of its long established education service and, to its further credit, an indication of the extent to which it is responsive to the field through its educational and social consultative network. More than this, it reflects the growing realisation that, despite more than 100 years of public education, there is an increasing number of adults in our society who cannot read or write or who have reading difficulties and who, because of the social stigma this puts on them, go to amazing lengths to hide their educational disadvantage. This realisation has also prompted the setting up of the Adult Literacy Resource Agency under the aegis of the National Institute of Adult Education to administer a grant of £1 million from the Department of Education and Science and the Scottish Education Department to help local education authorities and voluntary agencies to increase the provision for adult literacy.

There have been those, impressed with the pre-eminence of the spoken word, who have cast doubts on the importance of literacy in present-day society, and certainly there is evidence that reading skills have not always received the emphasis that they once had in the classroom. It is timely that the recent report of the Bullock Committee – *A language for life* – re-emphasises the essential need for literacy, and that seventeen of its recommendations are concerned with the need for greater effort in the field of adult literacy.

In his foreword to Peter Clyne's *The disadvantaged adult*, Professor Arthur Jones writes: '. . . the most striking feature of the record lies in the ingenuity and energy of devoted individuals or small groups who, having identified a need, have set out to try to meet it, often with no clear line of communication to a base of resources in the educational or welfare services.' This is certainly so in the field of adult literacy. The contributors to this book are all practitioners who, having perceived a need, have set out to try and meet it. Throughout the book they are punctilious in drawing attention to the tentative nature of their suggestions and to the inadequacy of knowledge and methods of teaching adults with reading difficulties.

The reader, however, should accept these qualifying statements as being illustrative of the deep understanding of the problems of adult literacy; the more you know – the more you realise how much more you need to know. The contributors are very experienced practitioners who, individually and in groups, have gathered together an impressive body of knowledge and methods of approach which have been tried, tested and refined, in which the reader can have confidence.

One of the most striking aspects of the various contributions, is the emphasis placed on the special approach to adults and their teaching. Accepting the adult student as he is, and at the point of learning at which he or she is, rather than where you or anyone else thinks he ought to be – is an axiom of all good adult education teachers. It is of vital importance in the field of adult literacy. However good the teacher of reading skills may be, if he cannot establish the right relationship with someone for whom, in the past, the educational system has failed, the results can be disastrous and can mean the final failure for the student. The implications of this for training schemes are considerable, whether they be for professional or for volunteer tutors. Similarly, it must permeate the organisation of statutory and voluntary adult literacy schemes. Such schemes must command adequate support resources if they are not to raise false expectations and feelings of ultimate rejection in those we seek to help.

The involvement and training of volunteers are an important ingredient in the attempt to tackle adult literacy, not simply as a means of augmenting the task force, but rather as a way of developing a caring community, willing to help those around us who need our help. To be successful, that help has to be effective, those who take up this work have to be trained. This book makes a notable contribution to the field of adult literacy, particularly as a reference handbook for trainers and for tutors, whether they be professionals or volunteers.

I commend it equally to administrators and elected members of local authorities, and all those who believe that we have a duty to educate and not just to continue the education of the educated.

W. A. Devereux
Director, Adult Literacy Resource Agency

Introduction

This book is designed to accompany the BBC Adult Literacy Project starting in Autumn 1975. The television programmes for adult non-readers will probably generate an increased demand for literacy provision. The radio series for tutors, which will be broadcast alongside the television programmes for adult illiterates, is designed to make some contribution to the work that must proceed in organising extra literacy provision and training efficient tutors.

This book aims to provide:

● advice and help to those who are about to start teaching an adult illiterate or those who are already engaged in teaching an individual or group of illiterates;

● advice and help to those about to organise provision for illiterates or those who have already established provision and wish to develop or make more effective that provision.

It is divided into three sections. The first section attempts to analyse the limited evidence that we have on the nature and causes of adult illiteracy and the kinds of skills tutors need in teaching adult non-readers. It contains four profiles of fictitious illiterate and semi-literate adults. The second section works through these four profiles and offers a variety of suggestions and alternative approaches for teaching and learning. The final section looks at the many problems organisers face in setting up and running literacy schemes.

From this brief description it is obvious that this book can serve the reader in a variety of ways. It is not designed to be read from cover to cover, instead it is hoped that it will provide a useful resource for the reader to draw upon. Our knowledge about the nature of illiteracy is at present so scant and our skills in teaching so comparatively underdeveloped that it would be presumptuous for us to offer directive and prescriptive models for teaching and learning. What little we *do* know suggests that adults learn in different ways. It is for the tutor and the student to discover the particular methods and approaches that are appropriate and effective in each case. The mini-exercises in the book are designed as an aid to the reader's own learning.

On a point of convention, the authors tend to use *he* to refer to the student and *she* to refer to the tutor. Our language makes it hard to avoid opting for one or the other and this choice reflects the fact that the majority of adult illiterates are men and the majority of tutors are at present women.

Students and tutors

This section is written by Ann Risman, Head of Adult Education services in Reading and Organiser of the Reading Literacy Scheme – Programme 2R. The section deals with information, advice and suggestions on: the nature of literacy, the characteristics of illiterates, the causes of illiteracy and the skills tutors need in teaching non-readers. The section also contains four fictitious profiles of illiterate and semi-literate adults compiled by Jenny Stevens, who was Deputy Director of the Cambridge House Literacy Scheme and is now a BBC Further Education Officer working on the BBC's Adult Literacy Project.

1. The nature and extent of the problem

> *I've learned the hard way that it doesn't matter how good you are at anything else, when they know you're no good at English, you've had it!*
> (Mrs T. aged 46, part-time factory worker)

The lady who spoke these words crept nervously into my evening class on basic English a few years ago. She, like so many others, had her own way of explaining and excusing the disability we commonly know as *illiteracy*, and was able, too, to describe very graphically all the prejudices and lack of sympathy most often directed against those who cannot read, write or spell to their own (or anyone else's) satisfaction.

The exasperated jibes, such as, 'Can't you read?' for instance are more than a little hurtful to those who indeed cannot. And is it really true, as many students tell me, that tradesmen and teachers, doctors, policemen and all officialdom treat those who cannot read or write as though they were simple minded or sub-normal? What a mystique the skill of reading must possess that a man must apparently run the gauntlet of derision before he even admits to wanting to acquire it! Yet perhaps in our time we have all laughed at those jokes of men saying 'Which is the Gents?' or taking a train to Land's End instead of Liverpool!

It should come as no surprise then that an adult who has severe difficulty with the reading, writing and spelling of his mother tongue will go to almost any lengths to conceal his lack of skills from the world at large and, in many cases, even from his family and friends. The young man who sat in a class of apprentices in a Yorkshire mill town, barely able to write his own name, told me that his mother filled in all his forms and read all his personal letters to him. The manager in his early thirties, articulate, immaculately dressed, whose spelling was so poor as to make his powers of written self-expression a cruel mockery of his fluent speech, had solved matters in the only way open to him.

> *I dictate everything to my secretary and rely on the personnel department to select someone with perfect spelling!*
> (Mr H. aged early 30's, office manager computer data)

In order to cope with the day-to-day demands of life, some individuals develop compensatory skills such as manual dexterity or an incredible aural memory. Famous indeed are those stories of boys leaving school able to assemble and dismantle intricate machinery without being able to read one word of the instruction manual, and of young men and women who have passed their driving test by learning the Highway Code off by heart. Nor is illiteracy a problem peculiar to the young, to be grown out of or shaken off with age. As the years go by when his children grow up and job responsibilities increase, the number of opportunities open to an individual who is illiterate or semi-literate generally decreases. His self-esteem, always at risk, assumes such monstrous importance that it must be protected at all costs.

The illiterate is a man who goes on a train journey not knowing whether he has been charged the proper fare, nor able to read the destination named on his ticket or the names of the stations through which he passes. (Jeffries).

'They kept asking me to be shop steward and I'd like to be, but I couldn't cope with the reading and writing you know.'

(guard, early 50's, British Rail)

It is incredibly difficult for you, the skilled reader, to imagine with any clarity, the precise plight of those who cannot read. As your eyes skim line after line of print extracting meaning from complex word combinations, have you ever paused to consider how often you use your own literacy skills and how vital they have been in your life so far?

Try to work out from this chart how often you use your own skills of reading and writing.

	More than once per day (score 10)	Once per day (score 8)	Once per month (score 4)	Rarely (score 2)
Reading a newspaper				
Reading a letter				
Reading any type of book				
Reading operating instructions for a machine				
Selecting goods by reading labels or catalogues				
Writing a letter				
Filling in an official form				
Writing a report, memo or instruction as part of your normal employment				
Total				
Final total				

What was your score? Remember that for an illiterate adult it would always be nil, and that many of the routine ways of giving and receiving information that we take absolutely for granted are beyond the scope of those who lack literacy skills. For most of us, too, many of the important milestones in life have been passed as a result of our ability to express ourselves fluently on paper – writing letters of application, or studying for and taking examinations. The gulf which exists between those who are functionally literate and can perform any task which requires skill in reading or writing and those who are illiterate or semi-literate is one which deserves the concern of all those who are involved in education at any level.

The illiterate adult

By all the categories most commonly accepted in this country an *illiterate adult* is one whose reading ability is roughly equivalent to that of a seven year old child (i.e. who has had two years' primary schooling). This is the concept of the *reading age* – used mainly by those who work with children in schools. Once a child has mastered the basic code of word shape and sound symbol, his reading development is linked to an increasingly complex structure of words and sentences. The concept of a reading age relates essentially to chronological age and to a standard that half the children of a particular age group could be expected to reach year by year. To say therefore that an adult reads as well (or as badly!) as a seven year old is a mode of comparison which leaves much to be desired. A reading age is useful mainly as a guide to those who plan reading development programmes and are searching for material of a particular readability level.

At what level then can an individual be judged illiterate? In practical terms an illiterate adult may recognise most of the letters of the alphabet but be unsure of their related sounds. He most probably will not be able to recognise more than a few simple words. Official print, e.g. application forms, is beyond him, all the daily newspapers are beyond him and it would be inconceivable that he could adequately cope with any job in which reading, writing, basic checking, or recording ability was needed. It is thought now that, *at the most conservative of estimates*, into this lowest category alone fall 0·5% of our population, over 160,000 adults. Many researchers would place the total much higher than this, though it it difficult to see how an accurate count of the illiterate adults in our community could ever be attempted.

The notion of illiteracy is in itself a complex concept. We can take no comfort from the fact that our country seems to have a much lower illiteracy rate than Africa, or Asia, or even the USA. Nor can we take the complacent view that illiteracy is a minority problem. Remember these statistics, for the most part, do not include the mentally handicapped, the educationally sub-normal and those for whom English is a second language. Recent studies have suggested that over the past few years the number of illiterates in this country has not declined and that to the total of 0·5% we must add countless millions, who though not completely illiterate, are unable, because of their *inadequate* literacy skills, to comprehend and cope with the mass of print which assails each one of us every day of our lives.

The semi-literate adult

Attention has lately been drawn to the projected level of literacy necessary to survive in this, one of the most complex, industrialised societies in the world, where every man's potential to live, work, feed and clothe his children and take full advantage of all the benefits of the Welfare State is limited by the level of his literacy skills.

It has been suggested by the United Nations Educational Scientific and Cultural Organisation (UNESCO) that, in order to function effectively and independently, a person must be able to read as well as a thirteen year old. Between the illiteracy level (of seven) and this suggested level of *functional literacy* are those who have been described as *semi-literate*. Able to read hesitantly but without fluency, unable to grasp the meaning of all but the simplest material and unable if they have not passed beyond a certain stage (generally thought to be equivalent to that of a nine year old) to *maintain* their standard without regular practice. For a semi-literate then the problem is to acquire literacy skills which will be *permanent* because they have been developed and reinforced to a sufficiently high level.

For even if a semi-literate reader can cope with the simpler daily newspapers, he will still be ill-equipped and totally disinclined to face the complex language of legal jargon and the mass of official documents, forms, etc., so necessary to him in everyday life.

Though figures have varied, at least one author estimates the total of illiterate and semi-literate adults as 'more than a million who are deficient in their basic education'. (Clyne).

Nor do we yet know enough about the precise combination of skills which make up literacy nor about the consequences of their imbalance (though this is thought to be a major factor in semi-literacy). If a student can speak well, read adequately but cannot express himself in writing, then this is a tragic lack of one of the skills which make up the communication process. The young wife who was driven to attempt suicide because she could read her soldier husband's letters from Ulster, but not reply to them, would seem to dramatically illustrate the dilemma in which many semi-literates find themselves. One man in his thirties who as one of the 'travelling people' had never received regular schooling in his entire life, walked into one of our local literacy classes a few weeks ago and summed up his situation in a very succinct fashion.

(Mr J. aged 38, factory worker)

The functionally literate adult

Why improve literacy skills to a point beyond mere survival? Consider one of the major motivating forces in life, satisfaction through work. In UNESCO terms, a functional literacy programme is taken to mean 'a comprehensive programme of education and training for illiterate (and sometimes semi-literate) adults with a literacy component built in'. It would be then, a work oriented programme with literacy teaching integrated into vocational training, as against simple literacy teaching leading on to separate vocational training. Although this UNESCO definition refers mainly to literacy schemes in under-developed countries, it has relevance for us, in Britain, too.

It is becoming increasingly difficult to isolate areas of unskilled employment which have not been overtaken by technology of one sort or another or by changes in the organisation of industry. How many illiterates can find employment and stay in it for any length of time? How many semi-literate workers are chained to unfulfilling jobs because they lack the more sophisticated literacy skills which are a written and unwritten entrée to supervisory and management levels.

We must remember too that the greater majority of jobs require not only a *basic* ability in reading and writing, but linguistic competence to a high level in certain specific tasks, e.g. letters, report writing, memos, minutes and a wide range of personnel relations work of all types. An examination qualification in English language is a basic requirement of many jobs. Training and retraining programmes are therefore insufficient without accompanying literacy help.

In so many concrete and easily illustrated ways it is necessary to read and write in order to survive, to have the power to receive messages – by reading – and send them – by writing. But any discussion of literacy levels cannot exclude the manifold benefits which proceed from functional literacy and from the acquisition of a wider range of communication skills. Notions of personal growth; the development of more complex mental functions such as the ability to generalise; the self-assurance which follows the certain knowledge that a reader has access (if he only had the time) to all the knowledge accumulated in the past. All these are inseparable companions of functional literacy.

(Newsom)

With such literacy comes the power to communicate with others in a variety of styles, formal and informal, casual and cordial, intimate and indignant, as befits the many roles any one of us plays in life as employer, parent, workmate, consumer etc. Only when literacy is a tool and not a master, does it become truly functional – to serve whatever purpose an individual may require at work or leisure, in social or economic circumstance.

Though McLuhanist doctrine may decry the value of print in our computerised age, technology has yet to find a substitute for literature – in my view, still the highest art to which literate people can aspire. It was by no careless hand that Huxley in portraying his *Brave New World* banned literature because it encouraged men to think, to feel and to question all that they saw around them! The notion of

Right: *'The level of reading skills required for participation in the affairs of modern society is far above that implied in earlier definitions of literacy.'*
(A language for life)

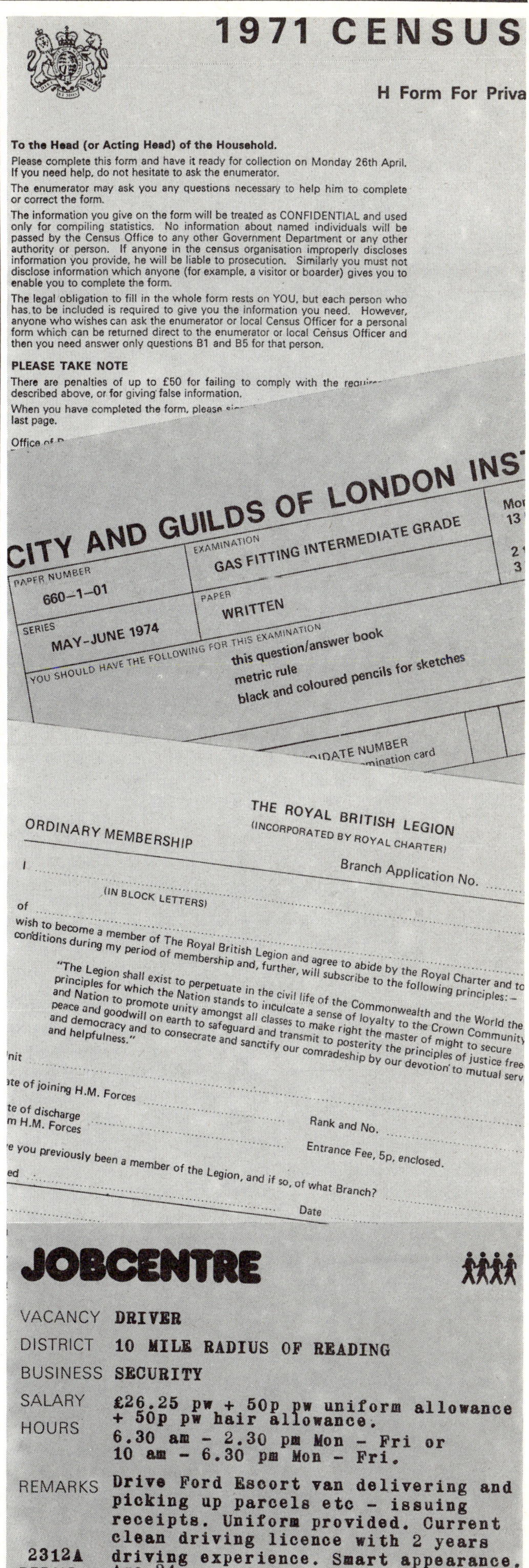

1971 CENSUS

H Form For Priva

To the Head (or Acting Head) of the Household.

Please complete this form and have it ready for collection on Monday 26th April. If you need help, do not hesitate to ask the enumerator.

The enumerator may ask you any questions necessary to help him to complete or correct the form.

The information you give on the form will be treated as CONFIDENTIAL and used only for compiling statistics. No information about named individuals will be passed by the Census Office to any other Government Department or any other authority or person. If anyone in the census organisation improperly discloses information you provide, he will be liable to prosecution. Similarly you must not disclose information which anyone (for example, a visitor or boarder) gives you to enable you to complete the form.

The legal obligation to fill in the whole form rests on YOU, but each person who has to be included is required to give you the information you need. However, anyone who wishes can ask the enumerator or local Census Officer for a personal form which can be returned direct to the enumerator or local Census Officer and then you need answer only questions B1 and B5 for that person.

PLEASE TAKE NOTE

There are penalties of up to £50 for failing to comply with the requirements described above, or for giving false information.

When you have completed the form, please sign the last page.

Office of P.

CITY AND GUILDS OF LONDON INST

PAPER NUMBER 660–1–01

EXAMINATION GAS FITTING INTERMEDIATE GRADE

SERIES MAY–JUNE 1974

PAPER WRITTEN

YOU SHOULD HAVE THE FOLLOWING FOR THIS EXAMINATION

this question/answer book
metric rule
black and coloured pencils for sketches

CANDIDATE NUMBER
examination card

ORDINARY MEMBERSHIP

THE ROYAL BRITISH LEGION
(INCORPORATED BY ROYAL CHARTER)

Branch Application No.

I

(IN BLOCK LETTERS)

of

wish to become a member of The Royal British Legion and agree to abide by the Royal Charter and to conditions during my period of membership and, further, will subscribe to the following principles: –

"The Legion shall exist to perpetuate in the civil life of the Commonwealth and the World the principles for which the Nation stands to inculcate a sense of loyalty to the Crown Community and Nation to promote unity amongst all classes to make right the master of might to secure peace and goodwill on earth to safeguard and transmit to posterity the principles of justice free and democracy and to consecrate and sanctify our comradeship by our devotion to mutual service and helpfulness."

Unit

Date of joining H.M. Forces

Date of discharge from H.M. Forces

Rank and No.

Entrance Fee, 5p, enclosed.

Have you previously been a member of the Legion, and if so, of what Branch?

Signed

Date

JOBCENTRE

VACANCY	**DRIVER**
DISTRICT	**10 MILE RADIUS OF READING**
BUSINESS	**SECURITY**
SALARY	**£26.25 pw + 50p pw uniform allowance + 50p pw hair allowance.**
HOURS	**6.30 am - 2.30 pm Mon - Fri or 10 am - 6.30 pm Mon - Fri.**
REMARKS	**Drive Ford Escort van delivering and picking up parcels etc - issuing receipts. Uniform provided. Current clean driving licence with 2 years driving experience. Smart appearance. Age 24+.**
REF NO. 2312A	

ED 101 (JC)

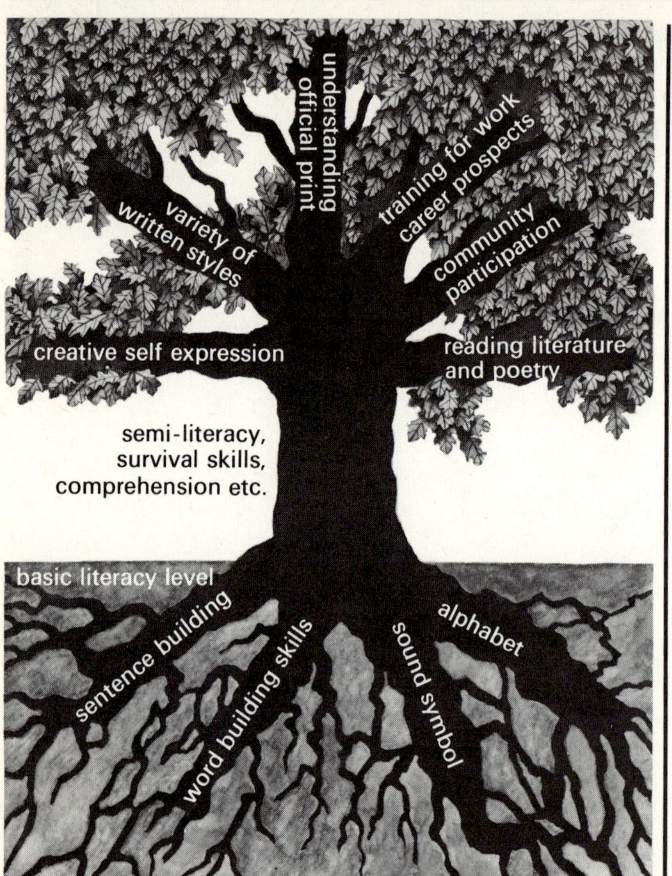

functional literacy includes the ability to read and write for emotional and aesthetic satisfaction just as much as the ability to decipher complex official prose and state facts in response to query. I return to the question, literacy for what? and end this section with a fragment from a Report from the UNESCO Conference in Paris 1965.

Adult literacy, an essential element in overall development, must be closely linked to economic, social priorities and to present and future manpower needs . . .

Rather than an end in itself, literacy should be a way of preparing man for a social, civic and economic role that goes far beyond the limits of rudimentary literacy training consisting merely in the teaching of reading and writing . . . it should lead not only to elementary general knowledge but to training for work, increased productivity, a greater participation in civic life and a better understanding of the surrounding world and should ultimately open the way to basic human culture!

Summary

The aims of any literacy programme must take into account the multiple use of literacy skills in our society so that individuals can:
- comprehend those areas of print which are necessary to acquiring the financial means for survival;
- develop a sensitivity towards words and written language which will enable choices of all types to be made;
- use language, read, written and spoken to communicate effectively with others and to maintain human relationships;
- use language as a means of emotional and intellectual growth necessary to self fulfilment and self esteem.

Left: *Literacy Tree.*

2. Profiles of four students

It is always easy when discussing aspects of provision of any service – educational or social – to lose sight of the individual among a mass of generalisations. These four profiles serve as a reminder that the word illiterate refers to an individual who often has little in common with another non-reader, apart from a difficulty with reading and writing.

Sean, Jackie, Murray and Michael are fictitious people drawn from the experience of the author who has worked and taught in literacy schemes for over four years. Although much of the information contained in the profiles could be gathered at a first interview, much of the detail could only be gathered by a tutor over a period of time. They have been so designed to give the reader a picture of an individual with specific needs and problems. They are referred to throughout the book and are the subjects of the section on teaching and learning. Each profile represents a student at a particular stage in learning, but each (and of course every student) needs an individualised approach to learning.

Sean O'Reilly is a cheerful, extrovert Irishman. He looks quite a lot older than his thirty-two years and speaks with a heavy Irish accent, although he has lived in England for eleven years.

He was born the fifth in a family of eight children in a rural part of County Cork. His father was a farm labourer who died when Sean was five. The family were very poor and Sean's mother had a hard job keeping her large family fed, clothed and housed. He can't remember very much about his father but he knows that his mother

is totally illiterate. He cannot ever remember seeing a book or a newspaper around the house. His three sisters received a good convent education and are apparently good at reading and writing. None of the five boys is literate and Sean attributes this to the family's general lack of interest in education as well as to the fact that all the boys missed quite a lot of schooling, doing seasonal work on neighbouring farms to supplement the family's meagre income.

Sean never liked school. Right from the start he found schoolwork difficult. His inability to master reading easily was not helped by the atmosphere at the school he attended. Classes were very large and contained a range of ages and abilities. Discipline was rigidly enforced. He vividly remembers being beaten for not being able to read a passage correctly and for making mistakes in his spelling. Absences enforced by economic necessity were looked forward to as a welcome release. As he grew older, he avoided going to school more and more often, spending days rabbit shooting. His mother was aware that his school attendance was irregular, but she was too busy to do anything about it, and in any case, having no education herself, saw little point in it. The school for its part seemed only too pleased to have rid itself of an unwilling student to whom learning did not come easily.

Sean continued working on farms until he was twenty-one when, bored with his way of life, he decided to follow his two older brothers to London. He got a job easily on a building site and after doing general labouring for a few months became a scaffolder, since when he has done a variety of jobs connected with the building trade and

Sean O'Reilly.

has apparently become very skilled at carpentry. He has never before used a rule but quickly learnt how to measure up, as well as to cope with simple arithmetical calculations. He soon found it advantageous to become self-employed, although doing so meant that he had to find an accountant to cope with his income tax and insurance. He has no way of knowing how reliable or how honest his accountant is. The contractor he works for at present has found him to be a hard, steady worker and has several times offered him the chance to become a foreman. This he has refused each time since promotion would involve filling in worksheets for ten others. But he would very much like to accept, and finds it increasingly hard to think up convincing reasons for refusing.

Although he is easy-going by nature, Sean is always concerned that his workmates should not find out about his illiteracy. He buys a paper every day and pretends to read it, although he can't understand a single word. So far he's been successful at getting out of tricky situations. If he's handed a joke to read he assumes he is meant to laugh, and duly does so.

Six years ago he married Susan, an Irish girl who was working as a hospital domestic. He told her that he couldn't read and write, but this didn't bother her as she knew plenty of boys from her own village who couldn't read either. She herself is very good at reading, although she reads little else apart from the newspaper and magazines. She writes quite a few letters, but says she's not a confident speller. They have two children, both girls, aged five and three. The eldest is highly intelligent and has been interested in books from a young age. Sean and Susan are anxious that their children do well at school and buy a lot of books for them. Susan regularly reads to the girls, but Sean has to pretend to read, making up stories to fit the pictures as he goes along. As the children know their favourite stories off by heart they frequently point out his mistakes.

Susan has always been sympathetic and supportive. She does all the necessary reading and writing for the family and subtly protects Sean socially if he is confronted with something to read and write. She is genuinely proud of his manual and wage-earning skills and loudly praises his expertise in home decorating. Since they heard of an opportunity for him to learn to read, she has been gently encouraging him to seek help and accompanied him to the first interview.

Sean did not know of the existence of adult education classes or of any of the independent literacy schemes. He had several times asked his wife to try and teach him, but she was reluctant, not being very sure how to set about it. Fortunately, the subject arose by chance during a chat with a sympathetic priest at his local church. The priest offered to help and discovered the whereabouts of a local literacy scheme. The priest explained how the scheme worked and with Sean's agreement made an appointment for him to meet one of the organisers.

When Sean attended his interview, immaculately dressed in his best suit, he was very nervous indeed. He was obviously ashamed of his illiteracy, but was even more embarrassed at the prospect of having to discuss it. It took quite a lot of relaxed conversation to encourage him to talk. His spoken vocabulary was not wide and one had to concentrate very hard with his strong accent. It was clear that he had a strong sense of humour. He has an armchair interest in many sports, particularly boxing. Most of his free time is spent with

Sean's attempts to write down the few letters of the alphabet he knows how to form.

AVAILABILITY FOR LESSONS

Best Time: ...evening – after 8.0 p.m. ....

Working Area: depends on site – moves round a lot ....

Working Hours: approx. 7.0 am – 6.30 pm ....

Best Place: ...away from home ....

Own Transport: ...no ....

Able to Travel by Public Transport: yes – with help first from wife.

Preferred Tutor: ..female ... young .... – not male .....

Information noted on Sean's availability for lessons collected by the interviewer to enable her to allocate the most appropriate tuition for him.

his family or drinking and dancing at the local clubs. His general knowledge was limited and he did not know that there was a river in London!

Sean spoke of the various difficulties he had encountered, and mentioned his continual fear of someone finding out and of making him feel foolish. He was worried that his children would find out and worse still, that they would shortly overtake him. He explained that he had told none of his friends about his problems, although he had recently discussed it with one of his brothers who, he discovered, had just enrolled at a literacy class in another part of London.

Sean was *totally illiterate* and could neither read nor write his own name or address. He had recently been taught the upper-case letters of the alphabet by his priest, but he was not familiar with the lower case letters, nor did he understand the difference between letters and words, using these terms interchangeably. He was quite oblivious of words around him and could not even distinguish between 'Ladies' and 'Gents'. Instead, he said, he usually waited to see who went in which door, having once made a mistake at Waterloo Station which he didn't intend to repeat. Writing obviously fascinated him and he held the pen like a paintbrush, slowly and painstakingly copying some letters. Although he had a great deal to master, Sean was obviously keen to learn to read and realised that it would be a lengthy struggle. He thought he would be happy if he could at least reach a level at which he would be able to understand a popular daily newspaper.

Jackie Baker turned out to be a blonde bombshell. Attractively dressed and immaculately made-up, she arrived for her interview set to enjoy a long chat. Her alertness and intelligence were immediately apparent. She was, in fact, not a complete stranger to the project since she had asked for help four years before. She had been allocated to one-to-one tuition, but in terms of actual learning, the arrangement hadn't been a success. Her tutor was a lively, busy and sensible woman around Jackie's own age, and although the two of them had got on famously, neither of them had stuck at the lessons regularly. Consequently progress had been slight. Now at the age of twenty-nine, she wanted to try again.

Jackie was the eldest of a large fairly close family. Her father was a painter and a decorator working mostly for himself. Her mother had done packing in a small factory before getting married. Both parents were able to cope with basic reading and writing, but apart from reading the local newspaper and writing the occasional letter to relations, they made little use of these skills. Jackie has four brothers and two sisters – aged between twenty-seven and fourteen – of these, two of the boys are not very good at reading and the fourteen year old is having some difficulty for which he receives special tuition at school. Jackie has taken it upon herself to encourage the youngest, pointing out the great difficulty she has experienced in being unable to read and write. Although the parents are aware that some of their children have literacy problems, they do not realise just how far off they are from being fluent readers. The parents felt that it was up to the school to do something about it, but they never went along to discuss their children's problems with the teachers. Jackie maintains that she does not want to blame her parents for their lack of interest, but she has no intention of letting the same situation develop in the case of her own children.

When she first started school, she did reasonably well, although she did not pick up reading immediately. Prone to asthma, her attacks became quite severe from about the age of seven when she spent six months away from school recuperating. When she returned to school after the worst bout she was well behind the rest of the class. Unfortunately, there was no remedial specialist available, and her own teacher had no time to give her the special help she needed to catch up. She spent an increasing amount of time painting and drawing and running messages. At the age of ten her inability to

HOLBORN READING SCALE

1. The dog got wet and Tom had to rub him dry. 509

2. He was a very good boy to give you some of his sweets. 600

3. My sister likes [*him*] me to open my book and read to her. 603

4. [*good*] Go away and hide behind that door where we found [*find*] you just now. 606

5. Please don't let anyone [*another*] spoil these [*those*] nice fresh flowers. 609

6. The string had eight [*n.a.*] knots [*n.a.*] in it which I had to untie [*n.a.*]. 700

7. Wine [*win*] is made from the juice of grapes which grow in warm countries. 703

A reading test showing the reading errors made by Jackie, (n.a. indicates no attempt made to read or work out words so marked).

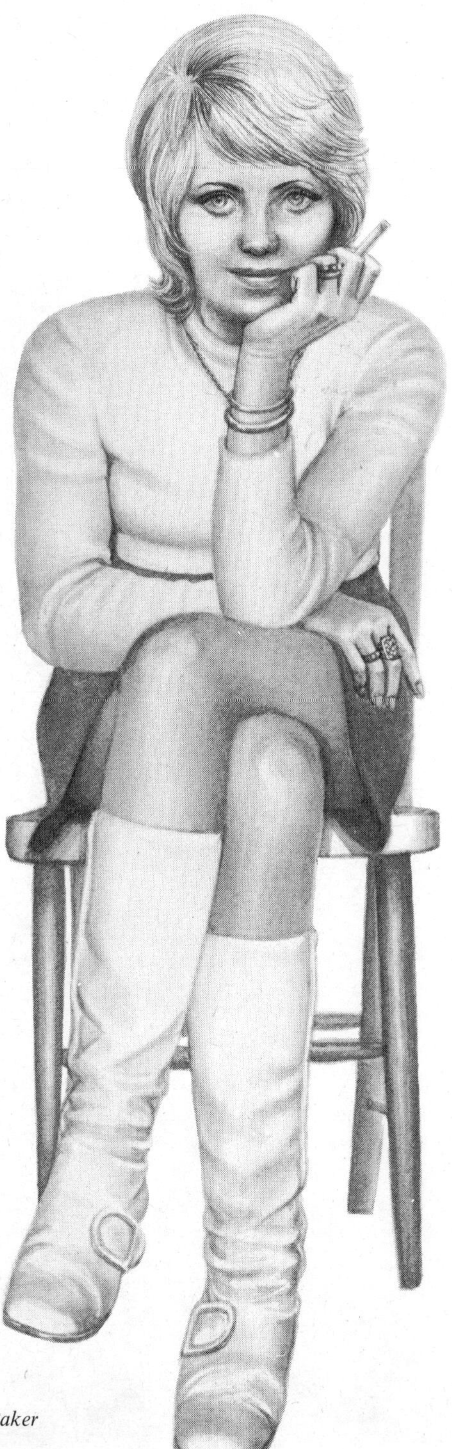

Jackie Baker

read made her the subject of ridicule from the other children. She began to dread being asked to read aloud in class, knowing that she would have to stumble through a passage. School became an increasingly unpleasant place. Her mother did not object when she pleaded to be allowed to stay at home and help in the house. Her mother was clearly disturbed to see her child in such an anxious state and was only too glad of her help with the younger children. The truancy officer called once or twice to discuss her absence, but her mother told them that Jackie's asthma had been getting worse again. She began secondary school where she made friends with a number of girls who also had difficulty with reading and writing. She and her friends frequently played truant and her leaving school at the age of fifteen was a mere technicality.

At fifteen she got a job on a factory assembly line. She found the job boring and tried several other similar ones. Then she went to work in a local dress shop, but she couldn't cope with filling out sales dockets. She tried a variety of similar jobs, never telling her employers that she couldn't read and write. They never asked her to fill in an application form, and as far as she was aware, no one ever found out about her difficulty. If it seemed likely that her problem would be discovered, she would leave.

At eighteen she married a young salesman whom she had met at a dance. He was very proficient at reading and writing, but he did not guess Jackie's secret. Eventually, just before the wedding, she plucked up enough courage to tell him, sure that he would not want to marry her once he knew. Although John was staggered by her revelation, to her relief he declared that it made no difference and suggested that after they were married he should try to teach her. This he has tried to do several times, but each time they lost patience with each other and the lesson ends up in a full scale argument.

Now that she is married and has her own family her illiteracy is increasingly becoming a burden. She is very keen that her own children (Heather, aged ten and Stephen, aged eight) should succeed in learning to read. Heather is doing well at school but Stephen has been having some difficulty with reading. Jackie would like to be able to help him but is unable to do so. Her husband is too busy to devote his time to listen to Stephen read for long, and to give him the encouragement he needs. Jackie has discussed the child's problem with the teacher and felt bound to admit her own inability to read. Her desire to help Stephen was in fact the main reason she decided to begin reading lessons again.

Recently she has gone back to work on a part-time basis. She drives for a firm delivering photographic materials. She has the same route to cover each day. If it changes at all, for example, if she gets a new customer, she gets help from her husband in identifying and locating the firm. She has a simple timesheet to complete which she can manage, and her employers have no idea that she is illiterate. She believes she would be sacked if they were to find out.

Jackie clearly finds her illiteracy a great burden. She desperately wants to be able to read and gets very irritable with herself for not being able to do so. She has tried studying her children's school books, but this hasn't helped her. Nonetheless, she believes that she needs a lot of pushing by a tutor and admits that she really dislikes having to concentrate for long periods. As she puts it, she would much rather have a chat than get down to work on a lesson.

A few of her friends know about her difficulty and most of them are sympathetic about it, but she takes great pains to prevent her children finding out and she hates having to tell them to ask their father for help with their school work.

She talked fluently and confidently at her interview and it was easy to establish a good rapport with her as she is friendly and outgoing. She maintained she could not read and write at all, but was not embarrassed about doing some reading and writing at the interview.

She could, in fact, write her own name in clear joined-up script. She said she could read her local road signs and place names and had passed her driving test without any trouble. Her husband had read 'The Highway Code' aloud to her, and she remembered it quite easily. She never uses public transport as she always gets lost and hates having to ask for directions. She can also cope with basic social sight words, e.g. look left, danger, police, exit etc. She glances through the newspaper each day and can usually work out the gist of her horoscope and the television programmes of the day. She is interested in domestic subjects and fashion, sometimes buying women's magazines to see the latest clothes, although most articles are too difficult for her to read. On a sentence reading test her *reading age is 7 years*. Her reading speed is very slow – too slow for comprehension, but she has learnt a little about breaking words up into sounds. She finds putting sounds together to form words very difficult. She can write a few simple three letter words, but little else.

The likelihood of her dropping out of lessons for a second time was discussed, but she said that this time she was determined to stick at it, as she felt that this was the last chance she had to become literate, and she definitely intended to persevere. She added, however, that she would appreciate having a teacher who would be firm with her and keep her up to the mark!

These words containing the common combinations of consonants and vowels were dictated to Jackie to get some idea of the nature of her difficulties
tap, man, rat, beg, red, pet, tin, lip, ink, lot, mug, cod, but, hub.

Murray Johnson

Murray Johnson was nineteen but looked several years younger. Thin and small, he wore a clutter of ultra-up-to-date clothing. His whole appearance suggested a concerted effort to appear tough and with-it, to compensate for his slight physique. He arrived accompanied by his father who was anxious to sit in on the interview. Murray looked relieved when his father was asked to wait in another room.

Had it not been for a probation officer's report it might have been quite difficult to assemble a picture of Murray's reading problem and its history. He was a reticent lad and accustomed to being taciturn with those in authority. The first impression was that he had been forced into coming along for an interview and would be glad to get it over with as quickly as possible. It was also obvious that the entire proceedings of the interview were likely to be thrashed out later by his father.

Murray was the youngest of four children, having two older sisters who were in their thirties – both married with families; and a married brother in his late twenties. Murray said he didn't know if his brothers and sisters were literate, but he knew his parents were. According to his probation officer's report, Murray's mother was highly intelligent but rather neurotic. Both parents were very ambitious for all their children and Murray had obviously been under considerable parental pressure since childhood to do well. They were particularly concerned about his inability to read, and spent a lot of time giving him coaching and going over his schoolwork with him. They had often visited the school to discuss his difficulties with his teachers.

Murray attended school regularly, but increasingly became difficult to deal with. He referred to himself with some pride, as one of the bad boys who was constantly in trouble. He said he hated everything about school: having to go when he didn't feel like it, the lessons, the teachers, the rules, everything. He was glad to leave at fifteen and his parents, despairing of his ever settling down, agreed. He could not remember much about his junior school days, but he remembered hating reading because he was not any good at it. He used to spend quite a lot of his time sitting at the back of his class, 'messing about'. He remembers one teacher who came to the school who took a particular interest in him. She used to spend about half-an-hour at lunch-time and after school helping him with his reading and he felt that he was at last getting somewhere. But then she left and that was that. When he started at secondary school he was sent to a local remedial clinic which he attended once a week

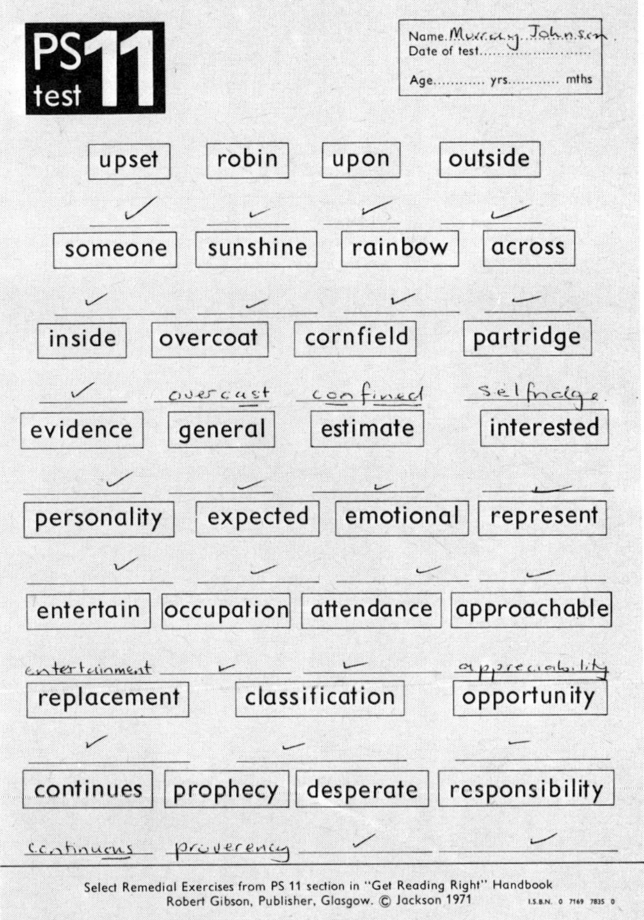

A multisyllable test from Stephen Jackson's PS tests described in 'Get Reading Right'. It was given to Murray to test his ability to read multisyllabic words. Ticks indicate the words he read correctly. The words he misread are written below the test word.

This list of words was dictated to Murray to identify some of his specific spelling difficulties: tap, man, rat, beg, red, pet, tin, lip, ink, pop, not, cod, but, mug, hub, lass, zig, bet, sop, cut, gull, kid, fed, rob, huff, yam, gab, jug, mend, lock, give, silk, ramp, tank, song, nod, rest, shelf, stuck, brush, twist, clash, blob, crisp, fled, frog, glum, grunt, plop, press, scamp, skill, spun, swift.

for two hours for three years. He resented having to do this, and maintains he didn't like the teacher, a highly experienced lady in her early sixties.

His first job on leaving school was in a warehouse, but this involved reading labels which he found tricky and he didn't like the dirtiness of the working conditions. After three months he left and became a van boy, but he got bored with that and didn't much like the people he had to work with. Next he tried gardening for the local council and stuck at that for a year. In the last three years he has had eleven different jobs, and is at present unemployed. He has registered at the employment exchange (he's been unemployed for six months) but the exchange has been having difficulty placing him because his choice of jobs is limited by his inability to read and write. Murray had little idea of what type of work he would really like to do, and in fact was not convinced that he really wants to work at all.

Four months ago Murray was caught trying to steal a motor bike. For this first offence he was put on probation for two years. The magistrate hearing his case suggested to the probation officer that some attempt be made to help Murray with his reading and spelling. For this reason he had been referred for tuition. The probation officer had discussed the question of lessons with Murray and had apparently felt that he was relatively interested in learning.

It was not easy to assess just how keen Murray was to have some help. He said he wouldn't mind 'having a go', but didn't have much idea how long the process would take. Surprisingly, he talked with some feeling about how difficult he had found it not being able to read. He confessed that when he left school, he'd thought it wouldn't matter, but he'd realised since how impossible it was to get a decent job if you couldn't read. He kept very quiet about his problem and would do anything rather than admit his problems to his employers or friends. He liked pop music and football, but he avoided joining clubs of any sort in case he was asked to fill in forms.

Murray was not at all unintelligent. It was apparent that where he had once found reading difficult, he had now become self-conscious about the problem and this would add to the difficulty of teaching him. He became more expansive as he realised that he was being talked to adult-to-adult and that his reading problem was being treated seriously and not as something that was just his own fault. He agreed to do some reading and spelling. His *reading age was 8½ years*. He tried to sound out unknown words with varying degrees of success. He'd obviously forgotten quite a lot, but he often guessed words intelligently, picking ones which fitted with the sense of the passage. He needed plenty of encouragement to try to decode long words and was inclined to want to skip them and say at once that he didn't know the word. When pushed gently he could frequently work out the word and obviously enjoyed the praise he received on so doing.

He could write his name and address and read most social sight words like 'Danger', 'Exit', 'Ladies', 'Gentlemen', and he could travel on public transport with ease. He said he sometimes looked at a newspaper but only tried to read the odd article that interested him – such as murder cases and sport.

He could complete a very simple form but his handwriting was chaotic. His spelling confirmed that he was confused about the different sounds and that he was ignorant of spelling rules. His hearing appeared to be good, but he found it difficult to split a word into its sound components before writing it down. Once having written it, he was never sure if the word was right or wrong. Lacking confidence, he was usually sure that it was wrong. At the end of the session he wanted to know how many he had got right, and was fascinated when his mistakes were discussed with him and some of his difficulties pinpointed.

Murray was pressed hard about his desire to master reading and writing. It was suggested that there was little point in his beginning lessons if he didn't really want to learn and wasn't prepared to give it a reasonable trial. The difficulties and the up-hill struggle ahead were outlined, but he declared that he would be prepared to give it a go for six months and then review the situation.

Michael Wells is a 43-year-old self-employed builder. He has recently been widowed and it is only since then that he has felt the full burden of his illiteracy. He has been running a very successful business for many years and employs eighteen men. He and his wife were very close and she had always helped him with his books, tax returns, specifications etc. No one apart from her ever knew that while he could read fairly fluently, he could barely write a short sentence.

Michael was the middle child of a family of three. His older brother and his younger sister are both clever and highly literate.

Michael Wells

His brother is an engineer and his sister is a top secretary. He would hate either of them to know about his poor literary skills. His parents were also, he recalls, competent at reading and spelling, but he thinks that to this day they do not realise the seriousness of his problem. It is something he has felt far too ashamed to discuss even with his immediate family.

Michael is a victim of circumstances. He would almost certainly have been literate but for the outbreak of war, when he was nearly eight years old. He does not remember having any particular trouble with reading until that time; but from then on his schooling was constantly interrupted and he was evacuated several times and so received fairly intermittent schooling. He didn't realise that he had a problem until he finally returned home at the end of the year and settled in again at the local school. He was then fourteen, but he couldn't cope with any of the written work which he was required to do. In the confusion of the first few post war years his problem remained undetected. Michael was acutely ashamed of his inability to spell all but the most basic words, and did his best to conceal it from both his teachers and his family. Thus he began an elaborate and life-long subterfuge to keep his problem secret.

When he left school he was lucky to be given a chance of a building apprenticeship with a friend of his father's. He did well being a hard worker and quick to learn. After six years he went to work for several other small firms and for the past thirteen years has worked for himself. He has built up a flourishing business and is never short of contracts.

When he was twenty-four he got married, but it took several years before he mustered sufficient courage to tell his wife about his difficulty. His decision to tell her was largely brought about because of his increasing difficulty in hiding his inability from her. He had spent several years avoiding doing any writing in her presence. If he had a form to complete, he would wait until she had gone out and then get to work with the dictionary on hand, looking up every word in turn. If he had to write a letter he would go to the library and borrow a book of sample business letters – look for an appropriate one and copy it out making any necessary adjustments to the text. His wife, when he finally told her, was amazed. She could not believe how bad he was until she dictated something to him to write down. When she saw the result she realised that he was not joking. It was largely through her support and encouragement that Michael felt able to launch out on his own in business, knowing that his wife was willing and able to help him do all the necessary paperwork.

He has two children aged 17 and 14, both of whom are academically bright, and look forward to going to university. Neither is aware of their father's difficulties and both Michael and his wife have always gone to great lengths to keep the secret from them. He feels that they would be very ashamed of him if they were ever to find out.

Eight months ago Michael's wife was killed in a road accident. He has had a difficult struggle since, not only to keep the family going, but above all to keep abreast with his business affairs. Apart from his wife, no one else, not even any of his close friends, knew of his difficulty. Recently he saw a television programme which offered help to people with literacy problems, and for the first time he realised that help was available. It took him some time to summon the courage to make inquiries, but so desperate was his need to overcome his difficulties that he managed to do so.

Michael is a very likeable person, accustomed to decision-making and possessing an air of confidence and independence. He is an intelligent man, interested in a wide variety of subjects. Well-dressed, quietly spoken, he was obviously controlling his nervousness at being in an unfamiliar situation. He found it difficult to relax at first, but admitted that he found it a surprising relief to be confiding in someone after years of concealing his difficulty. He was clearly very keen to learn, but worried about whether he was now too old to be able to do so. He was also still very shaken by the death of his wife.

His reading was no problem. He said he read the newspaper from cover to cover each day, and although he doesn't read many books (his reading speed is very slow) he has laboured through a number of books on football and archaeology – two of his main interests. His *reading age is about $10\frac{1}{2}$ years*. His spelling on the other hand is well behind his reading level, and he is capable of writing only short words of up to five letters. He appears to know no spelling rules, but usually recognises if he has mis-spelt a word. He lacks confidence to attempt to write long words without first looking them up in the dictionary. This is no easy matter since he is often unsure how to spell the first part of the word and often has to look up words under various letters before he locates the right one. He is also worried about using the correct grammar, and about using the right word in the right place. He would like some help in learning how to set letters out correctly and to fill in the forms which he regularly has to complete. He is especially anxious that his lessons should be in confidence, as he does not want anyone from his own district to learn of his difficulty.

The following passage was dictated to Michael to get some idea of his spelling difficulties.
Last week Tom King's erratic driving caused him to land up at a police station. He had been going along at speed when a police car stopped him. He pleaded that he was not drunk but the breathaliser test proved otherwise.

Last week Tom King
eratic driving coursed him
to land up at the police
station he had been
going along at speed when
a police car stoped him he
pedid that he was not
drunk but the brethalize
test proovd otherwise.

3. Characteristics and causes of illiteracy

'If the test of disadvantage is taken to be the extent to which integration into active society is prevented, the factors are found mainly to lie in three areas . . . personal capacity, social disadvantage and educational disadvantage . . . but it is also clear that these factors interact . . . different types of disadvantage tend to accumulate.'

(Adult Education – a plan for development)

Information is gradually being gathered on the background of illiterate and semi-literate students which will help us to better define both the causes of adult illiteracy and the best modes of teaching adult students.

Such information is necessary if literacy programmes are to be effectively organised and students well taught. At this time, however, it is important to realise that research into adult illiteracy in this country is in its infancy. There are no longitudinal studies to set against apparent trends, no samples from different types of area to offset the tentative conclusions of inner city schemes and no published body of material on standards, methods and results such as is common in the widely researched area of reading standards and progress among school children. The very small body of published research can therefore be listed and its relevance assessed in terms of data on the characteristics of adult students.

Existing research

Of the few surveys and studies now available, remarkably little data is of use in defining the characteristics of adult illiterates throughout the whole population.

Research interest in the problem began mainly after World War II though adult education classes in basic literacy date back to the Adult Schools of the eighteenth and nineteenth centuries. Indeed by 1840 'on the average about three quarters of the adult population had some knowledge of reading and about three fifths some knowledge of writing.' (T. Kelly)

Nevertheless, the 1919 Report in its history and survey of Adult Education documented the fact; 'a considerable portion of the attendants at the evening schools then existing (1851) were adults who desired to obtain as men the elementary education which they failed to receive as children.' (1919 Ministry of Reconstruction HMSO London. Adult Education Committee Final Report)

In 1945 after two World Wars and three quarters of a century of compulsory schooling Sir Cyril Burt published the results of his pre-war sample of 227 illiterate adults. He concluded that illiteracy still existed in Great Britain and that low IQ, absence from school, special disabilities of vision and hearing, motor difficulties, left-handedness and unstable emotional balance were characteristic of the sample he had observed and on statistics from Army samples.

W. D. Wall in 1945 and 1946 added to this body of work by information from his sample of 323 Army recruits. Wall concluded that intelligence was not totally linked with illiteracy but an important factor in reading backwardness, along with the kind, length, changes and interruptions of schooling, nervous temperament, left dominance and defects of eyesight and hearing.

In the years which followed the war, attention was directed to reading standards in schools and it was hoped that in the general apparent upward trend of reading ability, the incidence of adult illiteracy would gradually be eliminated in all those of 'normal' intelligence. Successive surveys, such as those published by the Ministry of Education 1957 and by the National Foundation for Educational Research (NFER) have indicated that this has been a vain hope: the number of adult illiterates in our country is not declining. In 1971 some attempt to trace the dimension of the problem nationally was attempted by the National Association for Remedial Education (NARE) in a study entitled *Adult illiteracy*. The NARE Sub-Committee surveyed certain characteristics of 1126 illiterates in a variety of establishments including penal institutions. Their two principal findings have since been called into dispute. Since 45 per cent of this sample was aged between 15 and 20 years and 32 per cent of the returns came from Penal Establishments (such as borstals), it is hardly surprising that the conclusion that illiteracy is a problem of the young has been called into question. Their second principal conclusion was that low intelligence was linked significantly with reading disability in 45 per cent of men and 54 per cent of women. Though no figures exist as yet to positively contradict these findings, it is important to state that these are opinions based on subjective guesses by tutors who had no common criteria of evaluation of intelligence and no common mode of testing for reading difficulty.

In 1973 a further survey was attempted by Michael Haviland. This study concentrates mainly on provision and provides useful information on existing classes and certain common aspects of funding and resources. And in 1974 another survey was compiled by T. W. Pascoe for NARE in *A register of facilities for adult non-readers within the United Kingdom*.

Despite these attempts at large scale surveys, detailed information from specific areas has been slow to emerge; information which is necessary to piece together the characteristics of illiterate students in different areas and to establish a common core of data. An attempt was made in 1972 to correlate some of the information gathered by the Cambridge House Literacy Scheme, Camberwell, London and to compare it with a sample group in a Local Authority Class. On this occasion testing methods and modes of seeking information were standardised. This study, by Jenny Stevens, is, as yet, unpublished.

Difficulty of using existing research on reading

Although a great deal of information is available from literacy projects in other parts of the world, especially in the under-developed countries, it is obviously of limited use. Different cultures, levels of literacy and schooling systems produce problems which differ not only from one country to another, but from one region to another. Who can compute, for instance, exactly how many children in this country, in Europe, in fact, all over the world, were affected by upsets to home and school during the years 1939 to 1945? They comprise thousands of our present over thirties age group. Who can trace the effects of changes in the curriculum policy of schools, of changes in legislation such as comprehensivisation or present cutbacks in teacher training or simply of methods which have altered the accepted pattern of literacy teaching in the past two decades? The situation in Cumbria is different from that in Cornwall, London's urban picture is different from that of Liverpool. Literacy in Britain cannot be compared with that in Bengal, Brazil or in Birmingham, Alabama, and the need for a British-based body of research is a vital one.

It may be tempting to try to transfer to the adult literacy field the expertise and research which has resulted from child development projects, but experience in other fields of adult learning would seem to indicate the danger of so doing. The information gathered during the years preceding school-leaving may not necessarily be of any use as an accurate prediction of adult standards. For example, one of my students left school with a reading age of 9 and managed to cope through his increased motivation and practice in his particular job because, his firm sent him on a course at the local college. Yet another who also left school with a reading age of 9 regressed into illiteracy because he had neither the opportunity nor necessity to practise his literacy skills. We now know that reading and writing, are skills soon lost in adulthood if they have not been thoroughly learned in the first place.

Our attitudes and personalities change as we grow older. The profiles of Jackie Baker and Michael Wells illustrate this well. Jackie left school semi-literate and her husband urged her to come forward for tuition. His help and acceptance of her difficulty were crucial in her attempt to try a second time to become literate.

Michael also left school semi-literate. He struggled for years, reluctant to admit the problem even to his family, and became so nervous and depressed that he was unable to concentrate for any length of time and continually blocked his own despairing efforts to master basic skills.

Information from other areas of adult learning would seem to indicate the difficulty of obtaining detailed data necessary for accurate research. Adults do not enjoy being tested. And, as attendance for tuition is voluntary, we risk losing the student for good if information-gathering is done in an over zealous way. While the army, prisons, borstals provide informative testing grounds for adult progress in this field, they are not typical of the entire population for obvious reasons.

With all these difficulties, it is clear that the comments which I shall make are based on a very *limited* amount of research information, from those students who have the opportunity and courage to come forward, on my personal experience and on the comments and experience of friends and colleagues who are currently involved in this work. They are intended mainly as *preliminary* guidelines for those who are seeking a means of better understanding and appreciating the particular problems faced by adult students.

Characteristics of adult illiterate and semi-literate students

The characteristics which are readily observable in any week's work in the adult literacy field, I have divided into the following categories: age/sex, physical factors, family background, social class, history of previous schooling, attitudes, work.

Age/sex. Information on the age at which help with reading is most often sought seems remarkably consistent. Three factors seem to emerge.

The young adult jaded after failed schooling is unlikely to seek tuition voluntarily and will often, as in our profiles Murray Johnson did, resist the well intentioned attempts of family and friends to get him to seek help.

So much depends on the links between adult education services (including literacy schemes) and the whole community, in particular schools, remedial departments, and employers, that it is easy to believe that this situation will alter when schemes become better established. There is little doubt, however, that some adolescents (and adults) have such unpleasant memories of their schooldays that they will not voluntarily undertake further tuition of any sort, no matter how great their need.

The family age group (25–40) is one in which motivation to seek help is provided by work and by marriage and children. Mothers wish to help children to read, fathers to seek promotion at work and both become additionally conscious of their inadequacies when children later seek help with homework.

❝ *It's beginning to get on my nerves when the kids say, 'Don't ask Dad, he can't spell!' They seem to think I'm an idiot or something!* ❞

(Mr J. aged 34, butcher)

Though motivation remains strong in the older age group (40–50) it seems to decline rapidly after that. This suggests not only that students may have accommodated to illiteracy, but that the process of disengagement so often discussed in relation to pre-retirement activities is also reflected in the area of literacy, a main mode of communication with others. We can add to this a decline in motivation prompted by the fear many students have that they are too old to learn.

There would seem, at the present time, to be slightly more men than women currently receiving help. It would be dangerous to draw any conclusions from any of the existing research about the proportion of male and female illiterates in the community because motivation is often linked strongly to work factors, and many of the existing samples have concentrated on male institutions. Added to these factors of motivation and sampling, we must add access to information about tuition. It is generally more difficult for women to acquire information if they are not at work – but when a number of articles appeared in women's magazines and on a women's television programme, a substantial number of housewives presented themselves for tuition.

Physical factors. It seems logical to assume that a childhood history of defects in eyesight or hearing would result in reading difficulty and indeed some adults who come forward for tuition do manifest such difficulties for which they have not sought help.

'I should wear glasses, but I can't afford them,' was what one student told me this year as I watched her squinting at the page. Hearing difficulties are less easy to determine and it is worth noting in passing that there is no professional specialist service on which adult education tutors can rely.

It is not easy to substantiate the widely claimed difficulties of left-handers from the small surveys available, and there is no information as yet on the percentage of students exhibiting cross-laterality (confusion of left and right hand) although some people believe this to be one factor which contributes to delayed progress in reading.

One observed characteristic which is only generally substantiated by subjective comments on attitude and personality are the number of students who have suffered and continue to suffer from illnesses related to nervous stress. Asthma, bronchial asthma, 'stomach nerves', dermatitis are frequently acknowledged illnesses. In our profiles Jackie Baker's asthma seems to have been a major cause of her difficulties at a crucial stage. Adult students complain of the continuation and recurrence of these illnesses and some attempt to rationalise them in relation to their literacy difficulties.

❝ *When the auditors come round at the end of the year, I start to get the rash on my hands again. I dread their finding out just how bad I am at reading and spelling.* ❞ (Mr T. office manager, age 29)

The inter-relation of physical and mental stress is sometimes very obvious in illiterate and semi-literate adult students and it is a nice point just how much one is cause and effect of the other.

Family. From all the research on reading difficulty in schools, it is not difficult to argue a most forcible case for the importance of certain factors of family background to literacy. The term *Cycle of Deprivation* is commonly used to describe the legacy of deprivation which passes down from parent to child and cannot be broken by intervention at only one point in the circle. If a child grows up deprived of, and unaccustomed to, books and libraries and opportunities to practise verbal skills, then this will affect his progress and he, in turn, unless intervention is made, will see no pleasure and relevance in reading and will pass this attitude on to his children. Researchers have plotted the crucial importance of parental interest; so much is a confirmation of commonsense observation.

The high incidence of parental or sibling illiteracy correlated by at least one research study, with the reading backwardness of individuals is frequently borne out by the high numbers of adult students who fail to recall the reading or writing practices of one of their parents. In our profiles on both Jackie and Sean, no books or stories were ever seen and none of Sean's five brothers were able to read at all. In Programme 2R – The Reading Borough Literacy Scheme – it is becoming increasingly common for our illiterate students to bring a member of his family along for literacy help.

Associated with literacy problems, there seems to be a high incidence of large family size. In one study done by the Army School of Preliminary Education, 50 per cent of their intake were from families of four or more children. The same close family bond which sometimes conceals the illiterate from society by protecting his interests can also be a threat to his self esteem. When children begin to ask for stories and to question their parents' refusal to help them, the fear of losing face in front of the children becomes one of the most powerful motivators. In my own area, one literacy group exists specifically to teach mothers through the reading material their own children are just beginning to tackle. Most students are uncertain as to whether their parents had discussed their reading problems with the school, regarding it as none of the family's business. Few can ever remember their parents having tried to help them with reading problems. In our profiles, Sean received no help from his mother, nor did Jackie. This conspiracy of silence and apparent disregard for the consequences of reading failure is one aspect of illiteracy which gives most cause for concern to teachers, for there is ample evidence that in order to achieve literacy at an early age, a child must be heavily dependent on his parents, their performance and standards, their attitudes towards books and on their concern that the child shall master reading skills. If they are too busy, too unconcerned or

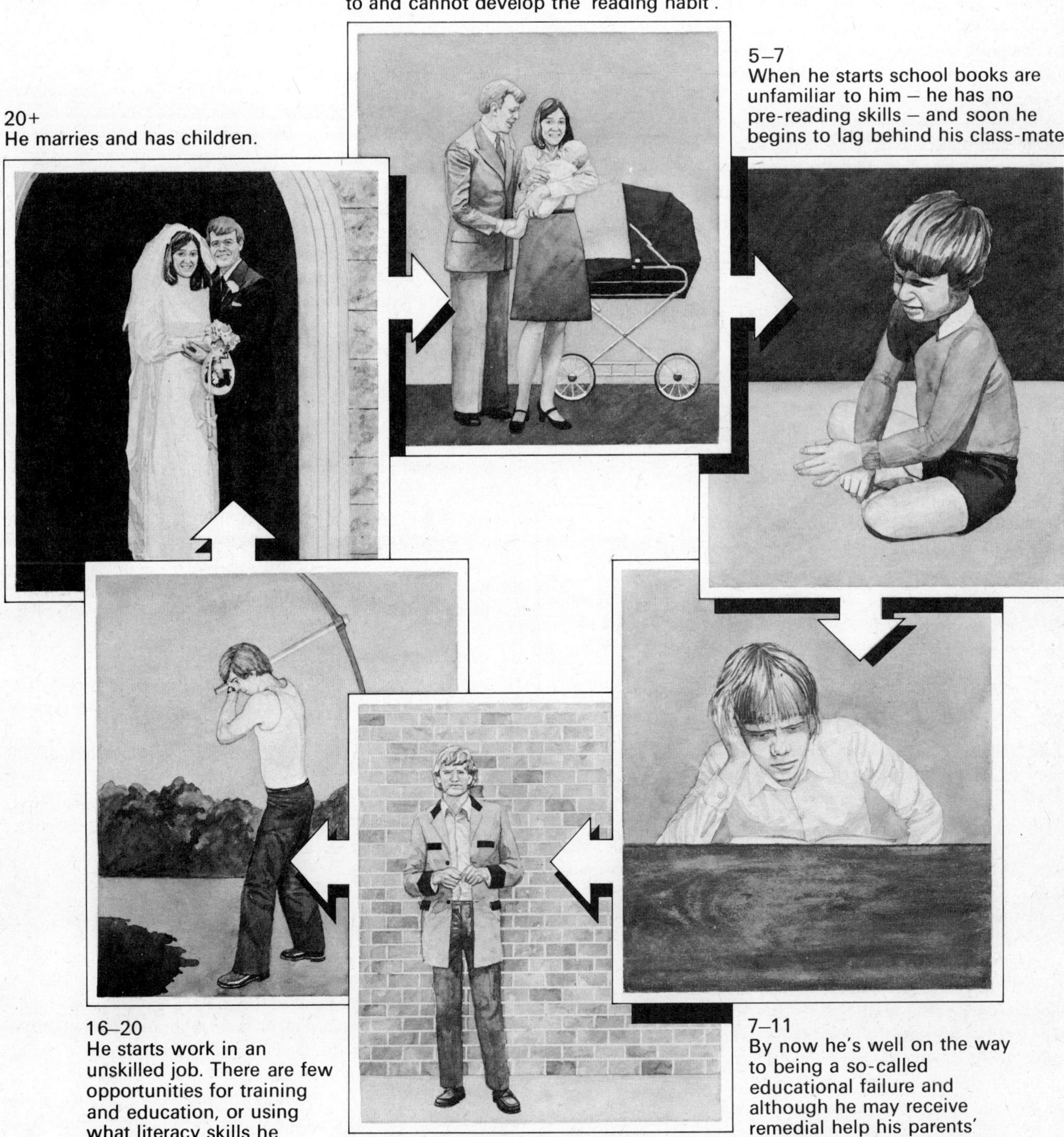

Cycle of deprivation

unable, then the child will begin at a disadvantage. For the unfortunate 0·5 per cent who, according to successive reading surveys go through the entire ten years of compulsory schooling without achieving the basic skills of reading and writing, there is little hope that they will be able to give their children any better start than they had themselves. Jackie and Sean are determined that their children shall not lack encouragement from home, but both are driven to a variety of devices to conceal their own deficiencies.

Social class. The relationship between social class and educational opportunity has been documented many times elsewhere. Illiteracy walks hand-in-hand as cause and effect of other deprivations such as poverty, homelessness, malnutrition, etc. Yet the students who come forward for tuition would belie the notion that this is only a problem of the poor or disadvantaged! We are at present only scratching the surface, giving help to those who will tolerate education again or who have been driven to desperation by some event which has threatened the revelation of their secret. Many students who could broadly be ascribed 'lower middle class' use much of their intelligence and ingenuity to protect their position by concealing their illiteracy and finding and developing other strengths to compensate for it. In our profiles, Sean buys newspapers and pretends to read them, composes impromptu stories to his children while looking at the illustrations, while Michael copies out business letters from the library. Both exhibit courage, intelligence and ingenuity in dealing with their problems. This should be an added reminder to all who believe that illiteracy can be equated with idiocy.

Schooling. Two basic patterns begin to emerge in relation to the educational history of present students. There is, on the one hand, a pattern of absence from school in the formative years and on the other, an accumulation of attitudes hostile to learning which has had its reciprocal effect in the low expectations teachers have held of recalcitrant and aggressive students.

❝ *We really were the bad lads. I never learned anything if I could help it.* ❞
(Mr J. salesman, age 29)

Many students suffered long absence from school with illness such as asthma and bronchitis frequently reported. When students, like Jackie Baker, return to school and fail to keep up with their group, an inevitable reaction sets in and absence is then compounded in many cases by parental collusion in truancy, particularly during the later years at school. Sean's long absences from school for seasonal farmwork were followed by truancy. Michael's school attendance was interrupted by the war and Jackie's absences with bronchial asthma became both cause and effect of her reading failure.

Many pupils have suffered neither absence nor behavioural difficulties: their reaction may be one of self-concealment and withdrawal. There is no doubt that it is still possible for an illiterate adult to have passed through the years 11–16 with no remedial help from anyone, either at home or at school. While evacuation and social dislocation

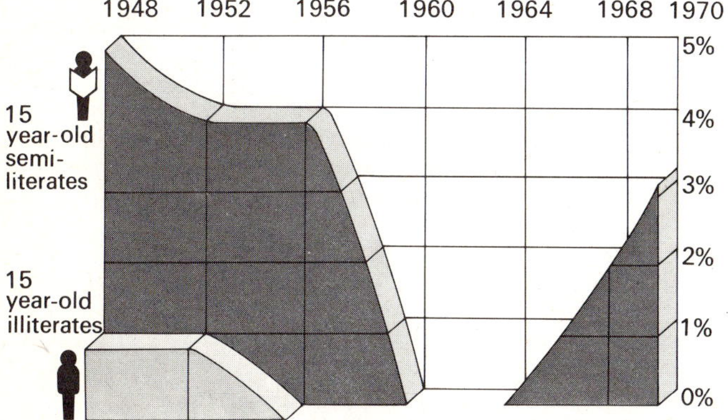

The number of 15-year-old school-leavers with high reading scores appears not to have improved in the last ten years – while the percentage of semi-literates seems actually to have risen dramatically. (Start and Wells).

due to war, was an obvious disturbance for all schoolchildren between 1939 and 1946, it is clear that after a rapid rise in standards after the war the graph of reading success does not show any encouraging picture in the past ten years of 'peace and plenty'.

It is always difficult to know what credence to give the many stories students tell of the horrors of their school life. Trenamen's research conclusion that 45 per cent of the adult population were resistant to the thought of beginning their education again must be a sobering reminder to all in this field that education has failed the student once already and the ingrained memories of large classes, boredom, restricting rules and regulations are not to be eradicated with age.

Work. Little research work has been done on the occupations of those who come forward for reading help. Here is a selection of the occupations I noted in my work in the Borough of Reading.
Females: – hotel maid, kitchen attendant, hospital worker, cleaner, part-time nursing assistant, sales assistant, waitress, cosmetics representative, factory worker.
Males: – factory operatives, self-employed building workers, storekeeper, motor mechanic, hospital workers, hospital ground staff, lorry driver, painter and decorator, panel beater.

Surprisingly few students are unemployed and many are coping with jobs which really demand a far higher literacy level than they are able to summon. It is a constant tribute to the initiative and resourcefulness of many students that they are able to get by. In our profiles, Jackie used to work on a boring assembly line job but has learned the Highway Code off by heart in order to pass her driving test. Michael has managed to run his own business in the building trade with the help of his wife. Sean, like so many others has had to turn down a chance of promotion because he feared the discovery of his illiteracy. Murray was unable to read warehouse labels so was unable to continue with his previous occupation, unskilled though it was. Murray, Sean and Jackie are all weary of the process of constantly changing jobs.

The relationship of work potential and literacy skills is an important one. The Department of Employment staff regularly encounter those who need assistance with application forms and, as they are briefed by many, many employers as to the importance of a good standard of reading and writing, it is difficult to find suitable employment for illiterate and semi-literate workers. And when they do find employment, however skilled they may be, their inadequate literacy prevents them from progressing to a higher level and much of the frustration which follows will affect their attitude towards learning and their ability to learn.

As yet, little is known either by the Department of Employment or by literacy schemes about the percentage of unemployed who are illiterate. People who cannot read take friends into the Job Centre to select from the self service section, many hold down jobs by sheer ingenuity alone.

Most students, for obvious reasons, do not seek help with reading and writing from their supervisor at work and it would seem that the subject is still taboo in many unions. One union leader told me quite firmly that 'it was a man's own business whether he could read or write and no-one else's affair to stir up trouble for him!' Another shop steward announced only half in jest, that if anyone saw him putting up one of our literacy posters on the noticeboard at work – he would be lynched.

It is hardly surprising in view of society's general attitudes towards the problem that few students confide their problem to their employer – they regard it quite rightly as a barrier to promotion – even to security. M. & E. Belbin in their experiments in retraining older adult workers comment on the difficulties of retraining the illiterate worker particularly in experiments using today's programmed learning methods. If a worker cannot read he is a safety risk and a security risk – to himself and to others. If he cannot even admit his difficulty to his family, his friends, his union or his employer, if he is denied promotion and considered unsuitable for retraining, there would seem to be little hope of progress for the illiterate student. This country cannot afford such luxuries with her vital manpower.

Attitudes. At interview, the illiterate student will invariably appear tense. Society has taught him to be so and the correlation between reading difficulty and personality disorder exhibited by nervous signs of stress is one that has often been noted. Dr Joyce Morris (1966) in her survey of Kent schoolchildren concluded that poor readers inevitably became nervous and depressed, while studies from the Army School of Education describe men who were exhibiting signs of emotional stress ascribed to reading failure.

The importance of research on counselling in relation to reading progress is important in this respect. If most adults suffer from attitudes and inhibitions which hamper their reading progress, then it would seem important that they feel able to succeed in the early stages of learning and that the tutor presents herself as someone on whom the illiterate can rely. However, until society revises its attitudes on illiteracy, there is little that the tutor can do except work patiently to restore the student's confidence in himself by success in his attempts to read and to express himself in writing.

What kind of information on a student do you think a tutor should have? What is essential, desirable but not essential or unnecessary? Are you prepared to justify your decision?

Summary of characteristics

It is evident from observation of adult students that illiteracy can be attributable to a number of causes – some of which are more rooted in circumstance than in congenital deficiency or environmental deprivation. Indeed, Sir Cyril Burt concluded that of the $3\frac{1}{4}$ million illiterate and semi-literate adults that *he* estimated to exist in this country – many could have been 'cured' by 'adequate methods of teaching in the early years and by skilled guidance continuing through adolescence.' Factors crucial to the development and maintenance of literacy would seem to be stable and linguistically capable family background, successful early learning, good eyesight and hearing, stable temperament, opportunities for special tuition at first at school and then at the place of work.

Two sets of characteristics are of importance in understanding and helping the illiterate student:

- age, family and work, background and general health
- past experience of learning

Present research is only of marginal help in accurately defining causes of illiteracy.

The adult illiterate as a student

It is obvious from the general picture presented of the students who at present seek literacy help that each one will approach the learning situation with a different set of expectations related to his past history and present background and attitudes.

Lessons will be boring, humiliating and unpleasant just as they were at school. Might this be Murray?

A few lessons will set the matter right. Might this be Jackie?

It is too late and I am far too old anyway. Might this be Michael?

How would *you* as a tutor, deal with the problems such students present? Which of these approaches do you think would be helpful:

- be encouraging and friendly;
- try to get to the root of the problem by asking a lot of questions;
- take firm control of the student and get him to get back to basics;
- give him a thorough and exhaustive test at the start;
- try to start off with a few small exercises which you know he could do;
- explain to him exactly what you are going to do, which methods you are going to use and so on;
- just start with an early reading book and take it from there.

Characteristics of adult learners

Added to the specific characteristics of the illiterate and semi-literate we must add those which are likely to occur because the student is an *adult* – and whatever his particular difficulty, he will begin to learn and re-learn in a way which all other adults do. He will also have the same difficulties other adult learners have, these can be described as follows:

Difficulties	*Reason*
Your student will forget things very easily.	His short term memory may be declining and unless he is given practice he will forget things from one week to the next.
Your student will often grasp things more slowly than you had imagined.	He is trying to reconcile what you say to all that he has observed in the past. His own fears and self doubts will put a block on new learning.
Your student will probably knows a good deal more about many topics than you do.	This is the biggest difference between child and adult non-readers and presents an obvious way of boosting self-esteem.
Your student may be very quiet and unforthcoming.	He is regarding the tutor warily because of past experience.
Your student may wish to chat incessantly.	He may dread the learning process or may be relieved to confide in someone at last.
Your student will not find it easy to adopt new habits (e.g. writing, spelling).	In so many cases his mistakes will have become ingrained over half a lifetime – it is easier to learn than to unlearn.
Your student may be far too nervous to concentrate for long.	Remember that helping him to cope with learning is as important as teaching him to read.
Your student will get very depressed at times.	Pressures from home and work weigh heavily at times and most students are, in any case, unaware of the plateaux of learning.
Your student may not like another member of the group.	Adult students set great store by group cohesion. Perhaps another member is taking up too much of your time.
Your student may not like you.	You may remind him of someone, a previous tutor? Perhaps he feels you are not genuinely interested in him? Alternative tutors are possible, after all.
Your student is tired after working all day and so are you.	He *will* be able to assimilate short and varied units of learning but will soon grow weary of relentless repetition and frustrating periods of difficulty without help.
Your student *will* leave if you don't meet his learning needs.	There are many reasons why students cannot and do not stay in a class – not all reflect on the tutor – remember that a friendly note will often renew contact with a student whose absence started by being unavoidable then stretched into indifference or reticence.

What would you do about the problems?

Research on the characteristic learning habits of adults gives important information about:

- *cognitive learning* or the acquisition of new knowledge;
- *affective or emotional learning* which describes the importance of taking into account the attitudes, values, and reactions which inhibit the learner.

4.Tutors

From what I have said before about the adult student, it will be obvious that the selection and training of tutors for adult literacy work is of the utmost importance. Most existing schemes agree that there is no shortage of potential tutors at present and that many people wish to give their services in what they regard as an area of need.

Tutor trainers. A small teaching force already exists amongst English specialists in further and adult education and among education specialists in Colleges of Education. This band prove the natural resource for tutor trainees together with existing tutor-organisers in the voluntary schemes whose expertise has been crucial in the campaign for adult literacy so far. Their particular need is for further research into teaching methods and studies of samples and for continual updating and consultation on training techniques.

Adult literacy group tutors. Teachers in primary education and in remedial departments of secondary education are often available for evening work. Most realise they need help adjusting to the particular needs of adult students and wish to be supplied with information on suitable methods and materials. Their expertise and patience are invaluable in the management of a small group of adults.

Volunteer tutors. The use of volunteers has a well established precedent. Men and women from many walks of life wish to be involved in literacy work and many have already given several years of devoted service to existing schemes. When a volunteer helper comes to a scheme for the first time, a training programme and informal discussion at regular intervals ought to be freely available as a way of offering support and allaying the feelings of apprehension which most volunteers naturally feel. Some schemes, such as the one in my own area, attempt a period of initial attachment to an established group supervised by an experienced tutor. Others feel that a volunteer helper ought to assist one particular student right from the very start. If you feel that you would like to help adult illiterate students, there are three questions you might like to think about: what must a tutor be? what must a tutor do? what must a tutor know?

What must a tutor be? What particular combinations of personality, attitude and professional expertise might reasonably be expected from someone who is to teach an adult to read?

While tutoring at a recent training course attended by literacy workers from all over the country, I posed this question and received a unanimous reply.

❛*Whether the tutor is a professional teacher or an untrained volunteer – personal qualities are the most important and first criteria for selection.*❜

I then asked the group to describe these personal qualities that, from their experiences, they considered to be all so important. Here is the list they supplied me with. Do you match up to this specification?

- sympathetic, empathetic, objective
- realistic, imaginative, capable of human understanding
- patient
- open minded
- flexible
- able to listen
- stable, resilient
- informal in approach, but able to give firm guidance.

Why are so saintly qualities so necessary you might ask? Mainly because, no matter how knowledgeable you may be in the teaching of reading, the real test is whether you are able to approach your student in a way which does not reinforce his frustration and low opinion of himself. If you are unable to imagine what it feels like to be illiterate in a literate society and make the mistake of bullying or patronising your student, you (as a tutor) will have failed him a second time. If you give him platitudes of encouragement instead of realistic targets and then watch him flounder, it will matter little that you are a master of diagnostic techniques or readability procedures, you will have failed him at a personal level – the most important level of all.

❛*I walked up and down outside the door for a good ten minutes trying to pluck up the courage to go in! I think I would have gone home if the tutor hadn't come out to get me! It was worse than going to the dentist's.*❜
(Mr W. aged 33, salesman, severe spelling difficulties)

What must a tutor do? The particular skills needed by a literacy tutor are not easy to define. Obviously, he must be literate – no trial and error methods of spelling, for instance! Social skills are of paramount importance too – in that the ability to maintain a tutor-pupil relationship or to successfully manage the learning of a small group of people so that they do not continually irritate each other, so they are encouraged by others but do not feel competitive towards them, is a skill of the highest order.

What must a tutor know? Anyone who wishes to teach an adult to read will need two areas of knowledge, first of adult education and in particular of 'education permanente' or 'lifelong learning' and secondly of reading. In other words an appreciation of the way in which adults learn as well as some appreciation of what there is to learn. You will almost certainly have to have:

- some knowledge of the techniques of reading to illiterate and semi-literate adults, together with the making of equipment, choice of reading materials and system of recording progress and diagnosing error (see Section two);
- some insight into the way in which adults learn and the particular methods that will help an adult to improve steadily and successfully – deriving pleasure and satisfaction from the start and carrying on in 'lifelong learning', developing new skills (see Section two);
- full knowledge of the organisation within which you work, its policy and funding, the accessibility of resources, facilities for specialist help and of the relationship of this organisation to the area it serves. (See Section three).

It has been proved over and over again that the enthusiasm and dedication which many volunteers bring to literary work, coupled with the very fact that they are not by profession a qualified teacher (therefore do not represent a regime which has failed the student once already) are powerful aids to adult learning. Naturally in order to be successful and to derive personal satisfaction from the work, a volunteer will need to feel not only that she is being supplied with information on teaching but that someone is available with whom she can discuss the problems of individual students. A monthly report card is hardly an adequate substitute for a face-to-face chat where problems both academic and personal can be discussed.

Here are five brief profiles of fictitious tutors drawn from my experience – recruiting and training – over a period of years.

Rhoda Curwen is 46. Her children are just about to leave home – one is already at university and the other, her daughter Lucy, is going to share a flat with a friend in London. Although Mrs Curwen has had a part-time clerical job for years, she feels the need of an extra interest now that the house seems so empty. Her husband is a civil servant, they are not short of money, and he has urged Rhoda to apply to the scheme after they had both seen a programme about illiteracy on the television. Mrs Curwen is quiet and patient – her motherly approach to her student is one which is working so far, she loves reading and is anxious to share her love of literature with her pupils.

Arthur Hobson is 53. He is married with three children (now married) and works in the local Job Centre. He is a sympathetic, humane man who feels distressed that so many workers are not being placed because of their poor literacy skills. His interests are football and gardening and reading which he prefers to watching television. A memo was sent down from the local Adult Education Officer about literacy classes and Mr Hobson rang up the Organiser to offer his help. He feels that 'everyone should be able to cope' at least and feels that it would be a tremendous achievement if he could move some of the difficult cases into suitable jobs by improving their literacy skills – by himself if necessary!

Here are three profiles of fictitious professional tutors:

Jose Graham is 28. Married. Two young children. Mrs Graham trained at a College of Education as a junior teacher and specialised in Reading Development. She taught for two years in the local junior school after leaving college and now is feeling rather depressed at home all day with two lively youngsters. She feels that she is becoming 'cabbage-like' and that evening work (when the children are in bed) is well within her capabilities. She lives in one of the better suburbs on the edge of town, her husband is a marketing manager, away quite a lot, but she has a considerable amount of entertaining to do when he is at home. Her main interests are the children, cooking and entertaining and she and her husband occasionally go car rallying when they can find someone to babysit. At the interview she said she would like some refresher training and some advice on materials and methods.

Evelyn Dann is 31. She has been working in the Remedial Department of the local comprehensive school for four years and has applied to the Adult Literacy Organiser mainly because she feels that adult literacy work would be a valuable extension of her experience, 'Who knows' she said 'it might even look good on an application form?' Miss Dann lives in a flat in the centre of town, owns her own car and is an enthusiastic musician, and a member of the local Amateur Operatic Society. She also attends Workers' Educational Association (WEA) classes and was a member of the Branch Committee last year. At the interview, she spoke convincingly of her concern for school leavers whom she had been unable to help and of the need for resources, of visual and auditory discrimination tests and of a firm professional control of class time. Miss Dann applied as a result of an advertisement for teachers in the local bulletin.

Martin Johns is 48. He came late into teaching and was, for many years, a production line worker in the car industry. As a young man he did war service in the Navy and remained as a member of the Navy Reserve until he entered teacher training college. After the war, he was unable to settle and moved from job to job until the wages paid by the car industry tempted him to stabilise himself when he had to provide for a wife, and family (four children). At the age of 40 he entered teacher training college and has now been teaching for five years in the local junior school. Although he specialised in physical education and woodwork, he has become increasingly involved in the teaching of reading and feels that adult literacy work would be an excellent opportunity for him – a return to the old days of working with adults and a chance to further himself in the teaching of reading.

These brief studies show how wide are the motivations and objectives of those who wish to teach illiterate adults. The professional teachers see something to their own advantage in the work. Is this not a powerful motivator for much of what we do? Jose Graham needs intellectual stimulus. Evelyn Dann hopes for promotion and

Martin Johns hopes that this, at last, will offer him job satisfaction as nothing else has. Our volunteer tutors also see a personal satisfaction in the work – Mrs Curwen to fill the gap left by her children and Arthur Hobson perhaps the unconscious wish to increase his own job satisfaction by having success in a way no one has yet been able to do.

Just as their motivations differ, so will their approach to the student and the objectives they hold.

Look back at the five tutor profiles again, then try to answer the following questions:
- which tutor(s) will have an approach most suitable to an adult relationship?
- which tutor is most likely to push the student too quickly?
- which of the five do you think, at face value, is most likely to persevere?
- who might be most upset by failure?

Could you assign one of the following particular objectives to each of the five tutors?
- to share the love of reading and good literature with someone who has not been able to appreciate it so far;
- to give a student the basic skills so that he can get about in life and not be so helpless
- to teach the student to read in a systematic way giving him every opportunity to improve his own skills
- to give help to someone who really needs it, who needs a second chance and the benefits of skilled help
- to help someone develop to their full potential.

Summary

The selection of adult literacy tutors depends on:
- factors of personality
- strength and quality of motivation
- relevant experience

Training programmes shared attempt to ensure that all tutors have:
- insight into the problems of the illiterate adult learner
- full knowledge of the organisation of adult literacy work in their own area
- knowledge of the techniques of teaching reading to adults and skill in their use.

Sources

JEFFRIES, SIR CHARLES *Illiteracy: a world problem* Pall Mall Press, 1967. p.13.

BURT, SIR CYRIL *The education of the illiterate adult, British Journal of educational Psychology* vol xv, I, February 1945. pp.20–27.

CLYNE, P. R. *The disadvantaged adult: educational and social needs of minority groups* Longman, cased and paperback 1973.

UNESCO *Report on the Evaluation of Functional Literacy Projects* University of London, 1969.

CENTRAL ADVISORY COUNCIL FOR EDUCATION (ENGLAND) *Half our future: a report* (Chairman, J. H. Newsom) HMSO, 1963.

UNESCO *Final report ED 217 World Conference of Ministers of Education on the Eradication of Illiteracy*, Paris 1965.

EDUCATION AND SCIENCE, DEPT. OF *Adult education: a plan for development* (Chairman, Sir Lionel Russell) HMSO, 1973. para. 279, p.78.

EDUCATION AND SCIENCE, DEPT. OF *A language for life* (Chairman, Sir Alan Bullock) HMSO, 1975, page 516.

KELLY, T. *History of adult education in Great Britain from the Middle Ages to the twentieth century* University of Liverpool, 1970. p.147.

ADULT EDUCATION COMMITTEE *Final report* HMSO, 1919. p.22.

WALL, W. D. *Reading backwardness among men in the army* in *British Journal of Educational Psychology* vol xv, I, February 1945. pp.28–40.

TRENAMEN, J. M. *Communication and comprehension* Longman, 1967. p.187.

PASCOE, T. W. *A register of facilities for adult non-readers within the United Kingdom* NARE, 1974.

Bibliography

CLYNE P. *The disadvantaged adult: educational and social needs of minority groups* Longman, cased and paperback, 1973.

HAVILAND R. M. *Provision for adult illiteracy in England* University of Reading, Centre for the Teaching of Reading, 1973.

REID J. F. *Reading: problems and practises: a selection of papers*, Ward Lock, cased and paperback, 1972.

ROGERS J. *Adults learning*, Penguin Books, 1971.

Teaching and learning

This section includes information, advice and suggestions on the first meeting, and approaches in teaching and learning methods, special problems, planning and evaluation, resources and information on the BBC Adult Literacy Project. The parts on teaching and learning, planning and evaluation and resources are written by Catherine Moorhouse, Central Director, ILEA Adult Literacy Schemes. The parts on first meeting and special problems are by Lee Pascal, a reading specialist. David Hargreaves wrote the final part on the BBC Adult Literacy Project.

1. The first meeting

❛At our first meeting I was terrified. I knew I had to create a relaxed situation but I didn't know what to say. We had a cup of coffee and started chatting. That worked all right until I found I didn't know how to bring the conversation round to what he'd come for. When he left I discovered I hadn't even made a date for our next meeting!❜
(A tutor)

❛When I got to the door I couldn't go further. I stood around for ever such a long time.❜
(A student)

❛I don't remember much about what we did first off. It weren't nearly as bad as I thought.❜
(A student)

Preparation for your first meeting should cover the personal and practical sides of the teaching situation. Your readiness in both these areas will instil a sense of confidence not only in your student, but in yourself as well. By using a structured, well thought out approach you will avoid tedium, wasted time and trauma.

Trepidation is a four-syllable word

Your student might reasonably be expected to feel apprehensive about your first meeting, but you too may feel anxious. This feeling in the tutor can cover the range from buoyant expectancy to stark terror. Naturally we all react differently to new experiences. However, if you keep a few points in mind, you can look forward to your first meeting with a sense of purpose, excitement and confidence. The image that you project and the skill you employ at the first meeting will influence what follows. Remember that you possess that magic skill. It is easy for you to undervalue the importance of your ability to read, write and spell. Think of all those occasions when *you* relied on a particular person's special skill and who generated tremendous confidence in you. A friend, who happened to be a weekend golfer, may have *taught* you the skills necessary to give you a handicap of 18. The scout troop leader may not have been a teacher but he possessed the magic skill of knowing how to tie a reef knot. You are someone who can turn squiggly lines called letters into meaningful patterns which communicate a world of information and ideas. You do possess the magic skill and it should give you some confidence for that first meeting.

Your confidence may also be heightened with practical preparation by considering the information you have been given about your student's specific difficulties. Whenever possible this information – tests or an interview record should be acquired before the first meeting as it will enable you to emphasise the positive elements and avoid tactless remarks and embarrassment. The student with a reading age of 15 and spelling age of 6 would no doubt resent being presented with a child's book and being asked to be careful with the difficult words! On the other hand, by asking a student to perform a task way beyond his capabilities you may shatter his confidence to such an extent that he will give up the idea of acquiring literacy skills as an impossible task.

What you always wanted to know about your student but were afraid to ask

You must try to glean as much information as possible from the literacy scheme you work with in so far as it applies to your teaching situation. You needn't concern yourself with your student's relationship with his budgerigar, but his relationship to his second form reading teacher may give you ideas about methods to adopt or avoid.

Why is your student having reading, writing or spelling difficulties? The reasons are varied and often give clues to indicate your approach. There are different reasons why Sean, Jackie, Murray and Michael failed to read, write or spell. Although you should bear in mind the shame and self recrimination your student may feel, a sense of justification can be an essential release of tension, worry and frustration for him.

The shame and cover-up ploys play an important part in Sean's attitude towards his illiteracy. There seem to be external factors to call upon as justification for his difficulties. The fact that through economic reasons he missed much of his schooling could provide you with the obvious, 'How can you be expected to know what you haven't been taught?' It is up to you whether you pose the question or not, but it is very important to let the implications of the question govern the approach and atmosphere of the first session.

Murray presents a complicated jigsaw of factors. He hated school and he hated reading and not being any good at it, but we have very little in the way of tangible reasons to account for his failure. Reading between the lines you might deduce that parental and school pressure may have influenced his lack of reading progress. If, in further conversation with Murray, your supposition is confirmed, you have a pretty good idea of what tack to take in your first meeting.

You might think that by lessening demands and lowering pressure the problem is on its way to being solved. However, wouldn't it be even more helpful for you to let someone like Murray establish his *own* demands? Perhaps for the first time in his life he will be in a position to dictate his requirements rather than having them thrown at him. What a relief for him to be able to say 'I would like' rather than 'What do you want from me?' Here, perhaps, the main theme of the lesson should be 'What can I do for you?'

What is the reading/spelling level of the student?
Often the information provided by a literacy scheme on this aspect simply gives the tutor a reading age and a spelling age. This, of course, is useful as a gross indication of standards, but it gives no direction in terms of specific difficulties. After a few lessons these specifics will become apparent, but it is helpful in terms of planning the first lesson, to get some idea about a student's difficulties. Keep in mind that question 'What can I do for you?' Ask your student what he finds particularly difficult. Responses can vary from 'everything' to 'oh, complicated things like words with ie and ei'. They may also give you an idea of any misconceptions that your student may have about language and may indicate methods to clear these up.

In so far as a specific reading assessment is concerned, choice of material can be considered wide open in terms of books, magazines, brochures, etc. However, considering the confidence factor, and given the reading age, it might well be beneficial to offer your student something to read that is at least a year below his reading age. You might prepare some reading material yourself. For Murray, for example, you might prepare something like:

The cop stopped me as I rode my bike on the street.

Being able to read at ease and in a relaxed fashion at the first meeting can do wonders in establishing the atmosphere for the course.

What would you prepare for Sean, Jackie or Michael?

Coffee, tea or . . .

You'll have noticed that the first indications of specific difficulties came from your questions 'What can I do for you?' and 'What do you find particularly difficult?' The use of direct, relevant questions is valid so long as the questioning is done in a relaxed and uninhibiting manner. Keep in mind that your nervousness at the first meeting may be minimal compared to your student's anxiety over this new situation. The associations he makes between illiteracy and general inadequacy, his initial fear and dislike of former learning situations and the challenge of a possibly demanding situation will, in all probability, cause your student to approach the first meeting with tremendous apprehension. How can you alleviate these fears and instil a sense of enthusiastic expectation in your student?

The association between illiteracy and general inadequacy.
Citing great historical figures who had reading and spelling difficulties – Da Vinci, Einstein, Hans Christian Andersen, Woodrow Wilson and contemporary personalities – Dr. Jonas Salk, Susan Hampshire, may offer some encouragement to your student. However, it may make far more of an impact if you can contrast his difficulty with his achievements. Getting your student to recognise that not only surviving, but succeeding in a literate society is a major accomplishment, you will start to dispel assumptions which mistakenly associate illiteracy with lack of intelligence. Dwell on your student's skills. In the profiles Jackie's driving, Sean's carpentry, and Michael's business acumen are considerable achievements for a non-reader in a literate society.

Murray's apparent lack of success can present difficulties in this disassociation exercise. The profile gives no indication of specific skills or talents, and the only interests revealed are pop music and football. You can highlight Murray's knowledge in this area. He may well find it incredible that you do not know the difference between hard rock and soul music! On the other hand, drawing out Murray's other interests will be beneficial not only in providing you with further disassociation factors, but in giving you material for the teaching situation as well.

The fear and dislike of former learning situations start to dissolve from the moment you begin to eastablish your relationship with your student. The traditional teacher-pupil : dominant-submissive relationship should give way to a sharing situation. The question 'What can I do for you?' is important here. Your student and you must feel that your situation is similar to that of a householder calling in a plumber. The plumber is called in to satisfy certain specific demands of the householder, perhaps fixing a dripping tap. The householder relies on the skill and knowledge of the plumber and yet it is the householder who establishes the demands. The plumber may indicate that the cistern needs a new washer as well and yet it is up to the householder to accept or reject the plumber's further service. So it is with you and your student. He establishes the demand – 'Help me to read and spell' and relies on your skill to assist him. He is in control of his expectations and when he feels he has gone far enough he has the right to withdraw. You may suggest extensions of these demands, but the student remains the decision-maker.

A relaxed setting will help dispel the memory of former, unhappy learning situations. In the one-to-one situation the use of lamps and tables can do a great deal to counteract the memory of glaring overhead lights and uncomfortable, unattractive desks. A cup of coffee and a cigarette is definitely not something that your student will connect with his fifth form English class! Casual clothes, first names and initial small talk can all contribute to the sharing situation. It is up to you which of these hints you will adopt or reject. Remember, in a sharing situation, the comfort must be mutual.

The challenge of a demanding situation.
In many ways we have already dealt with this problem. By establishing that *he* is going to state the demands and that *you* are going to help provide solutions, the student is no longer in a stressful situation. Work in which you and your student discover language patterns, rules and exceptions will be work that is shared. In this way a great deal of security can be built up from the beginning. The knowledge that you are going to be working with him and exerting as great an effort as he will be, is also a tremendous boost. A student may feel that the burden of learning rests solely on his shoulders. If you establish a supportive relationship the student can share that burden.

Today cat . . . tomorrow catachresis

'Learn a foreign language in six weeks' is a familiar advertisement. A total immersion course may enable you to get by in French or Dutch in six weeks but you will still sound like an Englishman. By the same token, a student may be able to get by after six weeks of concentrated literacy teaching, yet he will not feel native in a literate society. Your student's expectations should be realistic right from the onset or he will be shocked and depressed when, after six weeks, he realises that he still cannot master the *Radio Times*. All too often a student will start a course with the idea that as just about everyone can read, write and spell, it must be a fairly simple skill to acquire and the course shouldn't take more than a few weeks.

A great deal of tact is necessary in order to emphasise the length of time such a course may take without dampening your student's enthusiasm. Certainly, by making the lessons stimulating and exciting, you will lessen the desire to hasten their conclusion. However, preparation for a long term learning situation is essential from the start. Using the analogy of foreign language teaching could help. But you could also discuss the whole question of time in a much more direct and relevant fashion. Explain the complexities of the code that is called the alphabet and mention some of the different processes that are used when anyone reads or writes. Those are some of the skills he needs to master – that, if you like, is the bad news. The good news is the prospect that through working together, reading writing and spelling will, in time, become second nature to your student.

So far we have stressed the sharing aspect of the learning situation. This is all well and good so far as your student is concerned. He knows what he wants to get out of it, and he knows why he is involved.

You must be prepared to provide reasons for *your* willingness to share this experience as well. The motives of the 'do-gooder' are sometimes suspect. The questions 'Why are you teaching me?' and 'What's in it for you?' may not be stated, but their implications can be damaging. It may well be necessary to offer your reasons for teaching in order to clear the air and establish a comfortable working situation. These reasons can vary from having an interest in language and structure, to needing an evening a week away from the television to keep you alert and active. The last thing some students will want is another social worker. Their demands are specific and your involvement must be justified in specific terms.

Why do *you* want to help a student to read?

Something to take away

'Nothing succeeds like success' and that is never more true than for people whose experience of education is an experience of failure. It is important to offer success to your student right from the start. So far, in the first meeting, we have dealt with establishing the relationship and coping with fears, feelings and expectations. What about handling some practical, technical aspects as well? You can, at this meeting, tackle three practical points:

- find out what your students can cope with;
- find out what your student cannot cope with;
- give your student some success to take away.

As with any practical work at the first meeting, you must tread carefully and always justify the work through emphasising its importance in terms of future planning. It may seem a bit daunting to provide your student with a sense of success right from the start, but you can turn the learning of the word 'at' into a major achievement. Keep in mind the complexities of our language – learning the word 'at' involves blending two symbols of a code together in the correct order, saying them and understanding the meaning of the blended result. The implication of this achievement can cause genuine excitement and pride in your student.

Take no notice of the python . . .

Lamps, a table and chairs, coffee and cigarettes, or biscuits can combat the memories of former learning situations. Now let's look at the room as a comfortable work setting. A lamp on the table provides the dual function of making things easier to see as well as establishing a definite working area. This working area becomes important as you develop your relationship with your student especially when the temptation to discuss the state of the Liberal party or last night's football match arises. The atmosphere connected with the table should be concerned with reading, writing and spelling. A half-time coffee break in another area of the room can provide a time and place for social chat. Peripheral lighting should be subdued and noise and distractions should be kept (in so far as possible) to a minimum. Your work area offers the structure and security of a very special learning space.

Generally, a literacy scheme tries to arrange meeting places convenient to both tutor and student and usually one or the other provides a room in his home for the meetings. However, due to various circumstances, it may be necessary to meet in 'neutral' territory. The quiet back room of a pub, an office in a library or town hall and a room in a school are all examples of such meeting places. The hints and suggestions previously offered can, with some effort, all be adapted to these external settings.

I'll just sit here quietly and knit

So far we have attempted to define your role and that of your student. What about external influences which can assist or undermine the lesson situation? Often a student is prompted to take on a course in literacy by a relative, friend, boss or social worker. This third party must be recognised, assessed and directed right from the first meeting. Again, the overriding influence of the roles of such people must relate to the demands of your student. If he wishes his wife to help him with his homework then, by all means, include her in the work. If, on the other hand, your student wishes the sharing arrangement to exclude a third party, then you must, with tact, ensure that the learning atmosphere is private and exclusive.

A third party can play a useful role on both the practical and morale boosting levels of literacy learning. The basic philosophy of satisfying student's demands should be made clear and the help which the third party can provide should be outlined in specific terms. By keeping to these guidelines you will avoid the hazard of having the third party dictate demands or take over the work from your student.

Can you hear me at the back?

Much of this section seems to have been related to the one to one situation. However, by keeping our objectives and approach in mind, even specific points can be adapted to a group arrangement.

A group working at an adult education centre (posed by students enrolled on a variety of courses at Holloway Adult Education Institute).

There are, of course, special difficulties in a group situation, for example, in a group, one would not expect everyone to share a simple enthusiasm in, say, football, pop music or underwater archaeology, and allowances will have to be made for a diversity in interests, deficiencies and abilities. But without much difficulty you should be able to elect a theme for discussion and free writing which will stimulate and excite the group in a less personal, but perhaps more controversial fashion.

The streaming of a group can be based on specific needs rather than on the gross assessment derived from reading and spelling ages. There may be a temptation to arrange streams according to ethnic origins of the group, age ranges, outside interests or general personality traits (i.e. outgoing people set apart from the shy ones). But keep in mind that your main role is that of technician. It may be more convenient to arrange your groups on the basis of technical abilities and deficiencies. A streamed group may, for example, have difficulty with blending sounds together, or coping with a sight vocabulary. The advantages of this type of streaming are two-fold:

- the members of the group will require much the same general teaching material;
- they will all feel more or less in the same boat, so that the sharing situation can lend itself to mutual assistance.

Perhaps the main hazard to avoid in the group situation is the turning of the sharing situation from 'us' to 'you and them'. You may prefer not to stream or group your students. Some may feel demoralised when they realise they have been assigned to the 'bottom' group. There are advantages in having mixed groupings:

- students who have mastered a particular skill can help others;
- students can see what interesting work particular skills can lead on to.

Once your grouping or streaming has been provisionally organised you are ready for your first evening. Remember that question 'What can I do for you?' This applies as much to the group situation as it does to one to one. Students may naturally fear exposure in confessing their disabilities publicly, but there will usually be at least one who will be prepared to start talking about what he wants to learn.

So I got off at Scunthorpe instead

The fear of exposing his literacy difficulties is often diminished in a student when he realises, perhaps for the first time, that other intelligent, normal people suffer from the same disadvantage. Being surrounded by these people in a group can ease anxiety and lift a tremendous weight off the person who thought that he was an isolated character and in some way incomplete. For others, it can be a harrowing experience to reveal their reading and spelling problems, even in front of a group of similarly affected people. Here perhaps, you can borrow an idea from the Alcoholics Anonymous meetings in order to bring the problem out in the open and negate the shame and distress that the difficulty may arouse. Picking a student out from the group and saying 'How does it feel to be illiterate' is not exactly the most tactful approach, but you can get a discussion going which will reveal causes of illiteracy and social ploys, thus getting your students to share their experiences. You might start off with some of those stories about how some people get by – by tying a handkerchief around their fingers and feigning a hand injury to avoid having to write out a form or cheque. The familiar 'I've left my glasses at home' ploy may well spark off a group into a discussion of similar useful tricks used to avoid getting caught out. Former embarrassments (getting off the train at the wrong station) become shared experiences and the atmosphere lightens and develops into a situation where the group can relax.

A few simple games can also ease the tension but do make sure that the demands of the exercises are well below the lowest standard of literacy in the class. Thus, when working with a group of students totally unfamiliar with the alphabet or basic sight words, you can start off with an oral word association game, such as tennis–elbow–knee (going round the group in turn) making sure that each student

feels some measure of success in the exercise. A simple blackboard game where students call out the missing letters in words can also reduce tension. Divide the class in two and each team in turn tries to fill in the missing letters. Your students will begin gradually to feel less isolated in this sharing situation.

May I help you?

Students in a group need personal, individualised attention. If, as a tutor, you have the offer of extra help, do take it. Often tutors feel that what goes on within the four walls of their classrooms is a private affair between them and their students. Volunteers can provide an invaluable function in a group, not only as technical assistants, but as supportive elements as well. The cry 'I'm stuck' can be answered by a visit from a person who again possesses the magic of literacy and may be able to provide some alternative insight into a problem. Getting together with extra helpers well before the first meeting will enable you to iron out any conflicts of teaching philosophy and method and prepare the first meeting with positive assurance. At the first session their presence should be somewhat subdued as you do not want to inhibit the discussion of the students. They should be introduced, and their roles as assistants to the group explained. The volunteers can expand their functions as the class progresses, and provide valuable assistance in the area of reinforcement.

Welcome to the group

About seven of them had attended a class last year and they were real matey with the teacher. I felt a real fool. I didn't know what they were all going on about. (A student)

The problem of staggered enrolment and late entrants must be handled with diplomacy and understanding. Remember, dropping in on a group of people already involved and comfortable with each other can be a daunting experience. How can you make a newcomer feel at home and at ease when he joins a going concern? Singling him out at his first session with a boisterous 'Oh, you must be Mr Jones. Welcome to the group' is an impulse which might well be suppressed. The new student will, in all probability, want to slip in as quietly as possible and blend in with the other students. Having a few moments chat with him before the lesson and during the coffee break will enable you to put him at ease. Let him know about the work you are covering and give him special help in his first session and in the ones that follow. Once he feels secure in what is happening he will be able to enjoy his involvement with assurance and comfort.

Notes and a nightcap

With the first meeting over you now have the foundation needed for the preparation of the first lesson and indeed for much of what follows. Look back over it and examine closely what happened.

The fears, feelings and expectations of your student will, to some degree, have been exposed and these must be taken into account in order for you to provide specific morale boosting, confidence lifting and skill building exercises. Your student has revealed particular reading and spelling difficulties and you can now plan your first lesson based on one or two of these points.

A check list, covering your presentation, impact and success might well be in order, keeping in mind the questions posed at the beginning of this section, and adding a few more.

Which activities worked? Why did they work? How can you follow them up? Did the student ever lose interest? Why? How can you avoid that situation next lesson? What materials will you need next time? Was the lesson exciting? Was the student at ease? Were you relaxed? Did you all share in some success? By answering this series of questions you will be able to plan ahead in a confident and structured manner.

2. Methods and approaches

Teaching an illiterate

In this first section I want to explore some of the ways you might begin a teaching/learning programme with an illiterate student – a student like Sean O'Reilly. If Sean was your student you would obviously need to take into account all the information you have so far been given about him.

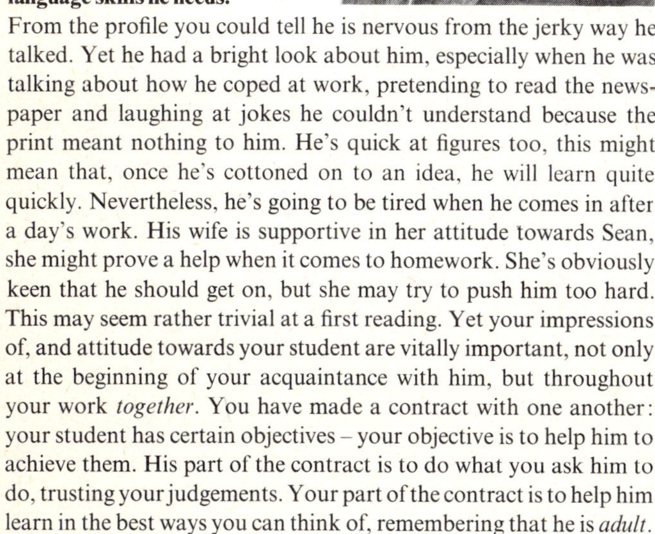

Look at the profile of Sean O'Reilly (on page 4) and note down all the points which you would consider relevant to the task of teaching Sean the language skills he needs.

From the profile you could tell he is nervous from the jerky way he talked. Yet he had a bright look about him, especially when he was talking about how he coped at work, pretending to read the newspaper and laughing at jokes he couldn't understand because the print meant nothing to him. He's quick at figures too, this might mean that, once he's cottoned on to an idea, he will learn quite quickly. Nevertheless, he's going to be tired when he comes in after a day's work. His wife is supportive in her attitude towards Sean, she might prove a help when it comes to homework. She's obviously keen that he should get on, but she may try to push him too hard. This may seem rather trivial at a first reading. Yet your impressions of, and attitude towards your student are vitally important, not only at the beginning of your acquaintance with him, but throughout your work *together*. You have made a contract with one another: your student has certain objectives – your objective is to help him to achieve them. His part of the contract is to do what you ask him to do, trusting your judgements. Your part of the contract is to help him learn in the best ways you can think of, remembering that he is *adult*.

It's tempting to base most of our ideas about learning and teaching basic skills like reading and writing on what we know about children, because it's during childhood that these skills are usually acquired. But, an adult learner, because he or she is adult, is very different from a child. He may need to experience the same learning *processes* to achieve the final skill, but the *presentation* will need to be different, otherwise the feelings of inadequacy and failure will only be confirmed. This is so important that it's worth considering the differences between children and adults as learners in more detail.

Adults as learners

The main difference between the child and the adult as learners is of great advantage to you as a tutor. *Adult learners are voluntary learners.* Unlike children in school, they are not a captive audience. Your student is coming because he really wishes to learn – and the wish must be strong if he's prepared to do so after a day's work. There are other qualities of adults as learners which are a positive asset to you as a tutor:

- your student has definite *aims* in coming;
- he has more *experience* of living and realises that he needs the *practical* skills of literacy;
- he is approaching a *realistic* solution to his problem.

As a result of his previous experiences of failure, he may be more impatient about learning and want to progress faster than he is really able to, but, *because he is adult* you will be able to discuss his feelings with him and explain the kinds of learning he needs to do, giving reasons as to why you want him to practise certain things in a certain way.

Many books have been written suggesting and discussing ways in which people learn and how we should teach to ensure that learning takes place. Basic learning is dependent on memory, so what we need to do is to make sure that our students *remember* the activities we do together. In the case of reading and writing, we have to remember and be able to *recall* the shapes and sounds of letters and words and to *reproduce* them either by pronunciation, or in writing. There are a few simple rules or laws about learning and remembering which it is useful to bear in mind when planning to teach something.

- *The law of experience* – doing something makes it likely that we will remember it. This means that it is important that you ensure that Sean, and any student, learns the *right* things in the *right* way at every step. First impressions are the most lasting.
- *The law of frequency* – the more often we do something, the more likely we are to remember it. This means that we should give our students frequent opportunities to *practise* the skills we are teaching them, so that there is no danger of them being only half-learned and therefore subsequently forgotten.
- *The law of recency* – the more recently we have done something, the more likely we are to be able to recall it. This links up with the law of frequency, and again means that plenty of opportunities for practice should be given, especially when something new is being taught. The time spent practising a particular aspect of learning can gradually decrease as your student's grasp of it becomes automatic, but it is a good idea to check periodically that nothing has been forgotten, e.g. at first, each lesson; later, once a fortnight; later still, once a month, and so on.
- *The law of enjoyment* – although placed last in this list, it is maybe the most important factor to consider. We all take pleasure in recalling experiences we've enjoyed, whereas we prefer not to think about unpleasant incidents. As you get to know your student you will discover the kind of activity he most enjoys and you can organise your teaching materials and lesson plans round these. For example, Sean is interested in boxing, so you can look for, and encourage him to help you, make reading materials based on this subject. He is 'fascinated' by writing, so you can use this enthusiasm in teaching him both a good hand and for helping him to learn spellings. If he really disliked writing, but enjoyed working with a tape recorder, you could make sure that you provided plenty of activities involving listening and recording, perhaps persuading him to write down what he has recorded.

The adult acquiring basic literacy skills

You need to think more deeply about how we learn in the case of adults who have had a problem in acquiring a set of skills normally associated with the teaching of children. Sean probably doubts whether he *can* learn; everything in his experience so far would seem to indicate to him that he cannot. Your first job really is to *prove to him that he can learn and remember*; he knows *what* he wants to learn and *why*, but he does not know *how* until you show him. Since, in learning to read and write, he will have to go through many of the processes and practices by which children learn and he might find this humiliating, it is important that you make it clear to him as an adult why you are asking him to do certain things.

Can you play draughts or chess? Can you change a plug, or perform some other practical skill? How would you teach someone else to do one of these activities? Write down what you would do to teach someone how to do one of these things.

You may have written something like this for fitting a plug:
1. unscrew the plug, show and explain the different parts;
2. connect the wires, explaining the connexions as you make them;
3. ask the other person to do it while you watch.
Teaching in this way what you are doing is bringing in *all* the different ways in which people learn – seeing, hearing, talking and doing, and exploiting them.

> '*I hear and I forget,*
> *I see and I remember,*
> *I do and I understand.* ' (Old Chinese saying)

You will enjoy playing draughts or chess when you understand the moves, and you will learn to understand them by making the moves. Sean, and students like him, have to realise that the same principles need to operate in learning to read and write, and that is why you may ask him to repeat tasks several times. The more often we try to play draughts, the more skilful we are likely to become as we practise the various strategies needed to win a game. Footballers or boxers practise for the same reason.

One of the delights of teaching an adult is that, by definition, he has had a lot of experience of living and has already acquired the basic language structures for reasoned thought. You can explain the learning process to him more easily than to a child, relying on his intellectual understanding to make it more acceptable.

Getting down to the job

Having thought about the basic principles of the *approach* we are going to use with a student like Sean, we now need to consider the *content* of what we are going to teach him in terms of his most immediate needs. What are these needs?

Look at Sean's case-study more closely and list what you feel his major needs would be, and compare them with what follows.

Sean's needs:
- he needs *success* – he's failed up to now. He's always afraid of being found out in his failure and he's undoubtedly afraid that he's going to fail with you.
- he 'could neither read nor write his own name or address'. Apart from the humiliation he must feel, how vulnerable he is! How does he know that his firm have his details correctly recorded. What happens if the postman delivers a registered letter and his wife is not there to sign for it?
- he knows the upper case letters of the alphabet, but not the lower case letters, and does not understand the difference between letters and words. Most printed language is therefore a complete mystery to him. This means that you should be careful not to use labels for different aspects of language, e.g. word, noun, verb, etc. without ensuring that Sean understands their meaning; otherwise you will further confuse him and undermine what little confidence he has.
- he cannot read the common signs he sees about him, such as 'LADIES' and 'GENTS'. These words are often included in a social sight vocabulary. These are the words we need to be able to read and understand in order to move around *confidently* and *competently*. You should teach these words to a student like Sean as soon as possible.
- Sean is fascinated by writing, so much of his learning may take place through this medium as he is more likely to remember activities he enjoys.
- his general knowledge, even about the city in which he lives, is limited. Therefore, you will be able to use reading materials connected with his environment – maps, street guides, simple reference books, etc.

A basic sight vocabulary of 220 words by E. W. Dolch
This list of words makes up from 50% to 75% of all ordinary reading matter. The words are arranged in order of difficulty. (This is a check list and should not be given to pupils.)

a	look	that	under	with	upon	fall	every
I	can	going	before	there*	give*	think	which
too	good	did	walk	about	once*	far	our
to	brown	who*	stop	after	together	found	want
two*	six	like	out	what	us	read	thank
the	be	come*	his	ask	tell	were*	better
in	today	had	make	sing	ate*	best	clean*
see	not	saw	your*	must	where	because*	been
into	little	no	ride	five	many*	grow	never
and	one*	long	help	myself	warm*	fast	those
up	black	yes	call	over	laugh*	off	write
blue*	my	an	here	cut	live*	draw	first
she	at	three	sleep	let	now	bring	these
yellow	all	this	cold	again	came	got	both*
he	so	around	will	new	buy*	always	shall
go	by	was*	pretty	well	very	much	own
you*	do	just	them	have*	hold	does*	hurt
we	are*	ten	when	how	would*	show	eight*
big	him	get	round	keep	hot	any*	wash
red	her	if	if	white	drink	try	full
jump	on	soon	funny	sit	light	kind	use
it	green	its	put*	made	their*	wish	done*
play	eat*	some*	take	went	pull*	carry	start
down	four*	from	of*	has	may	know	
for	said*	fly	say	seven	goes	only	
old	away	then	or	right	small	pick	
is	run	but	ran	why	find	don't*	
me	they*	as	work	please*	could*	gave	

*Denotes an awkward word for reading, i.e. those which students find most difficulty with since they cannot be worked out using the usual rules or generalisations. Words presenting particular difficulty are likely to vary with regional accents, e.g. words like *ask* may be difficult for those with a 'southern' accent but easier for those with 'northern' accent when it is pronounced with a short (a) sound.

- Sean would like to be able to read to his children. He might therefore find children's books acceptable reading material.
- he has a stated long term objective: 'to be able to read and understand a popular daily newspaper.'

Planning the content of Sean's lessons

Now that you know what Sean's most immediate needs are, and can see these in relation to his long term objective, you can begin to plan your lesson content. You cannot separate *what* you are going to teach from *how* you are going to teach it. You know that language learning takes place through the use of the eyes, the ears, the voice and the writing hand, and that it is a good idea to use these simultaneously. You know that he likes writing, so that won't be a problem. You know that he is almost totally illiterate, so you can start from the beginning. You know that he is Irish and has a heavy Irish accent despite having lived in England for eleven years. This is an important piece of information: it means that Sean is going to give some letters sound values which differ from those to which you are probably accustomed, e.g. Th will sound like t, consequently *three* will sound like *tree* and even if he is repeating such words given a conventional pronunciation by you, he will say them in his own fashion. Since his speech is the one area of language use in which he has any competence at all, it would be unwise to undermine it. You, the tutor, have to make the adjustment. Ideally, Sean's oral use of language will reinforce his learning of reading and spelling, so it is *his* conventions that must be used as the constant in your approach to him. And, since his sound discrimination habits differ from yours, it may be wise to emphasise the *visual* aspects of the material you present to him as there is no evidence that he sees letter shapes differently from you; they simply have no meaning for him so far.

There is more about problems in aural discrimination on page 27.
This is some of the early vocabulary you will need to use in teaching your student to read and write. Check that he understands each term.

Reading: letter, name of letter, speech sound of letter, small letter, capital letter, word, sentence, rhyme, vowel, consonant and full stop.
Writing of letters: left, right, up, down, first and last.

Sean's early lessons

At the end of his first hour of learning, Sean should be able to read something which at the beginning he could not. Using the information you have about Sean, you can try one of a number of choices.

The language experience approach in which you use Sean's own conversation as a starting point:

● ask him something about himself: his work, his interest in boxing, whatever comes to mind. You might elicit the following kind of response:

'I get up at seven o'clock.
Susan gets my breakfast.
If it's fine I go to work on the bike . . .' or

'Cassius Clay's the boy.
Cooper never matched up to him.'

● write down two or three sentences from what he says in clear, fairly large capitals with plenty of space between the words and sentences. (Perhaps Sean's earliest work might be done using capitals because he is familiar with them and might be encouraged by having his previous learning acknowledged. Ordinarily, one would use either lower case print or round writing – you will find more about this on page 29).
● tell him that you are going to read the first *sentence*, indicating it with your finger (remember, he does not know what a sentence is until you show him), and that you are going to point to each *word* with your finger. Read slowly, pointing to each word *so he can see it as a whole unit*, and so that he can follow your left to right movement with his eyes.
● ask him to read the sentence to you and point to each word as he reads. Encourage him to repeat reading the sentence until he does so fluently and at a reasonable speed.
● repeat this pattern for each of the three sentences until finally Sean can read them one after the other without hesitation.
● next write each sentence out again on separate strips of paper and ask him to match the separate strips with the original. (This could be done in the second session after you have asked him to practise reading the sentences in the intervening period.)
● give them to him out of order and without the original for reference and ask him to put them into the correct sequence and to read them.
● do similar exercises by cutting one sentence at a time into individual words and ask him first to match them to the original, then to read them.
● you can show these isolated words to Sean one at a time to see whether he can read them out of context. Remember to explain to him that what you are doing is trying to give him a concept of what a word is. This can become a game. Sean keeps the words he reads correctly and you keep the others and practise them with him until he knows them.

Alternative approach 1.
This approach has been successfully used by Mrs. Joan Kerridge of Bexley Tutorial Units for several years:

● have plenty of pictorial material around – magazines, colour supplements, do-it-yourself magazines etc. You will also need a plain scrap-type book or folder, scissors, felt-tip pen and glue;

● ask your student to choose a picture which he likes or which interests him in some way and to cut it out and paste it in his book;
● encourage him to talk about the picture and label the nouns for him (in the case of Sean, use capitals). Suggest he copies what you have written (begin on a double spread page so that the illustration is on one side and his writing on the other).
● write down a couple of the sentences he says about the picture. Read them to him and have him read them as described earlier.
● write the words separately on cards or slips of paper and make sure he can read them in isolation.
● do the matching exercises previously described. You can keep these words for future use, and others as you introduce them, in an envelope stuck into the back cover of Sean's book.

Alternative approach 2.
We know that Sean has had embarrassing experiences through not being able to read social sight words like 'LADIES' and 'GENTS'. Choose a few words that he is likely to see often and print these on cards, capitals on one side, lower case on the other. Teach these words using the methods already described.

● let him practise reading them, arranging them differently;
● write each word at least three times on separate pieces of paper or card. Now suggest that he tries to arrange them in different ways. You can show him what you mean. Of course there is no need to use all the cards at once.

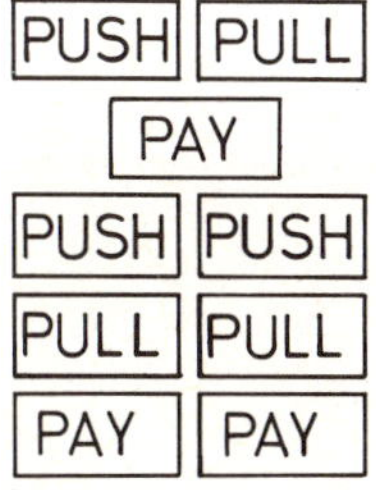

● Sean can have further reading practice with these words and you can talk about the different effects which can be achieved by changing the word order.

Alternative approach 3.
You know that Sean would really like to be able to read to his children, instead of having to pretend to read to them and consequently suffering their corrections. You could suggest in your first meeting that he brings one of his children's books along and teach him to read part of that, using some of the procedures described above. A book of short, simple poems might be ideal; you can work on one with him and he can present it to his children complete, thus having an opportunity to put his skill to immediate use, and to display his progress to his wife in an adult way, by reading to his children.

Alternative approach 4 – a survival kit for your student.
Start working on a survival kit with and for your student. Sean can't read or write his name and address. Teach him to do so using some of the following procedures.

● write down the words 'name and address' and teach your student to read these.
● on a strip of paper write: Name: Sean O'Reilly/SEAN O'REILLY Teach him that when he sees *name* he writes his name as you have written it. Teach him to read first his christian name, then his surname. Ask him to copy them.
● do the same with his address, treating it line by line.
● then compose a form like this – a postcard would do:

NAME:

ADDRESS:

and ask him to complete it, using the copy he has already made.
● chop his name up so that each part is on a separate piece of paper. Ask him to place them in the correct order, to read it and copy it.
● it may take him some time to spell each of his names, especially if they contain more than a few letters. Write each in large writing and encourage him to trace them with his finger.
● for homework, ask him to continue to practise writing his name from the copy and suggest that, when he feels he can do it, he turns the copy over and tries to write it from memory. Then he should compare what he has written with the copy.
● treat his address in a similar fashion until he can write both his name and address without hesitation. Then he can practise writing it on envelopes, etc.
● as some forms specify block capitals it may be best to encourage Sean to use these for form filling all the time at this stage. Later on, you can introduce him to different ways of recording this information and teach him to look out for the instruction 'block capitals please' and what it means, i.e. by the ordinary print style A, B, C etc.
● your student will need practice in basic form filling procedures throughout his time with you, gradually learning to recognise a request for, and to record, more information, e.g. birth date, nationality, age in years and months, age next birthday, etc. Collect samples of different kinds of forms, the Post Office is a useful source, and also mail order advertisements in newspapers. Grade these according to level of difficulty and practise each with him when you think he is ready to cope with them. You can build up a file of examples which he can keep for reference.

At an early stage your student might enjoy writing greetings cards to his family and friends – it is an important means of social contact and of expressing feelings of affection of which he has hitherto been deprived. These ideas can be extended to other areas of formal language – writing letters of application, enquiry, invitations, postcards, etc.

When to move on

How long will each stage take? This is at once the most natural question to ask and the most impossible to answer. All that can be said is: don't hurry your student. When you feel he is ready to move on and has thoroughly grasped what you have taught him so far, so that you can build upon his knowledge, then move on. This question becomes harder to answer as time goes on. People tend to learn in spurts with an interval of time between each area of progress. Time is needed to consolidate learning, and to mentally organise new learning in relation to previous learning. Rates of learning vary among people and you will learn to assess your student's capacities as you get to know him better.

The next steps

As soon as Sean has enjoyed some successful experience of reading you can start a more systematic approach in your teaching but, still as far as possible using the materials with which he is already familiar. To date, you have been using what is often called a *Look and Say* approach towards teaching reading, presenting words as *whole* units. It is an approach you will continue to use, in conjunction with other approaches when possible, but it is particularly valuable in the early stages of teaching reading to adults because it:

● allows for quick success;
● presents the most common words occurring in written language, many of which do not conform to any general pattern and so cannot be taught by a logical approach.

However, it would be uneconomical to rely exclusively on this approach for teaching adults. It involves the teaching of each word as a separate unit and it would take a long time to teach the thousand words of which 90 per cent of written language is made up. Many people do learn to read by this approach. However, they usually unconsciously begin to make generalisations about the speech sounds and sequences of letters, which they apply to unlock the pronunciation of any unfamiliar words they meet, e.g. c is usually pronounced (k) before a, o and u and any consonant (cat, cod, cup, cram, clip); and (s) before e, i, and y (cell, city, cycle). The problem for the non-literate adult is that this is often just what he has not managed to do, so we have to teach him that these relationships between speech sounds and sequences of letters do exist. The approach which emphasises such relationships is usually called *phonics*.

Teaching phonics can be compared with building a wall: you lay the basic foundations very carefully and then build upon the structures. The basic foundations in the case of a student like Sean are the shapes and most common sounds of the letters of the alphabet.

Some of the most common vowel letter sounds in English

Letter	Sound	Example		Sound	Example
a	(ă)	apple	u	(ŭ)	umbrella
	(ā)	apron		(yü)	united
	(ȯ)	ball		(ü)	ruby
	(ä)	father		(u̇)	push
e	(ĕ)	elephant		(ĭ)	gym
	(ē)	equal		(ī)	fly
i	(ĭ)	ink		(ē)	penny
	(ī)	five	a-e	(a)	cake
			e-e	(ē)	cede, athlete
o	(ŏ)	orange	i-e	(ī)	five
	(ō)	opener	o-e	(ō)	rope
	(ŭ)	mother	y-e	(ī)	type

Vowel diagraphs

Letter	Sound	Example		Sound	Example
ai	(ā)	sail	oy	(oi)	boy
ay	(ā)	tray	oo	(ü)	moon
au	(ȯ)	August		(u̇)	book
aw	(ȯ)	saw	ou	(âu̇)	out
ea	(ē)	meat		(ü)	soup
	(ĕ)	bread	ow	(au̇)	cow
	(ā)	steak		(ō)	snow
ee	(ē)	three, feet	ue	(yü)	statue
ei	(ē)	ceiling		(ü)	true
	(ā)	vein	ar	(är)	star
ey	(ē)	key		(ēr)	dollar
	(ā)	they	er	(êr)	her
ew	(ü)	grew		(ĕ)	letter
ew	(yü)	few	ir	(êr)	bird
ie	(ī)	pie	or	(êr)	world
oa	(ō)	boat		(ēr)	doctor
oe	(ō)	toe	ur	(êr)	Thursday
oi	(ȯi)	boil		(ēr)	Arthur

Other sounds

Letter	Sound	Example		Sound	Example
c	(k)	cat		(sh)	chef
	(s)	city			(French words)
		(before e, i, y, usually)	ed	(ĕd)	folded
				(d)	sailed
g	(g)	goat		(t)	jumped
	(j)	giraffe	igh	(ī)	light
		(before e, i, y usually)	eigh	(ā)	eight
			qu	(kw)	queen
ch	(ch)	chair		(k)	quay
	(k)	chord (Greek words)			

Early phonic work

We know that Sean has been taught to recognise the upper case alphabet, so that he knows the names of the letters, although he may no know the sequence in which they occur in the alphabet. He has acquired some information that will be very useful: the names of the individual letters are their only stable feature.

Their visual form can change:

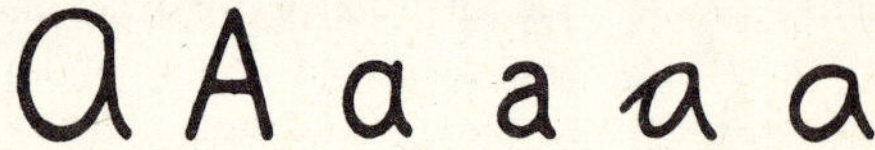

Their sound can vary: e.g.

cat   mi<u>c</u>e

apple   (ă)   Vowel <u>a</u> in fact has over

w<u>a</u>tch   (ŏ)   40 different sounds.

b<u>a</u>ll   (or)

st<u>a</u>r   (ar)

doll<u>a</u>r   (er)

b<u>a</u>n<u>a</u>n<u>a</u> (uh, ar, uh)

Their position varies in words, as in the examples above, and the words in which they occur can vary in *visual* presentation.

<pre>
              S
            T A
STAR   star T S   R
            A
            R
</pre>

Only the name of the individual letters remains unchanged. The pronunciation of the sounds is constant regardless of format. There are three aspects to learn about each letter then: the shape, both upper and lower case; the sound(s): the name.

N.B. In this book, the *sound* of a letter is shown in brackets e.g. (b) and the *name* of a letter is shown with a line e.g. <u>b</u>. You would not need to use these with students.

If you do not know which letters Sean understands by name, you can find out by asking him to read both the upper and lower case alphabets, first in sequence and then in random order.

There are various ways in which you can help your student to learn the features of each letter. It is useful to have sets of plastic lower case letters. The three-dimensional form of these helps to emphasise distinctive features. Here are some suggested activities:

● hold up individual plastic letters for visual identification.

● ask your student to close his eyes. Put a letter into his hand and ask him to identify it by feel alone. He will be able to feel the straight sides of M and the slanted sides of W for example.

● ask your student to put plastic letters in sequence as far as visual recognition has been taught. Alphabet sequence is important – for finding seats in cinemas and theatres, using telephone directories, later the dictionary, etc.

● make sets of alphabet cards – one upper case, one lower case. Ask your student to match them and name the letters.

● play alphabet battle. Deal a set of letters between you. Whoever has M puts it out and each of you in turn builds backwards or forwards in sequence. The winner is the one who puts out all his letters first. You can play this with the plastic letters in a box and vary the game so that you both have to *feel* for the letter you want. Always encourage your student to verbalise his activity, i.e. to *name* the letter as he puts it down.

● play 'before and after'. Ask your student to put plastic letters in sequence. Then ask him to pick up the letter *before* p, n, s etc. or *after* c, y, r etc. He *names* the letter as he picks it out. Do not mix 'before' and 'after' until your student is secure on both as separate exercises. This game can also be done verbally: 'Which letter comes before l?' etc.

● make cards showing the letters of the alphabet in groups of three, each set having a blank in either initial, medial (between the initial and final letters) or final position: e.g.

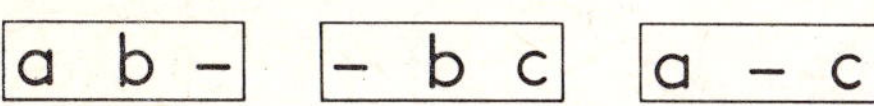

Ask your student to name adjacent letters as well as supplying the name of the missing letter; this helps to reinforce his learning of the alphabet sequence.

● adults are often fascinated by accounts of how each letter of the alphabet has developed, e.g. the letter A was originally the Phoenician symbol for ox (aleph). Through the years it has become inverted. The letter B was originally , the symbol for house (beth). Most libraries have books treating the development of writing, usually in the children's section. There are further

suggestions for developing efficient use of alphabet sequencing later on, (see page 35).

Although various authors suggest an order for presenting letters and sounds, these are usually intended merely as a general guide. The order of presentation of letters and sounds you adopt for your student will, of course, depend on what he already knows. If he knows nothing, you can choose to use the letters and sounds occurring most often in his language experience, social sight or other work as your starting point. The important thing is to:

● *plan* your work in advance;

● *record* the work you do with your student;

● *evaluate* your student's grasp of information and principles so that you can *structure* your work with him and *control* the learning situation.

These points will be treated in more detail in a later section on planning and evaluation.

Here are a few general points to bear in mind when considering the *sequence* of information you intend to teach a student like Sean who is almost a complete beginner:

● concentrate on the sounds of vowels and consonants at the *beginning* of words at first. They are easier to discriminate in this position, e.g. <u>a</u>pple, <u>b</u>at. Later you can show that they appear at the *end* of words, e.g. ba<u>t</u>, pa<u>n</u>, and in *medial* position, e.g. p<u>e</u>n, l<u>e</u>t.

● when introducing a new letter, concentrate upon its most common sound. Do not confuse your student at this early stage by telling him that <u>c</u> says (k) in cat and (s) in mice or that g and s have two sounds. This information is not useful to him at present.

● teach the short sounds of the vowels first, i.e. (ă) as in bat, (ĕ) as in egg, (ĭ) as in ink, (ŏ) as in orange, (ŭ) as in umbrella.

● as soon as your student knows a few consonants and short vowels you will want to start teaching him to *blend* the separate speech sounds into words (i.e. pronounce sounds together into a smooth sequence). This is often a stumbling point. Don't get discouraged if your student does not grasp the idea straight away. It is probably the most complex stage in learning to read. Once he's got the idea, like learning to ride a bike, he'll not forget, so it's worth approaching it in a relaxed way.

You will need to do lots of activities involving aural and visual discrimination to help your student learn the shape and speech sound of the individual letters and to discriminate between them. However, if you have a student who displays a particular kind of confusion, e.g. he finds difficulty in discriminating between sounds such as (b) and (p) and (d) and (t) it will probably be wise to *concentrate more on visual activities*, exploiting his strengths to solve the problem. Alternatively, if he confuses the appearance of letters such as <u>b</u> and <u>d</u>, or <u>p</u> and <u>q</u>, *concentrate more on their sounds*. This does not mean that you completely avoid treating his particular problem, but that you use his strongest learning ability to create the association between letter forms and speech sounds, which is the basis of reading, and then gradually build up his other strengths.

Exercises in aural discrimination

● read a list of words to your student, e.g. pit, pen, pink, puppy, puddle, and ask him to repeat the sound he hears at the beginning of each. Avoid giving words with an initial consonant blend in this exercise, e.g. place, at this stage; these can come later. Check that your student can echo the sound you have asked him to listen for; if he has difficulty in doing this, you may need to begin with *visual* discrimination exercises.

● ask your student to give you some words beginning with a particular sound, e.g. (dă, dĭ) – he might say damp or dig. It is advisable to attach a vowel sound to each consonant sound from the beginning, as there are very few consonants which can be pronounced in complete isolation and, of course, they never are pronounced in isolation in words. This approach will help your student to *blend* speech sounds together to form words later on in his reading activities.

● pose riddles, e.g. I'm thinking of a word beginning with:

(să) which means unhappy (sad)
(sŏ) they go with shoes (socks)
(sĭ) means a small drink of water (sip)

● which is the odd man out?
tug   table   tinker   dog   test
● which word begins with (pɪ)?
dog   bed   pin   bug
● I spy something beginning with (fĭ), etc.
● games involving producing words with a particular initial sound connected with names, places, food, flowers, etc.

Carol   Dover   peas   daisy
Cathy   Doncaster   potatoes   dahlia
Coral   Dudley   parsnips   daffodil

● make sets of cards on which are illustrated common objects and ask your student to arrange them in categories according to initial sounds. Be sure to provide illustrations which are not infantile; use unambiguous illustrations which can be given an adult appearance, e.g. a rabbit – rather than a Bugs Bunny type of illustration, find a real photograph or good drawing.
● use the material you have made in your language experience approach, or one of the alternative approaches, to point out particular sound families, e.g. 'I get up at <u>s</u>even o'clock. <u>S</u>usan get<u>s</u> my breakfa<u>s</u>t.'

The same practice can be derived from the noun labels in a picture your student has selected or from the children's book he has brought. You can then ask him to name some other words which begin with that sound.

Exercises in visual discrimination
● matching letter shapes

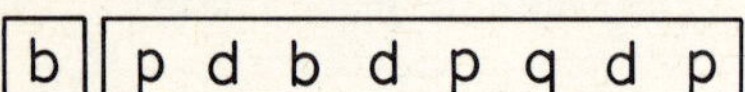

join up letters which look the same

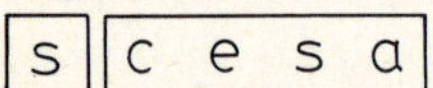

ring the letters that match the letter in the box.

● Daniels and Diack's Visual Discrimination Test, No. 4 in 'The Standard Reading Tests' is a useful basis for this kind of exercise. This is one of those tests.

● to help in teaching and reinforcing the relationship between upper case and lower case letters try cards like these:

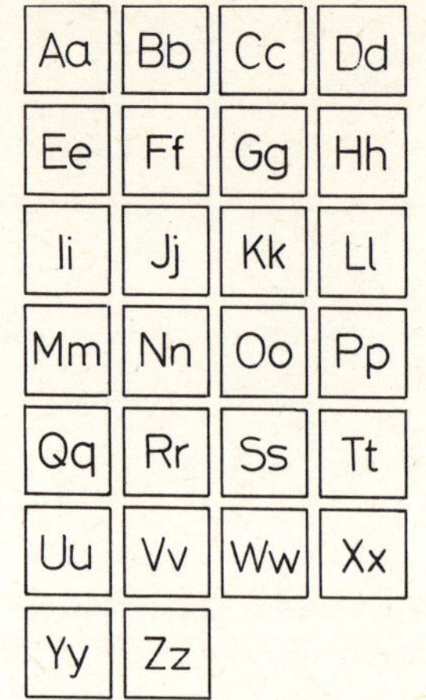

Initially, using these for reference:

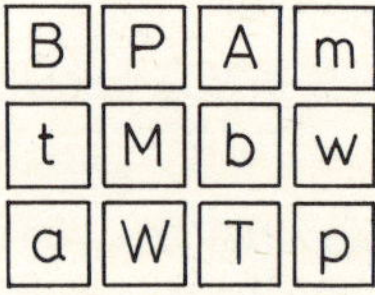

Join up the letters with the same name.

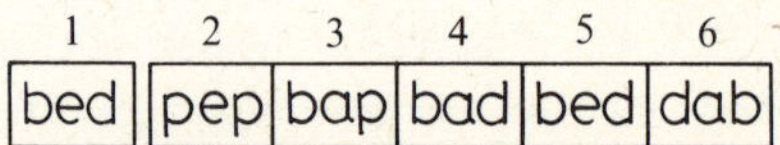

Ring the word which looks the same as 1.

Early exercises involving both visual and auditory discrimination
● pictures of objects requiring the student to identify the initial speech sound of the noun.
● pictures of objects requiring the student to match those beginning with the same speech sound, e.g. (p)

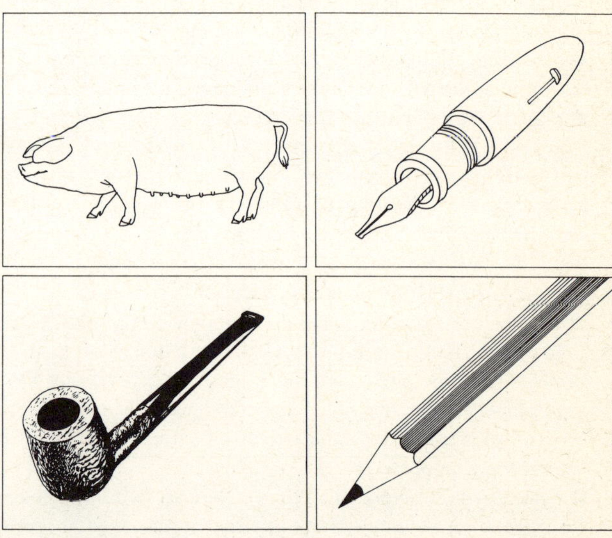

● joining letters with the same sound

B M P t
h N H n
m b r A
R a T p

● which of these letters says (t)?

d e p g c b t k

● phonic bingo – particularly useful with a group

a	e	i		a	i	i
o	u	a		o	e	u
e	i	u		u	o	a

Read out word lists, the student crosses out the appropriate vowel sound. This can be used as a game with the student aiming to get a line.

● which word begins with (p)?

dab   pad   bad

Each of these exercises can be done when your student has acquired a minimal amount of reading skill. The most he is required to recognise is an initial speech sound or a letter. These activities can be used in conjunction with your systematic introduction of new letters and sounds (derived from your language experience and other approaches). Be careful not to ask him to do something which you have not taught him, and which he does not know.

Early handwriting

Along with Sean's early auditory and visual work, you will need to work on handwriting. This will not be a problem with Sean because he is fascinated by it and you can encourage him to use it to reinforce his memory of letter shapes. If you have a student like Sean who, because he is interested in writing, may already be able to copy or to learn fairly easily, you will be able to ask him to copy his language experience and sight words from the beginning. He will then be able to connect the sound, shape and feel of writing each letter together.

If your student cannot write at all, you will need to adopt a procedure for teaching him to write each letter. This is most economically done by grouping letters involving similar strokes. Use a large felt tip pen to start with so that your student can really feel his movements. You may encourage him to trace letters first with his finger, prior to using a pen, so that this feeling sensation is a more direct experience, then let him trace the shape of letters you write for him with a felt tip pen. A felt tip pen is recommended because it moves over paper easily. Show him the movements involved and talk about them as you write, e.g. P 'down, up, right round'.

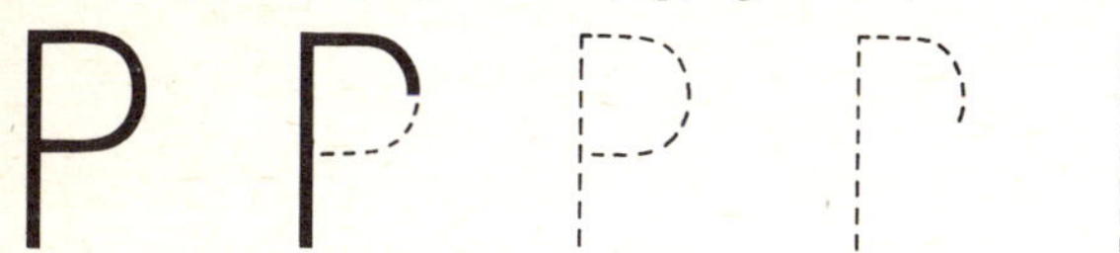

Check that he knows the meaning of these words, particularly *right* and *left*, and that he realises the direction in which writing moves. It is helpful with a left-handed student to show the strokes with *your* left hand – if you use large movements you will manage quite well. Right-handed writing *pulls* the pen across the paper, left-handed writing *pushes* the pen along and the feeling of letter shapes is quite different. Watch how your student holds his pen – he should not grip it too hard, nor should his fingers be too near the point or he will not be able to *see* the letters as he *writes* them, and a valuable learning connexion will be lost. Tell your student that you are going to try to lift the pen from his fingers as he writes. You should be able to do so quite easily if he is not gripping it too hard. Many older left-handed people have suffered in early schooldays when teachers or parents have tried to persuade, or even force them, to use the other hand. This may have had two damaging results:

● *confusion* over movements needed to shape letters because of the distinctions between the push and pull required by left- and right-hand writing respectively;

● *tension* associated with writing because it has been felt as a painful experience.

Some students suffer from a real pencil fear and dislike even lifting up a writing instrument because to do so recalls unpleasant past associations with writing. This is something you will have to work through together. Talk about it with your student, let him express his feelings and then discuss with him ways in which *he* thinks he might be able to overcome his fears. The larger the writing instrument, the more easily will your student be able to relax and to slide his *whole* hand over the paper.

It is vital that you take your student's *attitude* towards writing into account when planning the proportion of lesson time you will spend on it. He may resist it, feeling that it is reading which is his priority and that he is not going to need to write except at a form-filling level. You can explain that writing the letters and words that he is learning to read may assist his reading by reinforcing his sense of letter shapes, but if he *chooses* not to write, you should respect his wishes because he is an adult. You can raise the subject of writing again later.

Writing is a fatiguing experience for people unaccustomed to doing it. Indeed, with reading, it is one of our most complex neurological achievements, so periods of practice for students willing to do it should be *frequent* but *short*.

Print a b c *or round* a b c *writing?*

You will have to make a decision about the style of writing you wish to adopt. There are arguments for and against both styles. Consider them in the light of your own student and the habits he has already acquired. What may be best for one student may not be best for another. If your student has already acquired some competence in a particular style of writing, you may choose not to interfere with this. Why attack something which he has achieved to his satisfaction? On the other hand, if he can write, but writes badly, so that letter shapes are distorted to an extent that recognition is difficult, you may persuade him to adopt a new style. The main thing is *not to further undermine his confidence in any way*.

Arguments for teaching print writing

● it more closely approximates the writing of most printed materials.

● it is simpler to form, consisting of a limited number of strokes – up, down, round.

● the new writer can more quickly develop a legible style.

Arguments against teaching print writing

● because the strokes used to form some of the letters tend to be isolated by a beginner, and the pen is lifted from the paper during the formation of a single letter, it is difficult for a student to feel the shape of a letter or word as a complete unit, so that his writing does not do much to reinforce his reading.

● certain letters in the print style have more similarities than differences between them in their formation, and if a student is already visually confusing them when he reads, his writing will exacerbate rather than clarify his confusion, e.g.

b   d,   p   q,   s   z

● it is more difficult to write in the print style quickly *and* clearly.

● joining on has to be taught as a separate skill.

If you do use the print style, try to teach the letter shapes as far as possible so that your student does not lift his pen from the paper until he has completed each letter.

Arguments for round writing

● with the exception of x and t and sometimes f and z each letter is formed without lifting the pen from the paper and is therefore felt as a whole, flowing movement.

● distinctions between easily confused letters are easily made:

b   d   p   q   i   z   z   f   f

● joining on at a later stage is more easily achieved as the strokes for it are incorporated into most letters from the beginning.

● round writing helps students to see that letters making speech sounds are *blended* into words.

How to help your student write

● in the initial stages use unlined paper unless your student shows preference for lined paper. Unlined paper gives unrestricted space in which to move the pen.

● give him a large, thick felt tip marker or pen to use so that he can hold it without needing to grip it.

● in teaching the letters, group together those which involve similar strokes, e.g.

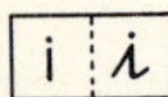

and encourage him to practise the writing patterns until his pen moves flowingly across the paper before isolating a particular letter for practice.

● write a large model of each letter as you teach it and encourage him to trace it over, first with the forefinger of his writing hand, then with his pen, so that he can feel its shape.

● some students seem to benefit from tracing letter shapes in the air using a whole arm movement. This gross pattern of movement may be a necessary exercise before your student can grasp the more refined movement required for writing on a page.

● encourage him to trace letter shapes with his forefinger on different surfaces, e.g. felt or the table, to enhance his feeling of the movements involved.

● when he is able to copy the model you have given him adequately, ask him to write it, first without the model, then with his eyes shut to see if his hand knows what to write.

● teach capital letters in the ordinary print symbols; round versions of these tend to be complicated and the block capital is perfectly acceptable.

It is often useful to show students the relationship between hand-writing and print by superimposing one upon the other using tracing paper, e.g.

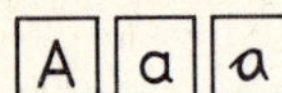

As Sean already knows the upper case alphabet letters, it would be best to use these as a starting point for teaching each lower case letter for reading and writing. Three sets of cards can be made, e.g.

and possibly a fourth set illustrating a word beginning with the sound of the letter. Various matching games and snap can be played with these.

Basic letter/sound relationships. A typical lesson with Sean while he is still in the early stages of learning basic letter sound relationships might be:

● alphabet snap using two sets of the cards similar to those described above.

● phonic work derived from language experience activities in the previous lesson, e.g.
'My brother Bill is almost as bad at reading as I am.' You might decide to concentrate on b this time. Ask Sean how many (b) sounds he can hear in the sentence.

● ask him if he knows which letter makes that sound. If he doesn't know, show him and underline the b's.

● ask him to give you some more words beginning with (b) or ask him if he can hear (b) in a selection of words, e.g. tap, bus, pump, bonny, upon, bus.

● read him some sentences and ask him to count the number of (b) sounds he can hear, e.g. 'The boxer's nose got bashed and bent' (NB Sean's interest in boxing) or 'The ball bounced into the goal and rebounded out'.

● if Sean's hearing discrimination is reasonably good, he may be able to do the following exercise involving listening and changing the initial sound of each word to b to make a new word:

cat —— bat	man —— ban
fit —— bit	west —— best
Lizzie —— busy	gutter —— butter

(Some students find this more difficult than others, it depends whether they are primarily auditory or visual learners, and how acute are their powers of sound discrimination. Avoid such exercises if your student has a lot of difficulty with them.)

● ask him to match b in a line of letters, e.g. b d p b g q

● show him a copy of the language experience sentence he can already read and ask him to circle the b's.

● use some of the printed materials you have in your own home, e.g. labels from food tins and packets, medicine bottles, pamphlets, picture papers, advertisements, old telephone directories and arrange these in phonic groups, e.g.

Bottle of bleach, biscuits, baby food, beer, brush, bed. You will be able to think of many more.

● draw a large b on a plain piece of paper so that Sean can watch your movements – this is important.

● ask him to trace it, to copy it, then to write it without a copy. Ask him to name it and tell you what sound it makes. (It is often effective to ask your student to name a letter *as* he writes it.)

Combining visual and auditory activities
Give Sean a sheet of pictures of objects and ask him to tell you which names begin with (b). Alternatively, ask him to write b underneath the appropriate picture.

In subsequent lessons you can repeat most of the exercises so far mentioned, introducing (b) in positions other than at the beginning of a word, e.g. rub, baby.

It is wise to separate the introduction of letters which are easily confused by a beginning reader, e.g. b and d, p and q, s and z are frequently *visually* confused. The speech sounds (d) and (t), (p) and (b) are frequently confused.

Later, as Sean's knowledge of letters increases, you can provide mixed exercises similar to those mentioned above, in which he has to discriminate between different speech sounds, e.g. (p) and (b), (d) and (t), and letter shapes, e.g. b and d.

What's happened to books?

There is a simple reason why it has not been suggested that you use any particular books with a beginner like Sean. There are few, if any, which are really suitable for *teaching* purposes with complete beginners. There are plenty of books on the market treating early reading skills but the majority of these are designed for children or backward adolescent readers.

Although the learning patterns included may be similar to those you are using, the usual language content and presentation is often unappealing to adults. An adult of 35+ *may* be prepared to accept a childlike approach but the younger adult is likely to reject it, because he is reminded of past failures, and because he feels that the approach assumes that he is backward in all respects, rather than in a specific area of achievement.

This does not mean that you will not use books with your student but that you are more likely to use them for purposes other than direct teaching. Books of photographs, pictures, do-it-yourself manuals full of clear diagrams, colour supplements and magazines, provide useful talking points and sources of language work. The subject and presentation is adult and therefore more acceptable.

If you feel that a student like Sean expects to have a reading book from the beginning, refer to the list of suggested materials given later in this section on resources.

Teaching a student with a reading age around seven years

Once a student like Sean has learned the basic letter shapes and their most common speech sounds, together with some social sight words and those he has learned from the language experience approach (or the alternative approaches), he will be at roughly the same age as a student like Jackie, i.e. with a reading age around seven years.

You will need to repeat the procedure used to assess Sean's achievements and particular problems with any student. Only by doing this will you be able to work out *what* your student *wants* to be taught, *what* you think he *needs* to be taught and *how* you are going to teach.

Look at the profile of Jackie Baker on page 6 and note down what you feel is important about her learning problems and her learning needs. Then compare what you have noted with what follows.

Jackie is obviously more out-going than Sean. She enjoys talking, has been able to tell some of her friends and her children's teacher of her problems and has sought help on her own initiative. She has already tried working with one tutor and failed in her own eyes, if not in those of the tutor. She has some insight into her learning problems and knows that she 'really dislikes having to concentrate for long periods', preferring chat to work.

These are useful pieces of information. Like Sean, she needs to *succeed* and not merely in the process of learning to read and write; she needs to succeed in developing a working relationship with her tutor so that she can *accept* teaching. Her chatter is probably a means of escaping from the task of solving her learning problems, not because she is idle, but more likely because she is *afraid* of showing up her inadequacies and afraid that she cannot make progress.

You will need to make an explicit contract with a student like Jackie. It must be clear to her that you are meeting together for a specific purpose and that, although you like her and enjoy chatting with her, the sharing of work must come first. Obviously, if she arrives feeling upset about something, you might waive the rule, but on the whole, she needs to see chatting with you about things in general as a reward for her efforts, or as a break from the lesson.

Talk to her about her difficulties in concentrating. Ask her about occasions when she has had no problem, when she has been really *interested* in a film or a television programme. Tell her that many people have the same problem and that you might perhaps both think about possible solutions.

One technique which sometimes works is to have a device such as a cooking timer to hand and to say: 'Let's spend ten minutes doing this and then we'll stop for a few minutes,' and set the timer. Its bell will go off at the end of the allotted time and she will be relieved with some respite. You could extend this idea later by suggesting that you both try to increase her concentration span by a few minutes at a time. She may eventually become so absorbed in some activities that the alarm bell, once an excuse to abandon effort, becomes an irritating interruption. It would be wise not to have the timer where she can see it or she will concentrate on watching the hand move round! Once her *stamina* for concentrated effort has become established, you can dispense with the device, only reverting to it when she is resisting something she needs to do.

Jackie's needs

Having decided upon a strategy for helping Jackie to overcome her problem in *approaching* learning, you now need to study the other information you have received about her to decide upon your teaching style and the content of her lessons:

- she can write her name in 'clear, joined-up writing'. As she has never been required to fill in a form, she probably cannot write her address, birthdate and other details.
- she has a range of interests relating to her roles as a woman, housewife and mother, which give clues to the type of reading matter you can use with her, e.g. family magazines, articles about child care, recipes, dressmaking and knitting patterns, information about allowances and supplements.

- she can read a little, but too slowly for comprehension. In other words, her struggle to identify words is such that by the time she reaches the end of the sentence, she has forgotten the beginning. You may have had a similar problem if you've ever started to learn a foreign language. This problem *has* to be solved, at least in part, early on in your lessons with her. There is no pleasure or interest to be gained from reading if it is a sheer mechanical act of barking at print without any meaning attached. It's a waste of time, and anyone could be excused for losing concentration under such circumstances. A tape recorder might be useful here, as a device on which Jackie can record her reading and then listen to what she has said. More detailed suggestions can be found in the section on resources.
- her main stumbling block in reading appears to be *blending*, the fusing of sequences of speech sounds to form words. This is a task that Sean also will need to practise.

Once the stage of blending is reached, a new dimension is added to the systematic work in phonics which you will be doing with both Sean and Jackie. So far with Sean, the emphasis has been on teaching him to *recognise* and *respond* to the *shape* of individual letters and to *recall* and *reproduce* the *speech sounds* these letters represent. Jackie is ready to learn that clusters of letters can be grouped together to form a meaningful pattern, i.e. a word. It is the spaces between words in speech or writing which help to indicate to us what the words are. As with Sean, you will need to check that Jackie understands what a word is and that she is able to discriminate between words she hears as well as between words she sees on a printed page.

❝ I asked a group of students recently to give me words beginning with (s). One suggested 'sraining' meaning it's raining. ❞   (A tutor)

Approaches to teaching Jackie

Jackie will want to progress quickly, the more so because she can already read a little, which is almost as frustrating as not being able to read at all. Also, this is her second attempt to learn as an adult, and she is likely to fear that she will fail again. Your motto with Jackie needs to be *economy* and *efficiency*. She needs the discipline of a systematic, structured approach in which you keep control of what she does. Therefore you need to bear the following principles in mind when working out *how* to teach her:

- teach her so that each new step she learns leads straight on to the next, e.g. you might start with short vowel a in your phonic work, then move on to the remaining short vowels e, i, o, u so that she begins to see there is a pattern;
- teach her so that in each new step she learns a way of coping with *as many words as possible*, i.e. show her that she can apply generalisations from one pattern of words to other words which conform to that pattern, e.g. the silent e patterns: date, bite, etc.;
- teach her so she can put her new skills to immediate use, selecting activities which *she* sees as important, e.g. writing a note to the children's school, shopping lists, instructions to the milkman, etc.

The content of Jackie's lesson

If you follow these principles, the content of your lessons with Jackie will include two main elements:

- language on topics which *interest* her;
- phonic work deriving from these *interest words* which will help her to make, and build up, generalisations about language.

The term *generalisation*, applied to acquiring and teaching reading skills, means that you teach students that there are certain recurrent patterns in the structure of many of the words which we use in speech, reading and writing. In reading, the speech sound represented by a letter or a group of letters in a word which has already been taught can be used to unlock the pronunciation of other words in which these particular letters recur, e.g. cat, bat, rat, sat, etc. Many of these patterns can also be applied to spelling, particularly in the early stages of learning.

An approach using phonic generalisations like this, in which the patterns of letters and speech sounds are emphasised and gradually built upon with more patterns, is both *efficient* and *economical*. It is *efficient* because it is systematic and your student can see his own learning increase. It is *economical* because he is learning strategies for coping with unfamiliar words when you are not there to help him. This has important implications for your student's sense of *achievement* and *independence*.

Unfortunately, not all the words in our hybrid language lend themselves to this phonic approach. Many of the approximately 15 per cent of words which do not fit into any phonic pattern are those which we need to use most frequently. However, if you remember that about 90 per cent of all reading and writing comprises only 1,000 words, there is no need to worry. You merely use a different procedure for teaching the awkward words in the language. Some of these are listed on pages 24 and 47.

Jackie, and any other student you might teach, will always need to know quickly whether her responses are right or wrong. She needs reinforcement of her correct responses with *praise*, and if she makes a mistake will need *reassurance* and *explanation*. If she makes a mistake, try to lift the responsibility from her shoulders. Say: 'I need to spend more time with you on that,' or 'I didn't explain that clearly enough, let me try again.' Needless to say, you will not expect her to do things which you've not taught her. However slow Jackie might be to grasp a point, she must *never* feel that she is incapable of succeeding or that you are blaming her; she is probably blaming herself enough already.

Jackie's early lessons

As with Sean, start with the abilities she already has. We know that she is a fluent talker. We know also that in her case it is important that her language work should be directed towards a learning experience from the beginning, otherwise she will use a chat as an evasion of learning. Here are some suggestions about the topics you might use as a starting point for a language experience approach with Jackie so that she is able to read and possibly write something new by the end of her first lesson:

Alternative approach 1.
● ask her about the type of note she sometimes needs to write to her children's school, for example, if they have been absent for some reason. Talk about what she might want to say and write it down in clear writing. For example:

> 8.5.75
>
> Dear Miss Smith,
> I kept Stephen at home yesterday because he had a cold.
> J. Baker

Follow the procedures for teaching Jackie to read and write this note as described earlier for Sean, dividing the main sentence into phrases to begin with. Suggest to Jackie that you together build up a file of the kind of letters she will need to write in connexion with the children, and which she can keep for reference. In the next lesson you can build upon this pattern by substituting different vocabulary and teaching the new words to Jackie, e.g.

I kept	Stephen	last week	he
	at home	because	
	Heather	yesterday	she
had a	headache	Monday	
	cold		

and continue to add choices, e.g. the days of the week.

By adopting this approach you will achieve several things:
● you will have provided Jackie with something which will seem useful to her. As she can already write, she will be able to copy the format you have given her until she is able to write the words from memory;
● you will have created some reading material which is connected with her needs and interests;
● you now have some reading material which can form a basis for your phonic work with Jackie;
● in addition to teaching her to read and write some words in sequence and in isolation, you have also, by substituting vocabulary, taught her something about sentence structure;
● you have included some of the words which we most frequently use and which do not fit into phonic patterns, e.g. some of the names of the days of the week, her children's names, last, because;
● you have produced material which can be extended quite naturally to encourage other skills Jackie needs;
● you can later teach her the convention of writing one's address and the date at the top of a letter and the formal 'Yours sincerely' ending;
● initially she can learn to write the date in numbers, but you can gradually teach her to read and write the names of the months of the year (this will be a useful link with her interest in horoscopes too);
● you can talk about the different forms she might need to complete in connexion with her family, e.g. to give permission for vaccination, to claim vitamin supplements, to buy from mail order firms (she is interested in cosmetics and fashions). This will involve learning how to use catalogues and follow instructions for measuring, etc.

Alternative approach 2.
Similar patterns of activity can be constructed from other starting points, still based on a language experience approach. You might make up shopping lists together, particularly if Christmas is approaching. The lists might be connected with food or with the presents she intends to buy. Either category will yield useful vocabulary. Collect advertisements for common food products, labels from food tins and packages. You will be able to make up several kinds of matching games from these, e.g.

● Snap – matching identical labels, or labels for a particular product produced by different manufacturers, e.g. Baked Beans – Heinz, Crosse & Blackwell, etc.
● matching labels from tins or packets to advertisements for the same product.
● grouping food labels or advertisements into phonic families according to the initial sound, e.g.
coffee carrots, cabbage,
cauliflower, coleslaw, custard.
● you could arrange household labels and advertisements into different categories, e.g. fruit, vegetables, meats, dairy foods, drinks, cleaning materials.

Again, this approach lends itself to a variety of extensions. You can discuss dishes which Jackie gives her family; any recipes she would like to learn; how she manages to keep within her housekeeping allowance, etc. A functionally illiterate person is a vulnerable consumer. It is impossible to shop around for good buys if you cannot read information about cut prices, details of weight and contents on the labels of pre-packaged foods, or newspaper and magazine articles giving advice about how to get the best for your money. You can spend a lesson shopping, or at least window shopping, together.

Alternative approach 3.
Jackie dislikes public transport because she gets lost easily. You could use her need to be able to understand directions, street names and street plans as your starting point:

●in order to show her that a street plan or map is a two-dimensional representation of a three-dimensional world, draw the layout of the room in which you are sitting for her.

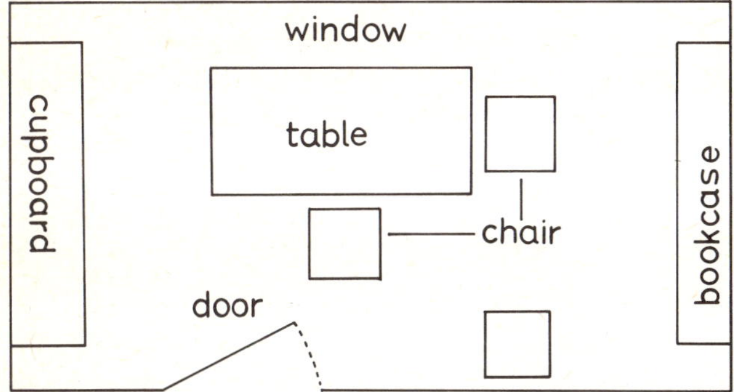

Then ask her to draw or describe her own sitting room for you so that you have two plans to compare. Then do a simple plan of the layout of your flat or one floor of your house, labelling the rooms;

●ask her to do the same for homework. Before she comes for the next lesson draw a simple map showing the location of her own home and the streets or roads immediately surrounding it. Discuss it with her and teach her the necessary vocabulary by the usual method, e.g. street, road, avenue, way, close, square;

●let her take it home with her so that she can compare the representation with the real thing. She might add a few features to it, such as shops, launderette, post office, etc.;

● prepare some simple maps labelled with the names of streets and amenities such as post office, police station, launderette, etc. Ask her to give you directions how to reach one of these from a particular point, using the map as a reference. Write down the verbal directions she gives and teach her to read them;

●in a subsequent lesson plan a short outing you will make together during your lesson the following week. Provide her with a simple map and ask her to work out your route there and back. It could be to your local library to collect some books for her for example;

●ask her to give you directions, for example, from your home to hers. Write down the questions you ask her, and when you have her answers as well, show her how you phrased your questions to get the answers you wanted (she has admitted she doesn't like asking for directions);

●play a game with her in which she asks you for directions, you give her these and she repeats them back. You can then check the accuracy of her recall on a map;

●you can continue activities of this nature alongside the other activities you will be doing with Jackie. Gradually introduce her to different kinds of street directions, bus and train maps and explain the symbol systems to her. As her reading efficiency increases, you will be able to teach her to use indexes, checking first that she knows the sequence of the alphabet. Always start any new activity at a simple level and build up her skills gradually, and with plenty of practice, so that she develops confidence in her own abilities.

Alternative approach 4.
Similar patterns of activity can be followed using horoscopes and details of television programmes as a starting point. Select a paper or magazine which gives horoscopes in simple language. Analyse the vocabularly used, it is likely to be fairly limited and repetitive, and teach her those words (she will also need to be able to recognise the names of the signs and the months of the year). She will then have an incentive to practise her reading every day.

If you begin by using television programme details, begin by writing down the names of the programmes she enjoys watching. She is probably able to read them as, when they appear on a television screen, there are visual and sound cues to assist her, but she may not be able to recognise them so easily in ordinary print. You can then move on to teaching her to recognise and spell the names of the six days of the week.

The next steps

Each of the activities so far described, and any others you may think of based upon Jackie's or your student's own interests and immediate needs, will provide you with a wealth of material which you can use as a resource when you feel the student is ready to commence some phonic work. You may choose to begin by concentrating on the words most frequently used in reading and spelling, teaching the awkward words among these (e.g. said, come, other) as sight vocabulary. The words fitting into phonic patterns can be taught in some of the activities already suggested for Sean.

●first of all, check that Jackie has thoroughly grasped the basic principles upon which phonic knowledge can be built. Although she has reached a reading age of over seven years, she may have forgotten some of the names and sounds of certain letters and you cannot build successfully upon shaky foundations. You can check by giving her the Alphabet Check shown below and by using some of the aural and visual discrimination exercises already described.

Alphabet check

E	W	d	H	y	J	m	F	i	P
D	A	L	v	g	C	o	q	R	s
f	e	k	w	j	M	n	T	V	x
I	h	b	O	X	p	t	Z	Q	U	K
Y	c	G	N	z	l	a	r	S	B	u

●ask your student to name letters *across* or *down* (you will also know if she understands directional instructions).

●ask her to match capital with small letters.

Once you are assured that her learning in these areas is secure you can start work on teaching her to *blend* the individual sounds into words in both reading and spelling activities.

Blending sounds into words
Jackie's problem with blending is perhaps the most common difficulty occurring amongst beginning readers. She will not stumble over every word because she already has a small sight vocabulary. This is why students will often read what might seem to be complicated words like 'demonstration' and 'fantastically' without hesitation but stumble over simple three letter words like 'pat'; the former have been learned as whole units, the latter have not.

● select a word that Jackie already knows by sight, e.g. hat

● write it like this and read it to her moving your finger under it as you read   ha t

Show her that <u>ha</u> in this word says (hă) or ask her 'what is left if we take the (t) away'?

● add some other words, e.g.

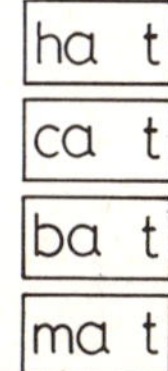

and follow the same procedure.

● make a set of cards like this:

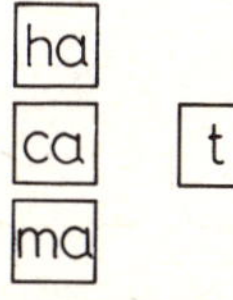

and ask her to attach the (t) to each one and to read the word.

It is very important that you present the vowel attached to the initial consonant in this way because:

● you need to teach *ha* as one unit of sound. If you separate the two letters the student is in danger of hearing *huh ă* and will not be able to appreciate the blend;

● visually this pattern ensures a left to right eye movement.

At the beginning of this work you need to concentrate on only one short vowel at a time, keeping the final consonant of the word constant as in the example just given and only varying the initial consonant. You can make sets of word building cards like this:

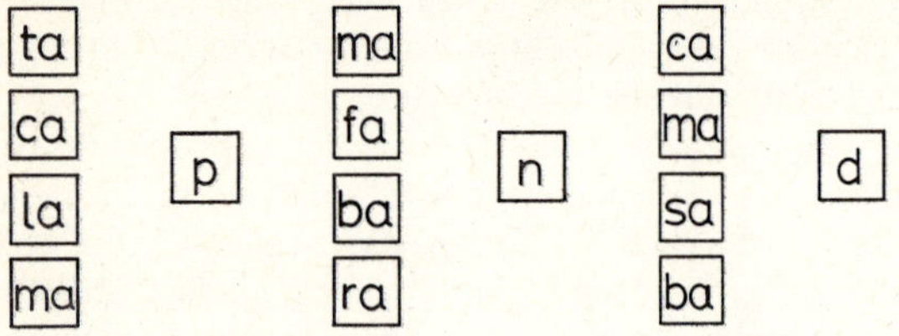

● reading and spelling can be practised together at this stage:
● take one of the blend cards, e.g.

ma and give Jackie a small pack of consonant cards

p n t d ; pronounce map, man, mat, mad and ask her to complete the word choosing the correct card from those in her hand;

● later, give her a pack of e.g. ma pa ca ta ra ;

place n on the table and ask her to complete the words man, pan, can, tan, ran;

● ask her to copy the words she makes using these cards and to read them to you;

● when she is competent at doing these activities, give her words to write down without the cards for reference.

It is better at this point not to ask her to spell the letters aloud. You are wanting her to think of (mă) as a single sound unit and, in spelling sound by sound, to feel it as a single writing unit. It would be inconsistent to ask her to spell words letter by letter now, *unless* she has already been taught by an alphabetic method requiring the naming of individual letters as part of reading and writing routines (often true of West Indian students). In this case you may need to continue with the habit already established to avoid confusion. However, if the student proves to have a difficulty in discriminating sounds you may need to emphasise the visual aspects of sound groups, associating these with letter names:

● encourage her to proof read whatever she writes to check that she has written what she intended to write. Tell her that we all have to do this, whether after filling in a form, writing a letter or anything else. You want to give her a chance to correct herself.

● present each of the short vowels a, e, i, o, u in this way, e.g. ma–p, se–t, bi–n, cu–b. You will usually find that your student grasps the idea more quickly as you progress through the vowels because he will begin to *transfer* his knowledge of one consonant-vowel pattern to others.

● when you have taught each of the vowels you can provide activities which give practice in distinguishing between them, both for reading and spelling. A rotating letter cube set is a useful device you can either buy or make, e.g.

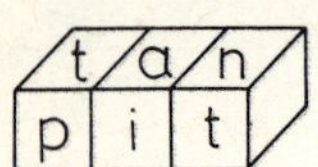

Ask your student to make different words:
● moving the final cube only;
● moving the first cube only;
● moving the middle cube only.

Remember, at this early stage of phonic blending you will be concentrating on single words. You will apply the same principles for blending words into phrases and sentences at a later date. Jackie will still be doing some language experience activities alongside phonic work. In this way she will be learning those words in the language she will need to use most frequently, e.g. said, done, which do not lend themselves to the phonic approach. Gradually, you will bring the two types of activity together to increase the scope of the material she is able to read.

Other early practice exercises in blending words

Remember to use illustrations that are adult in format. You might even ask your student to draw her own.

● provide exercises on the short vowels. When they have all been learned you can provide mixed exercises:

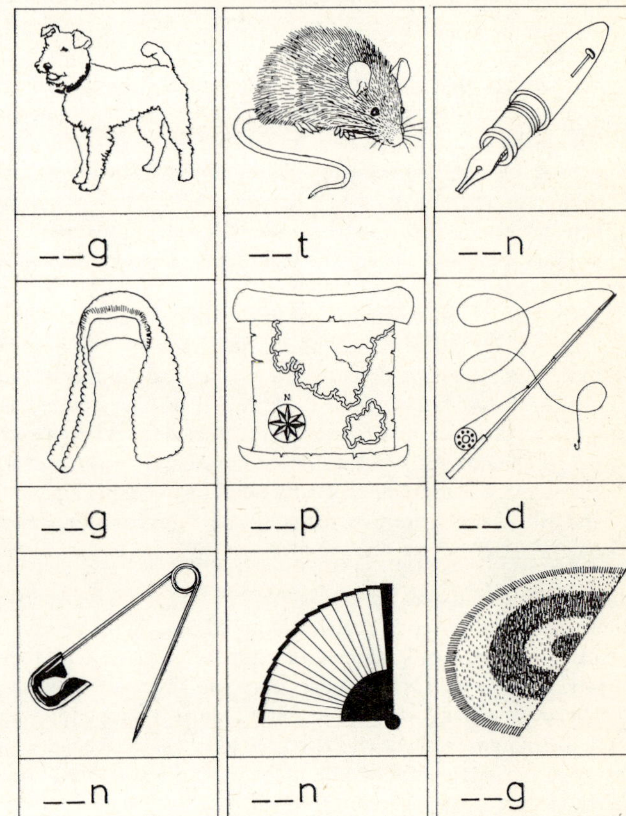

Vary exercises so that practice is given in completing initial and medial letter/sound connexions:

● when your student is ready, give her noun labelling exercises in which no spelling clues are provided.

If you have a student who needs particular practice in discriminating vowel sounds, try some of the following exercises, e.g.

Ask your student to pick out all those names of objects in which he hears (ă).

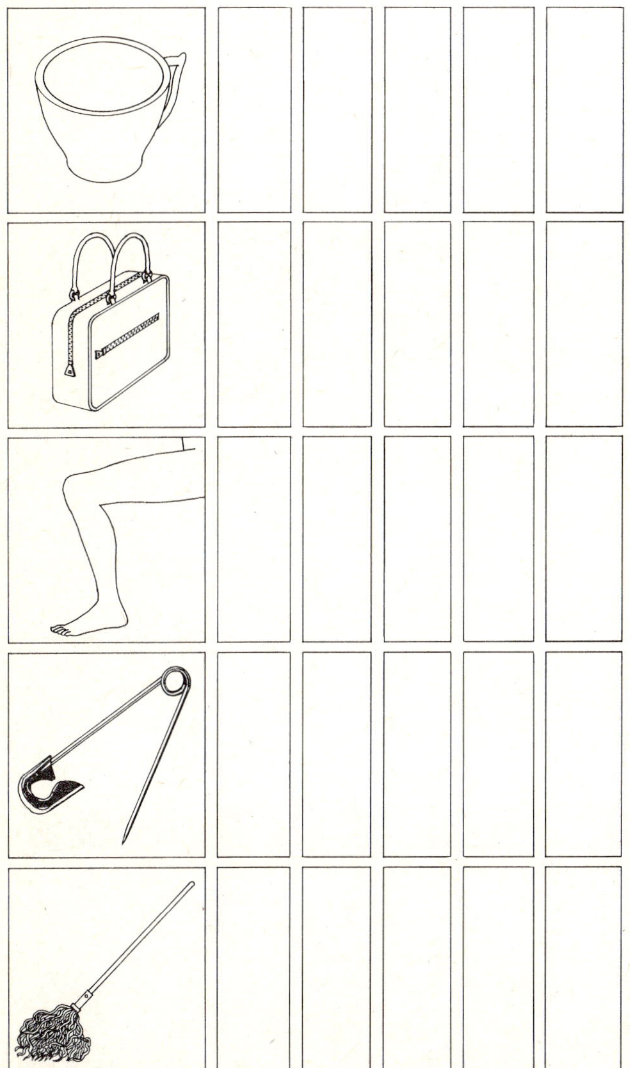

Ask your student to place a tick in the appropriate column to show the vowel heard in the name of the object.

Very simple crosswords – student fills in vowel to make words down and across:

Similar exercises can be constructed to give practice in discriminating between the sound of any initial or final consonant sounds which your student regularly confuses, e.g. (b) and (d)

Ask your student to write *initial* sound under the picture or construct a similar exercise where the student writes the *final* sound under the picture

● exercises in picking out rhyming words or the 'odd man out' in a set of rhyming words are still useful:

map   cob   rap   lap
mud   cud   rod   bud

● these can be extended to include practice in comprehension:

dog   cat   cup   fox

Which word does not fit in with the rest?

Practice in alphabet sequencing

One of your long term objectives is to teach Jackie how to use a dictionary, so you will need to continue to give her practice in alphabet sequencing, still concentrating on the initial letter of words for a while:

● pick out small groups of words that she has been using either in her language experience or phonic work, and ask her to arrange them in alphabetical order, e.g. and, cat, pay, tea, wig.

● a small card index file is useful; show her how to file words according to their first letter, explaining that this is the principle of office file systems;

● now that she knows all the short vowels, periodically ask her to sequence either plastic letters or alphabet cards and to pick out the vowels;

● show her a set of telephone directories; the alphabet is divided into quartiles (not quarters as they are not equal parts), the sections beginning with A, E, L and S. Ask her to arrange the plastic letters to show these, i.e.

A B C D
E F G H I J K
L M N O P Q R
S T U V Z

She can remember these with a mnemonic, e.g.
All Elephants Like Sweets
Give her practice in selecting the right directory for a name which you pronounce;
● suggest that she makes her own dictionary of 'awkward' words and that this is arranged alphabetically.

Reading and phonic skills

As both Jackie's sight vocabulary and her knowledge of the *strategies* she can use to sound out unfamiliar words increases, you will be able to give her more practice in reading phrases and sentences. She should be reading more confidently now, and at a faster rate so that she is able to comprehend the material. She may also have realised that she can often work out what a word might be from the words around it. We read what we *expect* to see a good deal of the time. You may not like the idea of guessing but what's the harm if the word is read correctly? You are not concerned with *how* Jackie produces the correct noises, it is only when she fails to do so that you need to think about how she is working out the word(s).

As her competence and confidence increases, she will need to sound out words less and less. She will either automatically respond to them at sight or use clues in the context to help her identify puzzling words, e.g. Jock shut the ———— and walked down the path. Obviously, you will want to provide her with reading practice material which enables her to make the *least* number of errors, so you still need to prepare it carefully. This is important whether you are using a book or your own materials. Check through whatever you are going to use *before* the lesson, note any word patterns which Jackie might not yet recognise and either teach her, or tell her what these are, before asking her to read. If she still hesitates over the word, read it for her, pointing to it as you read, so that the flow of meaning is not interrupted. Then ask her to repeat that phrase or sentence. Take care to provide plenty of *repetition* in her reading matter. Pictorial clues can be useful. They will help her to focus her thinking so that she reads along the right lines, and they give her the security of an instant feedback as to whether the reading response she is about to make *will* be right. Remember, it is better, and easier, to *prevent* her making mistakes than to correct a wrong response.

Teaching a semi-literate student

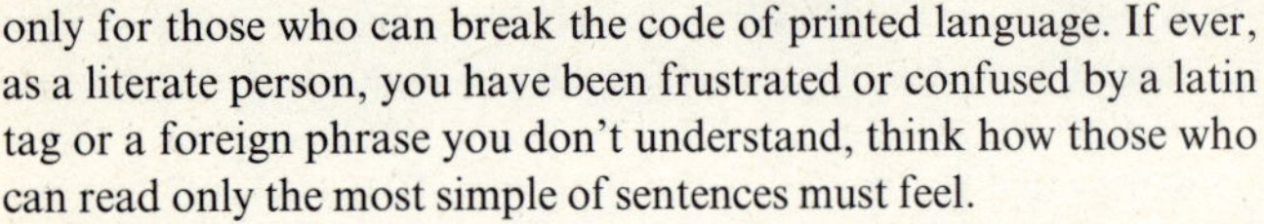

Although in terms of reading achievement, Murray Johnson is ahead of Jackie, he too presents a considerable challenge to his tutor. It seems that the whole of his schooling was a negative experience for him, almost certainly due to his difficulties in learning to read. School has increasingly less to offer a failing reader as he moves through the system. It is a verbal and print-dominated world which has meaning only for those who can break the code of printed language. If ever, as a literate person, you have been frustrated or confused by a latin tag or a foreign phrase you don't understand, think how those who can read only the most simple of sentences must feel.

Even when Murray did find a teacher who tried to help him, the assistance was short-lived. He became labelled as a remedial case and was sent to have teaching outside the school, which enhanced his feelings of failure. Home hasn't provided much support either, he's been just as much of a failure there. His parents' well-meaning attempts to bring him up to the level of achievement they considered adequate, can have been only recrimination in his eyes. The only way Murray could excel was to be a bad boy. That's how he felt at school, and probably at home too, and that's the image he now has of himself. Stealing a motor bike was probably the best thing he ever did:

from the point of view of his future, he's now got the chance to receive some help with his basic problem, and he's old enough now to see that literacy is an essential for getting a satisfying job. Even so, it's not going to be easy for him to *accept* and *maintain* a learning situation. He's never built up the habit required for such effort.

What does this tell you about how to approach your work with Murray? Certainly his experiences and relationship with you must not be a repetition of the pattern of his school experience.

He is 'nineteen but looked several years younger . . . His whole appearance suggested a concerted effort to appear tough and with-it, to compensate for his slight physique.'

Despite his childlike appearance, Murray is an adult. However tempting it might be to mother such a frail looking figure, this is not what Murray wants. He probably has had enough smothering already. He is a man and he must be approached as such. Discuss his situation with him, give him a part in making decisions about what he is to do and honour his choices. If possible, avoid contact with his anxious parents; your contract is with Murray and not with them.

Murray's needs
Murray's profile provides some useful information which will help you in planning your work with him: (see page 9)
● he has a reading age of $8\frac{1}{2}$ years, i.e. he reads at the level normally expected of a child of that age. His performance on the reading test shows that he has some sight vocabulary, has grasped the basic letter-sound relationships and certain phonic patterns, e.g. he recognised the prefix *over* but read *cast* instead of *coat*. Most of his errors on this test of reading single words are sensible guesses, making the most of his incomplete knowledge of phonic patterns. It is likely that if he met these same words in a sentence, he would read at least some of them correctly, by using clues in the context in which they occur. Remember the test was not a real reading situation, but words isolated from their context.
● his achievement on the spelling test reveals a general uncertainty about written language. He has problems in discriminating between, and spelling, short vowel sounds, some consonants including p and b, and some consonant blends. He obviously has very little knowledge of spelling patterns or generalisations. This is particularly clear in his errors in the spelling of the (k) sound in the words he was given in the test.
● his handwriting needs attention. He has chosen to write the test in capital letters, probably because he feels that this is his most legible form of writing. Notice the interesting lapse of writing style in his writing HOUFf, suggesting that writing has become such an unfamiliar activity for him that he is beginning to forget the distinctions between upper and lower case letters. His capital letters are ill formed and the words are cramped together, indicating that he does not really appreciate them as separate units of sounds in space. It is likely that his writing has deteriorated through lack of attention and practice.
● he finds long words difficult to read but is beginning to develop a strategy for tackling them when he cannot guess them from context. With encouragement, he is prepared to try and enjoys the challenge.
● he has stated interests in pop music, football and in reading about murders and sport.
● he knows what he would like to be able to write – forms of application to join clubs, and the type of writing he needs to be able to do to become employable.
● he knows his limitations. He is unused to sustained effort and to enjoying a learning situation. A short-term contract of six months might be a realistic arrangement in his case. It would give him the *choice* of opting out after not too long a period if he found that he still could not tolerate a learning situation.

It is interesting to see how much positive teaching information can be extracted from what, at first reading, is a searing account of Murray's problems. It becomes clear that, when still a fairly young child, Murray was on the point of solving his reading problem when his friendly teacher left, and the cycle of failure was really established. His progress probably stopped from that point, and time and neglect has ensured a regression to at least a year below his original achievement. He's lost what confidence he originally had. All this means that you need to set the level of your early work with Murray well below the level of his achievement on the tests. He needs to start at a level where he can be sure that he is making the correct response, in order to revise his earlier learning and to regain confidence.

If he is going to maintain his effort to conquer his reading and writing problems, he will need evidence that he is making progress, so your teaching should be systematic and structured into learning steps which he can see.

Murray's early lessons

As with Sean and Jackie, you need to start off with topics which engage his *interest* and activities which use the *abilities he has already acquired*. You can check on his grasp of basic letter/sound connexions by presenting him with some of the activities already suggested for Sean and Jackie (see page 30), adapting them into games, so that he does not feel the stress of a testing situation. You should also check that he knows basic concepts like vowel, consonant, etc. These activities can be incidental to other work you are doing, to provide a change or an opportunity of Murray to work on his own.

● crosswords

<table>
<tr><td style="background:black"></td><td>1
P</td><td>2
O</td><td>3
D</td><td style="background:black"></td></tr>
<tr><td>4
R</td><td style="background:black"></td><td>5
N</td><td>I</td><td>6
P</td></tr>
<tr><td>7
I</td><td>8
N</td><td style="background:black"></td><td>9
M</td><td>E</td></tr>
<tr><td>10
P</td><td>A</td><td>11
N</td><td style="background:black"></td><td>N</td></tr>
<tr><td style="background:black"></td><td>12
P</td><td>O</td><td>P</td><td style="background:black"></td></tr>
</table>

Help Murray read any clues with which he has difficulty.

Across	Down
1. Peas grow in it	2. Not off
5. Crabs do it	3. Not bright
7. Not out	4. To tear
9. You and ——	6. You write with it
10. You cook in it	8. A short sleep
12. —— goes the weasel	11. Not yes

● 'magic change' – change dog to cat one letter at a time

dog		pan
dot	or pan to jug	pun
cot		pug
cat		jug

An easier alternative would be to insert the consonants and ask Murray to insert vowels to form words, without using the clues.

Alternative approach 1.
You might choose to structure your work around Murray's interest in football. Some of the following activities will yield material which will be useful for your language work:

● find out the division and team in which he's interested. You can check his knowledge of alphabet sequence by collecting the names of the players in the team he supports, and the towns in its division, and asking him to arrange both these lists alphabetically;
● record the vocabulary he uses when talking about football, e.g. division, forward, defence, pitch, goal, tactics, cup tie, full back, kick off, shooting, equaliser, professional, penalty, supporters, tackle, goal average, foul, pass, throw, sign on, contract, sprinting, 'keep ball', training, offside;
● teach him to read and spell these words as sight vocabulary. Ask him to explain each term to you, write down his definitions and use them as reading material;
● help him to arrange this vocabulary in alphabetical order and suggest he records it in his own dictionary;
● ask him to draw a plan of a football pitch and to give instructions about how the game is played. Write these down, each sentence on a separate slip of paper. He can practise reading these. In a subsequent lesson you can ask him to arrange the strips of paper into a correct sequence;
● make up word and sentence completion exercises from this material, e.g.
A f––tb–ll p–tch is ––– yards l–ng and ––– yards w–de.
A football pitch is ––– yards long and ––– yards wide.
● use some of the vocabulary you have collected together as a starting point for extending Murray's inadequate knowledge of phonic patterns.

The next steps

It does not much matter in which order you present the various reading and spelling patterns. If you are going to make the most of Murray's interests, it would be better to look at the kind of language he is using and to create a sequence of activities based on this. It may mean that you treat certain language features, normally considered to be more difficult, earlier than others considered more simple. This is fine as long as you have a *reason* for introducing a particular pattern (i.e. because it recurs frequently in Murray's language use and in the materials you want to use with him), and as long as you *record* what you are doing so that you keep control of the situation.

The sequences of learning normally adopted for use with children are not necessarily those most suitable for an adult learner. You know best what your student needs and wants to achieve most and it is better to comply with his expectation than to follow slavishly some external authority.

What follows therefore are some illustrations of the types of activities you can practise with Murray which can be adapted for whichever language activity you select for attention. Some indication of possible problems to watch out for, and circumvent, will also be given. Neither the suggestions for activities, nor the problems you might encounter, will be exhaustive. The intention is to give you some idea of the pattern your planning of Murray's lessons might take.

Handwriting

Handwriting is likely to be the activity which Murray least enjoys at first. He may feel that it slows him down; that his hand cannot keep pace with the speed of his thinking; that the product is not worth the effort involved; that it is childish to practise copying. As has already been stated, handwriting is a valuable medium for the reinforcement of the visual recognition and recall of letter shapes. You may have to sell writing to Murray, countering his negative attitude towards writing with positive evidence of its value. Answer his objections by explaining that you want him to slow down his thinking so that his brain and his hand work in conjunction. Writing does improve with practice. It is often useful to be able to copy accurately and legibly, e.g. to take down directions, instructions, addresses, etc. Often, just writing these down helps you to remember them.

Try to be as economical as possible in working on Murray's writing. Group together letters involving similar strokes and encourage him to practice these (see page 30). Give him opportunities to practice joining letters into words as soon as possible (some are best left unjoined to another letter). Get ruled paper to help him with the proportions of letters. This is important, for example, when he writes <u>d</u>, he is likely to misread it as <u>a</u> when he is checking his work.

(If a student has visual difficulties in discriminating between the shapes of letters, it is sometimes helpful to suggest that he names the letters as he writes them, i.e. he tells his hand what to write.)

You will be able to give Murray plenty of writing practice when you are working with particular sounds, and in teaching him sight vocabulary. If he has difficulties with particular letters, let him trace your copy or provide an outline for him to follow, e.g. ♭ . Watch him while he writes to make sure that as far as possible he is using a left to right sequence of movements in forming letters. Students who have not been taught a writing system often practice strange contortions with their writing hand, and unless a definite pattern of writing movements is established the value of writing as a reinforcing activity will be lost.

Most of the writing Murray will be doing at this stage will involve either copying or word completion activities. You may encounter a student who can be persuaded to co-operate at this level but who will resist any other kind of writing, insisting that it's reading he has come for. You will between you have to make a decision. How much does he need to be able to write to function efficiently in his work and life in general? It may not be very much. If he is not going to use the skills you are encouraging him to develop, he will be unlikely to retain them. He may see writing and spelling as activities of secondary importance which he can tackle later when he has achieved a good level of reading efficiency. Your task is to strike a happy compromise between his demands and expectations, and what you feel he *needs* to do. Given his needs, the previous exercises will provide useful experience.

Combining syllables into words

Murray's performance on the reading test shows that he already has some knowledge of the components of syllables and how they combine to form words. That this knowledge is as yet very partial is evidenced by the errors he makes. One of your tasks will be to complete his grasp of the different kinds of syllables and you can do this fairly systematically, again using his own language as a basis.

Pick out words which he knows by sight and use the syllables contained in these for word building exercises:

● for　ward
　fork　back ward (s)
　form　north ward (s)　point out that '-ward' is usually at the
　fort　up ward　　　end of words to do with *directions*.
　ford　down ward

● you can then add endings or beginnings to these words to show how their meaning can be changed or extended:

　　　forward　ed
　　　forward　ing
　or　pro-fes-sion
　　　pro-fes-sion-al
　　　pro-fes-sion-al-ly
　un-pro-fes-sion-al-ly

| under | process | fester | mansion | (ally) |
| unhappy | programme | festivities | tension | dally |

● you will be able to show many of these syllables in different positions in words.

<u>pro</u>cess, im<u>pro</u>vise
<u>under</u>, <u>thunder</u>, <u>fun</u>

● group together words which share a common sound pattern:

tac-tic	kick	luck
pic-nic	sick	sock
fran-tic	back	

● make up exercises involving combining syllables to complete words:

fer
tend　　Which one do you __________ ?
pre　　Let's __________ that Chelsea's won the cup.
et
plete　We watched a __________ blaze across the sky.
com　　Would you __________ this form?

Depending upon your student's abilities, you can make such exercises as simple or as complex as you wish.

● syllable completion exercises, emphasising particular patterns to which you wish to draw attention, e.g.

You are making good – – –gress.
The miners marched in – – –test about their low wages.
The workman was – – –moted to foreman.

All these activities lend themselves to further language work involving the use of prefixes and suffixes. This will extend Murray's reading ability and add to his vocabulary, use of language structures and general knowledge. Remember, people with literacy problems have been cut off from an important source of information, i.e. the printed word. Find out the subjects about which Murray would like to know more and structure some of your language work around these.
Play oral word building exercises together, e.g. 'beginnings and endings':

tele	phone			meter
tele	gram	or	thermo	meter
tele	vision		thermo	stat
tele	pathy			statistics

Murray's vocabulary may initially be very limited, but by doing and discussing activities like these, you will be extending it and whetting his curiosity about words.

Blending sounds into syllables

Although Murray seems to have grasped the concept of a syllable and is able to combine some of these into words, he may encounter problems in blending together the sounds composing some of the new syllable patterns which you introduce to him. Sometimes, it is a particular letter which causes the problem, e.g. consonant blends containing (l) and (r) as in (pl)ace and (pr)ivate often prove a stumbling block. If you have a student who has a general difficulty in blending consonant sounds together, and who needs specific teaching to overcome the problem, it is best to concentrate on words containing blends in final position first. These are usually easier to grasp,

he(lp), li(ft), ba(nk), fe(lt), ra(mp) ju(st), mi(nt), la(nd), pu(lp),
pi(ts), fi(lch), a(sk), bu(lb), e(lm), ke(pt), li(sp), a(ct), etc.

● build up the blend from a simple syllable your student already knows then change the initial consonant:

la(mp)　da(mp)　ca(mp)
then change the vowel:
li(mp), pi(mp), ra(mp), bu(mp), ju(mp), lu(mp), hu(mp), pu(mp), ru(mp).

● give further practice with rhyming exercises such as 'odd man out':
bump, jump, *lamp*, pump, hump

● you can use the same approach for teaching the blending of initial consonant sounds:

(bl)ed, (dr)ug, (sk)id, (sm)ug, (sn)ug, (sp)ot, (st)op, (tr)ip, (str)ip,
(pl)an, (sl)it, (sw)im, (fl)at, (fr)et, etc.

● gradually build up sounds:

```
    ram              rip
c   ram          t   rip
    cram  p          s   trip
    cramp  s             strip  s
```

If you find that your student is having problems when reading in discriminating between two easily confused consonant blends or digraphs, the following types of exercises show how the distinctions between them can be emphasised: (cl) or (cr)?

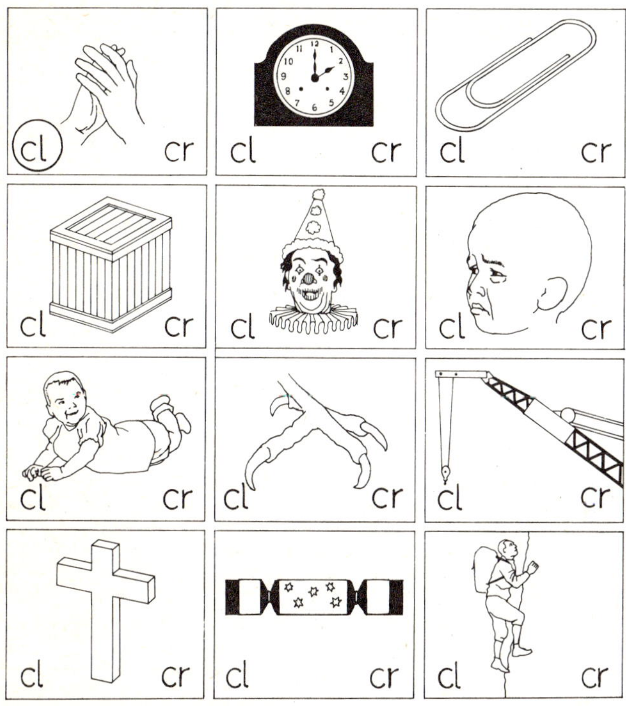

Ask your student to circle the initial sound he hears when naming the picture.
● similar exercises can be constructed for distinguishing between (bl) and (br), (pl) and (pr), etc.

Similarly, if your student needs explicit teaching to read other phonic patterns:
● (ar) (star), (er) (fern, letter), (ir) (bird), (or) (fork), (ur) (Thursday), vowel digraphs and diphthongs oo, ee, ea, oi, oy, ou, ow, etc.
● silent –e syllables (cake, five, etc.)
● suffixes -(ing), -(ed), -(er), -(sion), -(tion), -(ment), etc.
● prefixes (un)-, (dis)-, (pre)-, (pro)-, etc.

Use the same gradual introduction, emphasising the distinctive features of a particular sound by comparing it with other sounds and providing plenty of practice opportunities.

Phonic blends

These need not be taught in any particular order but as the need and occasion arises.

Final Blends

gulp	gust	lump	lint	gilt	gild
gift	gasp	rasp	hasp	fund	risk
rank	film	filch	felt	fast	dust
welt	dint	dent	deft	bunk	bunt
bump	rump	bulb	bond	best	bend
belt	belch	bask	bank	band	hand
last	held	helm	hilt	hurt	hump
hunt	jump	just	kept	kilt	lamp
land	lend	lent	lest	limp	lint
list	mask	mast		melt	mint
mist	nest	pant	past	pelt	pest
pulp	punt	rant	rend	pent	rest
romp	rust	sand	sent	silk	sulk
task	tend	tent	test	tilt	tint
ramp	tuft	tusk	vamp	vast	vest

waft	weft	weld	welt	wend	went
west	wilt	wind	wisp	yelp	zest
bits	hops	bats	bets	dots	pots
pits	pats	nuts	pets	gets	hats
hits	hips	mats	nets	pops	pips
pups	rips	rats	ruts	rots	raps
saps	sips	sops	sups	sits	sets
tips	tops	taps	tots	vats	wits
wets	yaps				

Initial Blends

bled	bred	blot	blab	drip	drop
drug	drum	flap	flat	fled	flip
flit	flog	flop	fret	frog	from
glad	glen	glib	glum	glut	grab
grab	gram	grim	grin	grip	grit
grub	plan	plot	plus	prod	prop
skid	skim	skin	skip	slab	slag
slam	slap	slat	sled	slid	slim
slip	slit	slop	slat	slug	slum
smug	smut	snag	snap	snip	snub
snug	span	spat	sped	spin	spit
spot	spun	stag	stem	step	stub
stud	stun	swim	tram	trap	trim
trip	trod	trot	twig	when	whet
whip	whit				

Initial and Final Blends

brand	brunt	brush	brink	brant	branch
bland	blank	blast	blest	blend	blink
blond	bluff	blunt	blush	dress	drench
drank	drink	drift	drill	drunk	dwelt
flank	flash	flask	flesh	flint	floss
fluff	flush	frank	fresh	frill	frisk
frost	gland	glass	glint	gloss	graft
grand	grant	grasp	grass	grill	gruff
grunt	grist	plant	plash	prank	press
skimp	skulk	slant	slept	slink	slump
slink	spend	spent	spilt	stamp	stand
stilt	stint	stunt	swift	tramp	trench
swish	trust	twist	whelp	which	

Sally and Ralph de S. Childs.

●invent mixed exercises involving the use of sounds, syllables, words and concepts you have recently taught, e.g.

Nouns and suffixes

licking	cases
kicking	sweets
milking	stamps
packing	cows
sucking	footballs

Ask your student to match cards together to make phrases.

Rhyming families

licking	singing	filling
ticking	ringing	spilling
sticking	flinging	willing
tricking	stinging	killing

Jumble cards and ask your student to place them into groups according to rhyme.

Always move from the most simple to the more complex examples of a sound's occurrence in words. The same approach can be used for teaching the spelling of particular sounds.

The period of time you will need to spend on the explicit teaching of phonic patterns will depend on your student's motivation and rate of learning. As his confidence increases and as he has more reading experience, he will begin to make phonic generalisations and learn sight vocabulary unaided. Your task will be to provide him with materials and language experiences which widen his vocabulary and his knowledge of sentence structure, develop his powers of comprehension and extend his interests.

Reading

The learning and teaching of reading skills is never completed. Once your student has mastered the basic mechanics of reading, a new and endless range of objectives is open to you. These include the materials with which your student might want or need to become familiar and the *reading strategies or styles* demanded by them. An efficient reader adjusts his reading skills to his purpose in reading and the demands of the text. He may relish a novel, savouring every word. He may read an exciting detective story very quickly in order to discover 'who done it'. He may study a technical manual very slowly and carefully in order to absorb information and instructions. He may read in order to collect information in note-form in preparation for a project or for a meeting. He may skim through a reference book very quickly, looking for a particular piece of information, out of necessity or curiosity; he may read critically, following a thread of thought, or an argument, in order to record his own comments. This is only a limited list to illustrate various reading activities.

You need to give your student experience in these different styles of reading partly because of their *utility* value, also to show him that as a literate person he has a *choice* in not only *what* he reads but *how* he reads, depending upon the purpose for which he is reading and the time available to him. Collect together reading materials which require the use of different reading skills, e.g.

● instructions – recipes, or instructions on household products (e.g. paint remover), instructions on how to do things (e.g. changing a fuse, a car wheel, mending a puncture). The sequence of instructions is important. Emphasise this by giving practice exercises, e.g. Hanging instructions for wallpaper

● place instructions out of order and ask your student to put them into the correct sequence, using the illustrations as a guide.

● sentence completion exercises, e.g.

allow .... to drain into ....

● check that vocabulary is understood, e.g. butt joints, overlap, adhesive, fungicide.

● ask questions to test comprehension of information given, e.g.

Why should you allow extra at the top and bottom ends when cutting a length of wallpaper?

How can you get rid of air bubbles when you have pasted the paper on to the wall?

What is a butt joint?

What do you need to do if you have to overlap lengths of paper?

Why should you not let children or pets drink the contents of the water trough?

● Work with comparisons. Completion exercise:

big	bigger	biggest
....	smaller	....
great	....	greatest
....	fatter	....
....	....	thinnest
dark	....	....
....	colder	....

● *jumbled pairs*

fish		mash
salt		onions
tripe	and	bacon
sausage		chips
egg		pepper

Ask your student to join up the things which go together.

● choosing from a menu

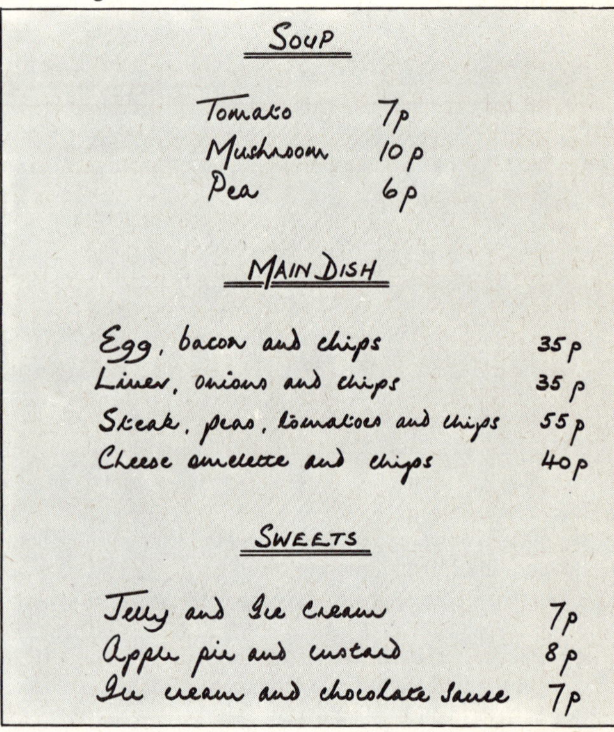

A range of exercises can be developed around the theme of eating out.

Hanging Instructions – Ready Pasted Vymura

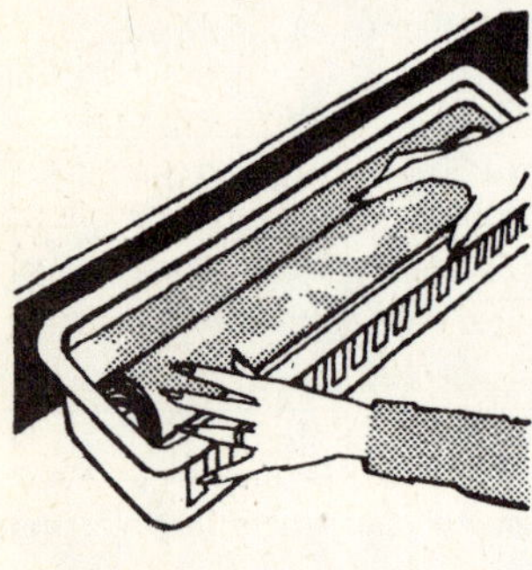

Shade rolls. Cut a length of Ready Pasted VYMURA, leaving extra at top and bottom of wall for trimming. Starting at bottom roll loosely (pattern inwards). Place in trough ¾ full of cold water.

Soak for 1 minute excluding air bubbles. Remove carefully, paste side to wall. Allow excess water to drain into trough. Position on wall.

Remove excess water from face with sponge rinsed frequently in clean, warm water. Smooth out all air bubbles and trim excess VYMURA from top and bottom.

Hang subsequent lengths with butt joints. Roll joints using a seam roller. Where an overlap is unavoidable use Dufix, Copydex or a similar adhesive.

The adhesive on this wallcovering contains a fungicide. Do not allow children or pets to drink the contents of the water trough. Wash your hands after using the product.

The possibilities are infinite. The main thing is to decide *which* particular aspect of language you wish to draw to the attention of your student and then to use your imagination in thinking out different ways of presenting it. Anything goes, as long as you know what you are aiming to achieve, and your student does too.

Collect jokes, cartoons, articles and stories which will appeal to your student's sense of humour and interests. If he's not yet able to read them himself, read them to him.

Newspaper headlines are a good source of ambiguity, e.g. 'Four Thousand Men Walk Out Over Woman' (*The Times*, 1969). They provide discussion points and illustrate that words by themselves have little meaning. It is their combination into sequence that constructs the message. Periodically change roles with your student, so that he is the instructor using words to teach you how to do something.

A list of suggested reading books appears in a later section. Find one which is simple enough for your student to read without difficulty so that he can comprehend and enjoy the text without the irritation of stumbling over particular words.

If you had to choose a selection of books for Murray, which ones from the lists on page 62 would you want to examine and think about?

Activities which involve reading and comprehending figures as well as words will give you an opportunity to check your student's grasp of basic numeracy skills, i.e. addition, subtraction, multiplication, division, weights and measures. He needs to be able to use some of these skills in everyday life for example, when shopping, to check bills, to budget etc. which involve simple mental calculations. These skills are best taught in the context of a practical situation, e.g. adding up the cost of a list of items, giving change, using scales, measuring objects etc. Check that the vocabulary of computation is understood, e.g. add, take away, inch, ounce etc. Dice games, shove h'appenny, billiards, darts, snooker etc. all require the use of, and give practice in, basic numeracy skills. Many commercial games are produced that can provide practice in numeracy skills.

Teaching a student with spelling difficulties

Michael Wells is an example of someone who has used all of his assets to the full and who has coped, not merely adequately, but successfully, despite a literacy problem. He probably feels, like Mae West, that he has moved up 'wrong by wrong', but his achievement is a fact which you must constantly emphasise. Had not his schooling been interrupted during a crucial period of his childhood he probably would have learned to write and spell almost as well as he reads. As long as his wife was alive, he was able to keep his lack of competence in writing private. Now he is in danger of this becoming public, not only to his children and the rest of his family, but within his business. His personal, social and economic security are threatened and it is likely that he will bring his anxieties with him to his lessons. You will have to contain his impatience to progress quickly and at the same time satisfy his desire to leave each lesson with an extra skill.

Your early lessons with Michael

In your first couple of lessons with Michael you might ask him to tell you about the sort of writing he needs to do and the words and phrases he needs to use in connexion with his business. Write these words and phrases on separate pieces of card and *show him how to learn them*. The following procedure might be useful for him to adopt for these words, and others he will encounter which cannot be spelled according to their sound:

- pronounce the word and name the letters,
- copy the word, saying each letter as it is written (students who find writing difficult may need to trace the word before copying it);
- pronounce the word and name the letters again;
- write the word without looking at the copy;
- check that the word has been written correctly. When writing, a complete word is not seen until it is written, and it is easy for even competent writers to make a 'slip of the pen', so proof reading is important;
- record the word in a personal dictionary.

You will need to give fairly frequent checks that words learned in this way are remembered – at first every week, then once a fortnight, later once a month, and so on. If you are using Michael's own language as the basis for your work, this will happen quite naturally anyway. Think about the type of writing he will need to do in connexion with his business: ordering materials and equipment; writing letters enquiring for information about new products and processes; complaining about late delivery dates; to customers answering queries and complaints; letters to solicitors in connexion with his employees; matters concerning his bank account, VAT, etc. Structure your work around his requirements in these areas, teaching him to spell the necessary words as they arise by the procedure described above, e.g. ordering equipment or drawing up a specification for a customer.

This method is a good way of ensuring that Michael enjoys some immediate success in his lessons, but it would be a slow and uneconomical way of teaching him to spell all the words he needs to know. What you need to do is to show him that most of the words we write conform to regular patterns of spelling, and that generalisations about how particular syllables and sounds are *usually* spelled can be made by building up his knowledge through *logic* and the *laws of probability* in spelling, using the vocabulary he is collecting in his letter file.

The buoy and the none tolled hymn they had scene and herd a pear of bear feat in the haul.

Most people who spell well do so without much, if any, reference to spelling rules or generalisations. They have reliable visual memories and just know what words look like and how they feel when written If they are not sure, they usually know enough to hazard a good guess, or to use a dictionary. Good spellers, on the whole, are born rather than made, so you need to be realistic about your ambitions for Michael's achievement in this respect of language use. It may be impossible for you to turn him into a good speller but you *can* teach him *strategies* for tackling the spelling of words.

Michael reads fairly fluently at an automatic, sight level, without needing to analyse words into their sound and syllabic components. Yet, if he is going to learn to spell reasonably well before not too long, he must learn to recognise the phonic bases of most of the words in our language. Many of the activities previously described, emphasising the blending of sounds into syllables, discriminating between easily confused sounds, etc. are useful as spelling activities. The right to left sequence of sound symbols is just as important in spelling as in reading; the spelling of a sound often depends on the sounds following it.

Teaching spelling strategies

Once you and Michael have gathered together and practised some sight spelling, as recommended for his first lessons, you can start using these words to build up spelling patterns. As in teaching reading, there is no particular sequence of spelling concepts you must follow, but obviously it would be wise to progress from the simple to the more complex.

Most of this section will concentrate upon the teaching of spelling, because this is Michael's specific problem. However, it is not intended to imply that other important language activities, e.g. reading, free writing, etc. should be excluded. The spelling course you plan for Michael should both derive from, and extend, these other activities, so that what he learns is always in the context of a real and relevant situation. Unless you plan your lessons accordingly to this principle, there is a danger that Michael will not *transfer* the knowledge and skills he acquires in the more formal spelling activities, to other situations where he needs to apply his learning. Thus, you need to regard the suggestions which follow merely as *possibilities* for structuring your work in such a way as to ensure that Michael's most immediate requirements are satisfied.

The emphasis upon syllables, described earlier in connexion with reading activities, is equally useful for spelling. Give Murray and Michael plenty of practice in spelling simple syllables. Initially, they can work with letter cards, putting sounds together, e.g.

| ch | i | p | | f | ee | t |

This helps students to appreciate the importance of the sequence of sounds in spelling. Always ask your student to read what he has spelled, to check that he has written what he intended to write. When writing, you don't see the word till you've written it so this is important. It is often helpful to have cards on vowels and blends in contrasting colours, emphasising their distinctive features. (But do make sure your student is not colour blind before adopting this strategy.) Gradually progress to dictating short phrases and sentences, introducing simple punctuation as the need arises. Always explain what you are going to do so that your student is prepared for the demands you are making upon him. It is important that you use a rational system for correcting any errors he might make. First, always encourage him to check his work himself. Then, if there is a mistake in a word which conforms to a pattern you have studied together, remind him of the pattern and help him to see where he has gone wrong and how to put it right. If there is a word which he can't be expected to know, show him how to spell it by writing a copy for him before you dictate.

> *Our queer language*
> When the English tongue we speak,
> Why is 'break' not rhymed with 'freak'?
> Will you tell me why it's true
> We say 'sew' but likewise 'few'?
> And the maker of a verse
> Cannot cap his 'horse' with 'worse'?
> 'Beard' sounds not the same as 'heard';
> 'Cord' is different from 'word';
> 'Cow' is 'cow' but 'low' is 'low',
> 'Shoe is never rhymed with 'foe',
> Think of 'hose' and 'whose' and 'lose',
> And think of 'goose' and yet of 'choose',
> Think of 'comb' and 'tomb' and 'bomb';
> 'Doll' and 'roll' and 'home' and 'some';
> And since 'pay' is rhymed with 'say',
> Why not 'paid' with 'said', I pray?
> We have 'blood' and 'food' and 'good',
> Wherefore 'done' but 'gone' and 'lone'?
> Is there any reason known?
> And, in short, it seems to me
> Sounds and letters disagree.
>
> (author unknown)

Fortunately, our spelling is not nearly so arbitrary as might seem from the verse above, *once we have enough experience* of 'our queer language' and know how sounds are *generally* spelled or, if they do not conform to a general pattern, how they are *probably* spelled. The spelling errors that a particular student makes are usually due either to *incomplete* knowledge of spelling generalisations, the *misapplication* of generalisations to parts of words, or complete ignorance of spelling probabilities. Look at the following examples of spellings

which could be produced for two simple words by a writer without this knowledge:

(ă)		(ĕ)	
day	(pay)	let	(bet)
da	(aorta)	leat	(weather)
dey	(they)	leit	(heifer)
dei	(veil)	liet	(friend)
dea	(great)	leot	(leopard)
dai	(rain)	lait	(said)
deigh	(neighbour)	lat	(many)
deh	(eh)	lut	(buried)
de	(fiancé)	layt	(says)
dee	(fiancée)	luet	(guess)
dez	(rendezvous)	+ others	
det	(ballet)		
dua	(persuade)		
due	(suede)		
dau	(gauge)		
dae	(phaeton)		
+ others			

Impossible! you say. Yes, quite true if you have any preconceptions at all about English spelling. You have gained these preconceptions through years of reading. You know the spelling rule that, when writing (k), if you are required to spell (kŭp) you write cup; if (kǐt) you write kit – and without conscious thinking. Look at Murray's performance on the spelling test again on page 9.

He spells two words correctly, but obviously more by accident than judgement, or they may be words he knows by sight. He has some knowledge of *possibilities* in spelling, but no idea of *probabilities*. When presented with a word he has not learned in this way, he knows that *c*, *k* and *ck* all say (k) but he has no idea *when* to use each. Are you going to teach him to spell every word as a sight word, and especially when it's already clear that he does not learn too successfully this way? A thousand words, each taught separately as sight words will see both of you going grey (probably prematurely).

About 85 per cent of English words fall into phonic patterns for spelling, and you can use *logic and the laws of probability* to teach these. The remaining 15 per cent are historically phonetic spellings and were originally phonically constructed, e.g. night – the *gh* was originally pronounced like the *ch* in the Scottish word loch. Many awkward words like this can be taught and remembered by reference to their origin. The book *Spelling* by G. H. Vallins, published by Andre Deutsch, gives a wealth of information about the *method* in our mad English spelling.

An approach to spelling
Obviously, you are going to have to do some homework yourself before teaching the method to students like Murray and Michael, but don't despair! Remember, you're streets ahead in your own spelling accomplishments, and you need be only a few steps ahead in teaching them an approach to spelling. The important thing is to *select* what you are going to teach carefully, concentrating on word patterns that it is important that they should each spell at least reasonably correctly. Thus, the spelling programme you offer a student will be individually structured according to his most urgent needs, and based on the writing vocabulary he requires to use. The examples which follow are *examples* only, you will be able to find your own words to suit your student.

Be realistic! It's not disastrous to spell *horrible* as *horable*; the word is still recognisable in context and there will be no difficulty in understanding what is meant. Therefore, it is a good mistake. But, if *pin* is spelled as *pen* and *share* is spelled as *chair*, there could be problems of confusion in meaning, and consequent embarrassment for your student. This does not mean that you countenance low standards. You set the level of the standard you expect Murray and

Michael to reach according to your knowledge of their abilities and achievements so far, and the achievement potential these seem to indicate. What is an acceptable mistake in one student's writing may be unacceptable in another's. Your criteria, should be:
- What are his capabilities to date?
- What have I taught him and what can I expect him to know by now?
- Which mistakes can I afford to ignore *for the present*, if not for ever?

Most of us discovered how to spell words during childhood. As our reading experience increased, we unconsciously made generalisations about spelling patterns, which most of the time serve us quite well even if, like Pooh's, our spelling is a bit 'wobbly' at times. We have to help Murray, Michael, and any adult we may teach, to *discover* these patterns too, and this process can begin almost as soon as they have grasped the basic letter-sound relationships.

As a literate individual you have cracked the complicated language code involved in reading and writing. Without necessarily knowing the multitude of spelling rules and generalisations, you nevertheless put them into practice all the time. The next section offers a guide to spelling rules and is intended as a reference for you as you begin to teach your student. Dip into it as and when the need arises with your student.

The first examples of spelling patterns for (k) are intended to illustrate an approach which can be applied to the teaching of other spelling patterns.

Look at some of the possibilities for spelling the (k) sound, the sound with which Murray displays so much confusion on his spelling test:

• at the beginning of a word	• at the end of a word
c as in cake	ck as in rack
k as in kite	ke as in rake
ch as in chemistry	k as in pink
qu as in quay	c as in picnic
	que as in antique

If you study this list, which is not complete, and think about the kind of words we use most often in writing, you will see that some patterns recur more frequently than others in spelling this sound at the beginnings and ends of words (the medial spellings have been deliberately omitted at this point). The number of words using the spellings *ch*, *qu*, and *que* is comparatively few and those words can be taught as sight words. It is upon the more frequent spelling patterns which you need to concentrate, because by doing so you will enable Murray or Michael to spell *more* words.

You will need to break down each pattern you wish to teach into very small learning steps, providing plenty of practice in each and ensuring that you do not teach a more difficult pattern until the preceding steps are learned and understood. Your spelling activities need not be practised in isolation from other reading and writing work. You can provide the appropriate practice within these other activities. It is often said that poor spellers ought to read a great deal as this will help their spelling. This is a dubious expectation. It will help if a student has a good visual memory, but otherwise is not likely to have much effect on spelling. Fortunately, it is important that your student has plenty of reading experience on other grounds, and reading may help to reinforce his consciousness of the structure of words.

Here is an example of how the generalisations about the spelling of the (k) sound can be illustrated and presented:

Step 1.
    cab
    cod
    cup
- first ask your student what he notices about these words – they all begin with the same letter c;

- then ask him what sound that letter makes – (k);
- explain that this sound can be spelled in different ways;
- ask him to look at the first two letters and ask which letters follow c – a, o and u. If your student says 'vowels' ask him which vowels;
- then ask him to explain the spelling rule which tells us how to spell (k) before a, o and u.
- repeat the exercise to show that (k) is spelled c before l and r, e.g.
cram
clamp
crane
close
- pronounce some words, e.g. cat, kit, cab, king, and ask your student to say 'yes' if he would use c to spell the (k) sound;
- provide some reading practice with sentences including words beginning with c.
- suggest to your student that he copies these words into his 'personal dictionary' under c or (k).

Step 2.
- follow the same pattern of questioning with these words to elicit that (k) is spelled k before e and i.
kit
keg
kite
keep
- then compare the lists

cab	kit
cod	keg
cup	kite
came	key
code	king
etc.	etc.

(k) before a, o, u and consonants is *usually* spelled c.
(k) before e, i (and y) is usually spelled k.
- give practice in *using* these generalisations, e.g.

–up	–od	
–it	–eg	c or k?
–at	–ab	

- try questions like:

Shall we have a –up of tea or –offee?
May I borrow your –ey to open the door?
A baby goat is called a –id; a baby –at is –alled a –itten.

- similarly, give practice in the (k) consonant blends, i.e. cr, cl. If Michael shows any confusion about these, put the two blends on separate cards, e.g.

| cr | | cl |

and pronounce a series of words, asking him to pick up, or point to, the card which represents the blend he hears, e.g.
class, crib, climb, crevice,
cranny, clip, clanging, etc.
- then provide word and sentence completion exercises, e.g.

Please ––ose the door behind you.

The plasterer mended the ––acks with Polyfilla.

Before teaching further generalisations about the spelling of the (k) sound, you may well choose to treat some simple generalisations about other sounds. However, to illustrate the complete process of building up knowledge about spelling patterns, or generalisations, we will develop the (k) sequence of spelling patterns further.

Step 3.
When Murray and Michael have grasped these first generalisations about the spelling of (k) at the beginning of a word, introduce the

following generalisations about the spelling of (k) at the end of a one-syllable word *after* a short vowel. (You will need to check that the description short vowel is remembered and understood; if not spend some time in revision.)

lock
black
sick
luck
deck

● read these words. Ask your student what is the last sound he hears in each – (k)
● ask him how it is spelled – (ck). Two letters making one sound (i.e. a diagraph).
● show the c̲ and k̲ lists with the c̲k̲ list to provide comparison and discuss the fact that c̲k̲ occurs at the *end* of the words; it can never occur at the beginning.

cab	kit	lock
cod	keg	black
cup	kite	luck
came	key	deck
code	Kyron	sick

● again, give plenty of reading practice to emphasise the visual pattern of the words, and play rhyming games, collecting words that fit into the pattern. Dictate words, phrases and short sentences, e.g.

back, luck, sock, tick,
black, jack, tick tack
Pack the spuds in a sack.

Step 4.
If your student seems confused about the sound of words like bank, explain that n̲ before (k) sounds like n̲g̲ (bangk); he should make the adjustment for spelling purposes quite easily.

bank
blink
sunk
honk

Step 5.
● you may have to delay treating the spelling of (k) after a long vowel if your student is not sure of it for reading yet, but it is the next step in this series of generalisations.

cake
like
poke
puke
(eke)

It is at this point that the differences between reading and spelling as activities becomes most apparent. Murray and Michael will have grasped that, when they encounter the silent e̲ pattern in reading, for example in cake and like etc., in most cases the first vowel says its name, and that it is the presence of the final e̲ which is the reason for this. In spelling words like cake, the (k) sound is *spelled* k̲e̲. It is best taught as this pattern, otherwise there will be confusion between this and c̲k̲. For this reason, it is a good idea to delay teaching this generalisation until your student responds automatically to reading that particular pattern of letters. Make word cards, or lists, to aid in teaching this step, e.g.

       pan   pane
or   pan e or pān̸e̸

crossing through the e to indicate that it is silent, and marking the vowel a̲ long.

● give practice in reading, and in sentence completion, e.g.

and

● eventually, you will be able to make up exercises requiring the use of each of these four generalisations.
● the final (k) generalisations can be dealt with at a much later stage:
● (k) between two short vowels in a two-syllable word is spelled c̲k̲ as in cricket, bucket, etc.
● (k) at the end of an unaccented syllable is spelled c̲ – frantic, arsenic, etc.
(*accent* means stress or emphasis in pronouncing a syllable of a word, e.g. blan'ket: *blan* is an accented syllable; *ket* is an unaccented syllable).
● in words of more than one syllable, (k) before a consonant is spelled c̲ – picnic, lactic.
But for the moment, and perhaps always, treat these as sight spellings because the formulation of the generalisations is both lengthy and abstract. (k) spelled q̲u̲ as in quay; q̲u̲e̲ as in antique and c̲h̲ as in chemistry, can be explained as foreign imports into the language. q̲u̲e̲ is a French ending; c̲h̲ only occurs in words derived from Greek (with the exception of ache, which is the result of a mistake made by Dr. Johnson). There is no need to dwell upon these patterns, as they are not in frequent usage, and you may choose to ignore them altogether.

Some other spelling generalisations and possible approaches

Most of the basic spelling generalisations can be built up as illustrated in the (k) example, first demonstrated individually, then compared with other patterns and put to use in sentences and paragraphs. It is helpful to group together generalisations conforming to similar patterns when they have each been taught separately, e.g.

The shortest vowels have the longest ending
● stiff hill lass (pass etc. + buzz, fizz later on)
  huff bell kiss (grass, later on)
one-syllable words with a short vowel followed by (f, l, s) tend to double those letters.
exceptions: bus us has pus
                    gas of his
● tack, back, sick, lock, duck.
one-syllable words with a short vowel followed by (k) spell that sound c̲k̲
exceptions: tic, sac
● badge, wedge, ridge, lodge, fudge
one-syllable words with a short vowel followed by (j) spell that sound d̲g̲e̲
● hatch, fetch, hitch, notch, hutch
one-syllable words with a short vowel followed by (ch) spell that sound t̲c̲h̲
exceptions: which, rich, such, much

The suffix generalisations
These can be taught as visual patterns initially, but this is not a reliable strategy in the long term for students whose visual memory is known not to be dependable. It would be better to treat each generalisation separately, showing the logical reasons for its existence.
● adding suffixes. Explain suffixes as a letter, or a group of letters, added to a word to change the way we use it. No spelling change is needed if the suffix begins with a consonant, if the base word ends in two consonants or in two vowels followed by one consonant, e.g. black-ness, prefer-ment, looking, handed, etc.
● double the final consonant of *one-syllable* words with *one short vowel* followed by *one consonant* before a suffix beginning with *a vowel*. e.g.,   bat + ing = batting,
                hop + er = hopper.
exceptions: living, having, giving, loving, etc.
● drop the final *e* of silent e words before a suffix beginning with a vowel, e.g. hate + ing = hating.
exceptions: a) words where final *e* is dropped when a *consonant* suffix is attached.

true + ly	= truly		
due + ly	= duly		
nine + th	= ninth		Truly, Mr. Duly, your ninth
argue + ment	= argument		argument is wholly awful,
whole + ly	= wholly		and that's the truth.
awe + ful	= awful		
true + th	= truth		

        b) words which retain silent *e*, despite a vowel suffix, to ensure that the meaning remains clear.

dye + ing	= dyeing		
singe + ing	= singeing		
mile + age	= mileage		sometimes
acre + age	= acreage		
free + ed	= freed		3 *e*'s together don't occur in English.
free + er	= freer		

If you adopt a logical approach towards spelling words with suffixes, you will need to emphasise:
● the broad meaning of each suffix.
● the letter pattern of each suffix.
● that they always occur at the *end* of words.
● that if a suffix is removed either a word remains, or a unit of meaning.
e.g.

bu/s	*s* is not a suffix here
train/s	suffix *s* = plural
box/es	suffix *es* = plural
r/ing	*ing* is not a suffix here
ring/ing	*ing* is a suffix here = is/was *doing*
r/ed	*ed* is not a suffix here
bor/ed	*ed* is a suffix here = past tense; the silent *e* of *bore* has been dropped.
hope/ful	suffix *ful* = full of
work/er	suffix *er* = a doer
attach/ment	suffix *ment* turns verb into noun
happi/ly	suffix *ly* turns adjective into adverb
giv/ing	suffix *ing* requires the dropping of silent *e* leaving giv etc.

The reason for the need for emphasis on the form and meaning of suffixes becomes apparent when you consider the following:

pact (noun)	mist (noun)
packed (verb)	missed (verb) etc.

If you have shown your student something of how language is *structured*, he will have a frame of reference for understanding the distinctions between these words, and will thus be able to *control* his own written language structures.

Point out each type of suffix as it occurs in reading activities first, then show how it is added to words in spelling. The spelling of a suffix never changes; the spelling of the word to which it is attached sometimes does. Take care to introduce and establish each pattern separately at first, only mixing with other patterns or introducing new elements or exceptions when your student has confidently grasped the previous steps.

add, double, drop, change

add	*add*	*double*	*drop*	*change*
suffix	*suffix*	*final consonant*	*e*	*y*
hands	looking	batting	raving	cried
coats	sailing	filling	hoped	fried
books	failed	hopped	shaker	lied
pencils	peering	dripped	coping	died
	rower	mopping	duped	*but**
	mewing	fatter	wiper	crying
				flying

+ ment	+ er			
ness	ist			
etc.	etc.			

*(because two i's don't occur together in English).

Plurals
● Exercises turning words, phrases, then sentences into the plural, based on your student's own usage. Treat the plural *-es* after the more frequent plural *s* e.g.

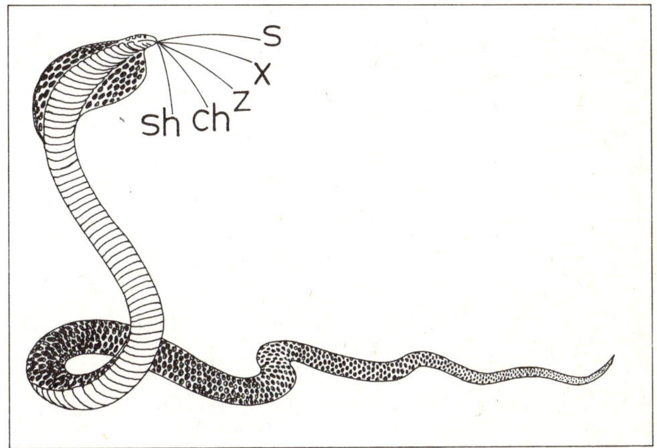

glass + (s) = glasses
box + (s) = boxes
buzz + (s) = buzzes
church + (s) = churches
ash + (s) = ashes

then deal with other plurals e.g. children, mice, geese, etc.
● *add, double, drop, change*
Do plenty of oral work with these, especially at the beginning, emphasising the patterns by questions.

wrap + ing	Is it a *one-syllable* word?	
build + er +	Has it *one short vowel*?	add
brick + ed	Followed by *one consonant*?	
	Does the *suffix begin with a vowel*?	

            if yes = double

or

WORD	suf.	1 syl	1 v	1 con	v suf	ADD or DOUBLE?
brick	ing	✓	✓	✗	✓	ADD
hand	s	✓	✓	✗	✗	ADD
black	ness	✓	✓	✗	✗	ADD
hop	er	✓	✓	✓	✓	DOUBLE
fit	ing					
back	ed					
hope	ful					

and later

WORD	suf.	ADD	DOUBLE	DROP	CHANGE
brick	ed	✓			
dry	ing	✓			
fill	er	✓			
crane	s	✓			
rope	ed			✓	
sit	ing		✓		
dry	ed				✓

later still exercises involving all the generalisations.

Include each pattern in dictated sentences, sentence completion exercises, etc. At first, limit these to one pattern, gradually mixing in new patterns as your student learns them. Always encourage him to give a reason for his answer in the early stages, to reinforce his grasp of the generalisation involved, so that you can be sure he knows what he is doing.

In this way you are encouraging him to have control over language, instead, as has hitherto been the case, language having control over him.

Long vowel sounds. The spelling of long vowel sounds can be treated equally systematically. Again, it is important to show that their spelling varies according to their position in words, e.g.

Most usual spelling of long vowel sounds			
long vowel	Initial	Medial	Final
(ā)	<u>a</u> apex	<u>a-e</u> tape	<u>ay</u> day
(ē)	<u>e</u> equal	<u>ee</u> feet <u>e-e</u> athlete (2 syl)	ee three
(ī)	<u>i</u> icon	<u>i-e</u> five	<u>y</u> fly (<u>ie</u> pie)
(ō)	<u>o</u> open	<u>o-e</u> rope	1. <u>ow</u> snow 2. (<u>o</u> potato, piano – Mexican & Italian words)
(ū)	<u>u</u> unit	<u>u-e</u> cube	1. <u>ue</u> statue 2. (<u>ew</u> stew)

The more advanced vowel digraphs and diphthongs (diphthong = 2 vowels brought together whose sounds blend into one syllable: oi, oy; ou, ow) can also be linked together according to their position in words, e.g.

Digraph or Diphthong	Initial	Medial	Final
(au), (aw)	<u>au</u> August	<u>au</u> Paul	<u>aw</u> saw
(ai)	<u>ai</u> ail	<u>ai</u> faint paint (<u>ai</u> is common before 2 consonants)	
(oi), (oy)	oil	coil	b<u>oy</u>
(ou), (ow)	<u>ou</u> 1. out <u>ow</u> 2. owl	<u>ou</u> 1. stout <u>ow</u> 2. town	<u>ow</u> now

(ow = common before <u>n</u> and <u>l</u>)

Final stable syllable patterns	
ta<u>ble</u>	bub<u>ble</u>
cy<u>cle</u>	fid<u>dle</u>
i<u>dle</u>	baf<u>fle</u>
tri<u>fle</u>	wrig<u>gle</u>
an<u>gle</u>	tac<u>kle</u>
an<u>kle</u>	tip<u>ple</u>

These syllables can cause confusion because the vowel sound is not spelled in the expected place. They are labelled as *final* because they occur at the end, or towards the ends of words with suffixes added, e.g. baffling; *stable* because the pattern does not vary ble, cle, dle, etc. Make syllable cards to show your student how these words are structured, e.g.

ta ble		bub ble
bu gle		**tac kle**

exceptions to the spelling pattern: label, triple.

Spelling choices.
The spelling generalisations mentioned so far do not include *all* those which one of your students might need to know, but they cover the most *frequent* patterns used in writing (see also page 26). Since some of the words which we often use in writing do not conform to these patterns, because they are derived from other languages, or their spelling form (but not their pronunciation) has changed over the years, you will need to introduce your student to other spelling possibilities and to show how a dictionary can help him to make a choice between these. This is where the *laws of probability* enter the picture. Take, for example, the sound (f). The most obvious choice for the spelling of this sound is <u>f</u> or <u>ff</u>. But there are a few words of Greek origin which spell that sound <u>ph</u> – telephone, <u>ph</u>oney, <u>ph</u>onetic, etc. There is also <u>gh</u> as in cou<u>gh</u> and rou<u>gh</u>. If your student learns that <u>f</u> or <u>ff</u> are the most *probable* spellings of (f), that <u>ph</u> and <u>gh</u> respectively are further *possibilities*, then the dictionary can be of use to him, because he'll have some idea of *where* to look for a word he's not sure of how to spell.

Developing dictionary skills
We know that Michael is in the habit of using a dictionary but it would be a good idea to check his speed and efficiency by doing some of the activities previously described, and, by giving him practice in locating simple words in the four quartiles, i.e.

A —— D (1st)
E —— K (2nd)
L —— R (3rd)
S —— Z (4th)

Show him a dictionary page and point out *guide words* which are an aid to locating words quickly provided that alphabet sequence is understood.

Make up a few dictionary sheets, e.g.

mine	300	minute
ministry		miracle

and show approximately where different words fit in, e.g. mingle, mirror, and explain that he would be able to find these with the help of the guide words.

According to the capabilities of your student, you can systematically extend his knowledge of the dictionary to include other aspects which may be useful to him, e.g. pronunciation symbols, parts of speech, definitions, etc.

Encourage your student to refer to the dictionary whenever he's in doubt about a word, so that he becomes familiar with the format of this reference tool. There will be plenty of opportunities for the use of the dictionary, both in the work you do based on his present interests, and the other subjects you introduce to extend his knowledge and interests to wider fields. There will be chances to add to his working vocabulary throughout your work. Words are tools of *communication and thinking*. The accuracy, flexibility, scope and subtlety of thought depends directly on the same qualities of this vocabulary. Words themselves can be stimulants to thought. Try some of the activities below as oral exercises, then encourage your student to record the words you produce together, and include them in subsequent language activities which you plan:

● discuss synonyms: collect words into categories for similar meaning, e.g. *old*, aged, elderly, antique, decrepit, ancient, etc. You could arrange them in descending order and talk about the qualities they suggest.

● discuss antonyms: collect groups of words opposite in meaning and discuss their precision, e.g.

easy – difficult, hard, complicated, intricate, etc.

● make up your own definitions of common words, e.g. table, and discuss them. Check in a dictionary afterwards and compare your results.

● try word building through word derivations, e.g.

telephone	bicycle	tricycle
television	bisect	trisect
telegram	biennial	triangle
telegraph	biped	tripartite
telepathy		
telecommunications		

● collect words with interesting histories or meanings, e.g.

derived from the names of people – boycott, sandwich, wellington, cardigan, macadam, Rachmanism.

biscuit (French 'bis cuit' – twice cooked)
precocious (French 'pre-cooked')

navvy – originally 'inland navigators' – nineteenth century canal builders.

● collect slang, idioms, and proverbs.
'a load of Old Codd's Wallop' – Mr. Codd invented the original 'pop' bottle in the last century. The brewers liked the idea but despised the tame contents, hence the description.

● group idioms, e.g. head, foot, heart.

off his head
head over heels in love
give him his head

put your foot in it
foot it fast

best foot forward

heart broken
touch the heart of
soft hearted

● collect proverbs, and discuss their meaning.
● use of prepositions, e.g. make after, away with, for, off, off with, over, up, up to.
● try word building games, e.g.

t	r	e
n	a	d
l	p	g

2 letter words = 1 point
3 letter words = 2 points
4 letter words = 5 points
5 + letter words = 10 points

Rules: Words can be made by moving from one letter square to another, on the same principle as the game of draughts.
Evening newspapers and some daily newspapers often feature word building games. It is worth collecting these.
● collect surnames – Miller, Fletcher, Bowman, Smith, Hill, Robertson – categorise according to derivations from people, places or occupation.
● collect compound words, e.g. handbag, scrapyard, overcoat.
● collect homophones – words that *sound* the same but have different spelling and meanings, e.g. threw/through, pair/pare/pear.
● collect homographs – words that are *spelled* the same but have several meanings, e.g. fair, just, exhibition, mediocre, etc.
● collecting word referents (subtle variations in meaning according to context) is a useful activity, e.g.

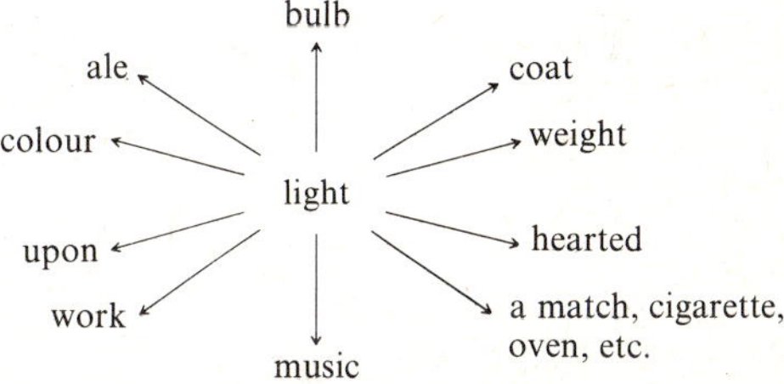

● collect words which have entered common usage fairly recently, e.g. escalate, viable, hijack, mugging, etc.
● try exercises requiring direct reference to a dictionary, e.g.
Carbon is a ....
Dick dressed <u>immaculately</u> for the dinner.
The possibilities are infinite and you will know the level of difficulty with which your student can cope. Activities such as these will increase Michael's vocabulary, appreciation of word usages, meaning, knowledge of word structures, and will reinforce many of your spelling activities by enhancing his consciousness of letter and sound sequences in words.

Difficult words
There are some words with which even reasonably competent writers experience confusion and difficulty in remembering, e.g. their, there; were, where; to, too, two, etc. The only solution is to find a way by which your student can remember them, either in the form of mnemonic sentence or by a series of associations, e.g.
● there/their and were/where
● here ⎫
  there ⎬ places
  where ⎭
heir – inherits *possessions*
Their – *possessions* belonging to *them*.
● to/too/two
too (more than you want of something, therefore an extra <u>o</u>)
two

associate <u>w</u> in swan with t<u>w</u>o

● son/sun
A sOn is a bOy.
● stationery/stationary
stationEry   } associate the two words.
   Envelopes
● principle/principal
princiPAL
   Promotes Adult Learning
● hear/here
we hear with our ears
● separate
sePARate into PARts.
● necessary
one collar, two socks   i.e. one c and two s's.

Other problematical spelling patterns

● e elephant   ea head.
Most of the words in which (ĕ) is spelled ea are short, common words connected with everyday life. Unfortunately, there are as many short words spelled with e.

(ĕ) spelled ea ; the most often used words

dead	dread	deaf	breadth	breast	meadow
head	spread	dealt	health	heavy	treadle
lead	stead	sweat	wealth	ready	heaven
read	tread	death	realm	steady	pleasant
bread	thread	breath	meant	weapon	measure

Select the words in this group which your student most needs to know how to spell and put them into sentences. If he knows that ea is a spelling choice for (ĕ), he can check in the dictionary when he is in doubt.

● -ary or -ery?
Only a few words end in -ery, the most common of which are:
cemetery   distillery   monastery   confectionery
millinery   stationery   dysentery
Spell the rest with -ary.

● ie or ei?
Write i before e
Except after c
or when sounded like tree.
As in neighbour and weigh,
And except seize and seizure,
And also leisure,
Weird, height and either,
Forfeit and neither.

Have a piece of pie
You can't believe a lie
In a siege an army sits before a city.

● y or ey?
Not many words in frequent usage end in ey. Choose those your student needs to know from the list below and teach him these. Any other words ending with the short sound of i or e are spelled with a y:

attorney	money	hockey	volley	chimney
honey	monkey	abbey	kidney	parsley
barley	turkey	Surrey	jockey	journey
asprey	hackney	trolley	covey	lamprey
motley	pulley	alley	lackey	
valley	medley	tourney	flunkey	

● ey says (ă) in the following words:
convey   obey
survey   prey
purvey   they

You will find that your student will need to use only a small number of these words, so group them into sentences or phrases to help him remember them.

A brief guide to selected spelling rules and generalisations

No, no. How many times do I have to tell you – horse before cow except after pig.

● q is always followed by u and at least one other vowel, e.g. quit, queen, quarrel.
● y and x are never doubled.
● no word in English ends in v or j (spiv and raj are not English words). They end in ve whether the vowel is long or short, e.g. gave, have, love.
● one-syllable words in which the vowel says its name usually end in consonant -e, e.g. cāke, fīve, cove, muse; exceptions: long ē is most often spelled ee e.g. feet.
● the (k) sound at the end of a one-syllable word after one short vowel is nearly always spelled ck e.g. back, deck, sick, clock, muck. Exceptions: sac, tic.
● the (ch) sound at the end of a one-syllable word after one short vowel is nearly always spelled tch e.g. patch, fetch, pitch, blotch, clutch. Exceptions: such, much, rich, which.
● the (j) sound at the end of a one-syllable word after one short vowel is spelled dge, e.g. badge, edge, bridge, lodge, fudge.
● the (f, l, s, z) sounds are usually doubled when spelled at the end of one-syllable words after one short vowel, e.g. stiff, hell, fuss, buzz. Exceptions: us, bus, gas, if, off, this, yest, plus, nil, pal.
● (ŏ) after w is usually spelled a e.g. wander, watch, wasp.
● (ĕr) after w is usually spelled o e.g. work, worth, word.
● ti, ci, and si are three spellings most frequently used to say (sh) at the beginning of all syllables except the first.
e.g.   national, patient, palatial, infectious,
         gracious, ancient, musician, financial,
         session, admission, mansion, division.
(exceptions – ship, as a suffix, e.g. worship.)
● i comes before e when it is pronounced (ē), except when it follows (c) – or when sounded like (ā) as in neighbour, weigh.
e.g.   brief, field, priest,
         receive, deceive, ceiling.
(exceptions – neither, foreign, sovereign, seized, counterfeit, and forfeited, leisure.
● all and well followed by another syllable only have one l
e.g.   also, already, although, welcome, welfare.
● oa almost always only occurs as a spelling in one-syllable words,
e.g.   roast, boat, oats.
● to keep the hard sound for g, follow it with a u when spelling (g) before i or e
e.g.   guess, guide, guest.
● igh, ough, and augh are usually followed by t
e.g.   might, bought, caught.

Plurals

● most plurals are formed by adding s e.g. animals, hands.
● nouns ending in s, x, z, ch, sh, add es to form the plural e.g. buses, boxes, buzzes, churches, lashes.
● nouns ending in vowel -y combinations are made plural by adding s e.g. toys, keys.

● nouns ending in consonant -y are made plural by changing y to i and adding es, e.g. lady, ladies.
● nouns ending in vowel -o combinations are made plural by adding s, e.g. radios, studios.
● nouns ending in consonant -o combination *usually* add es, e.g. potatoes, volcanoes, but words from Italian connected with music add s e.g. pianos, solos. It is wise to use a dictionary for these words.
● *most* nouns ending in f or fe form their plurals by adding s, e.g. roofs, chiefs. Some change the final f to a v before adding -es to form the plural, e.g. leaf, leaves; knife, knives.

Suffixes
● *double* the final consonant before adding a suffix beginning with a vowel to one-syllable words ending in one short vowel followed by one consonant, e.g.:

drop   dropping   dropped
fit   fitter   fittest
man   mannish
flip   flipper   flipping

Exceptions: fix, box, mix – x never doubles in English.

● add suffixes beginning with a consonant, e.g.
sadly, hatless, sinful
● double the final syllable in two- or three-syllable words, if the final syllable is stressed, e.g. confer, conferring, begin, beginning, but visit, visited; benefit, benefited.
● words ending in el or al double l before adding a suffix regardless of accent, e.g. quarrel, signalled, metallic.
● usually *drop* the final e on words when adding a suffix beginning with a vowel, e.g. late + er = later.
● retain the final e on words when adding suffixes beginning with a consonant, e.g. hope + less = hopeless.
● change final y to i when adding suffixes *except* when the suffix begins with i or when y has a vowel in front of it, e.g.

try   tried   trying
rely   relied   reliably   relying
play   playing   played   player

● use -est as the suffix when comparing three or more things, e.g. tallest, nicest, oldest.
● use -ist for people (nouns) who do things, e.g. artist, humanist, violinist.
● the sound (n) as a verb suffix is spelled en, e.g. ripen, deaden.
● the sound (n) indicating a person, nationality or religion is spelled -an, e.g. American, Lutheran.
● use -ous as the suffix when the word is an adjective, e.g. dangerous, marvellous (-ous at the end of a word usually means 'full of'). Use -us as the suffix when the word is a noun, e.g. sinus, crocus.
● -ise, -ize? Use -ise most of the time, -ize is becoming defunct. Only two common words end in -yse: analyse, paralyse. Only two common words end in -ize: prize, capsize.
● usually use -er as a suffix for one-syllable words meaning a person who 'does', e.g. diner, jumper, runner.
● use ar to form an adjective, e.g. singular, regular, popular. Use or for words of two or more syllables meaning a person or thing that 'does', e.g. actor, editor, incinerator.
● -ceed, -sede, -cede.
three -ceed words – succeed, exceed, proceed,
one -sede – supersede.
All others – cede, e.g. intercede, antecede, precede.
If you proceed at this rate, you will succeed in exceeding the speed limit.
● -able or -ible ending.
use -able:
after root words, e.g. available, dependable.

after root words ending in e,
e.g. desirable, believable, usable (drop e).
after i, e.g. reliable, sociable.
when other forms of the root word have a dominant a vowel, e.g. irritable, durable, abominable.
after a hard c or g, e.g. educable, practicable, navigable.
(exceptions – formidable, inevitable, memorable, probable, portable, indomitable, insuperable)
Use -ible:
after non-word roots, e.g. audible, horrible, possible.
when the root has an immediate ion form, e.g. digestible, suggestible, convertible.
after a root ending in ns or miss, e.g. responsible, comprehensible, permissible.
after a soft c or g, e.g. legible, negligible, forcible, invincible.
(exceptions – contemptible, resistible, collapsible, flexible)
● -ery or -ary ending. Words ending in -ery are often obvious, e.g. very, brewery, flattery, bakery, nursery.
If in doubt use -ary, e.g. dictionary, secretary, commentary, stationary (halt).
(seven words ending in -ery that might cause trouble – distillery, confectionery, millinery, cemetery, dysentery, monastery, stationery (paper)).
● full and till added to the end of another word drop one l, e.g. useful, handful, until.

Pronunciation
● silent -e at the end of a word usually makes the preceding vowel long (say its alphabetic name).
e.g. cake, Pete, time, home, puke, compose, concave, etc.
● a following w is usually pronounced (ŏ), e.g. wander, watch.
● o following w is usually pronounced (er), e.g. work, worth. Exceptions: worry, worried, wore;
● when c is followed by e, i, or y, it says (s). Otherwise it says (k).
centre, ceiling, circle, cycle,
cottage, cave, cream, curious, clever;
● when g is followed by i, e, or y, it says (j). Otherwise it says (g), as in gold, e.g.
gentle, giant, gymnastic,
gallon, gold, guide, glass, grow;
(exceptions – get, begin, girl, give, gear, geese, gift, girth, geyser, giddy);
● a single vowel in the middle of a syllable is usually short, e.g. hot, pic-nic;
● a vowel at the end of a syllable is usually long, e.g. pi-lot, ba-con;
● when a vowel comes before a double consonant, it is almost always short, e.g. super, supper;
● when two consonants stand between two vowels, the syllables usually divide between the two consonants, e.g. blan-ket, nap-kin, ten-nis, but-ter;
● when one consonant stands between two vowels, the syllables may divide before or after the consonant, e.g. be-long, man-ic;
● when three consonants stand between two vowels, the syllables divide between a blend and the other consonant, e.g. cap-stan, hand-some;
● when ed comes at the end of a word, it adds a syllable only if it is preceded by d or t, e.g. dented, folded (otherwise: shipped, walked, etc.);
● a compound word is divided between the words making it up, e.g. hand-bag, bath-room, air-port;
● prefixes and suffixes are usually pronounced separately from the rest of the word, regardless of the rules already described, e.g. con-tent-ed, cold-est;
● if a word of more than one syllable ends in le the consonant preceding the le begins the last syllable: e.g.

ta-ble   bu-gle
bab-ble   strug-gle.

3.
Special problems

So far in this book we have discussed ideal teaching locations such as your home, the student's home or neutral territory. Now let's take a look at some less than ideal locations which may, if not dealt with, hamper the teaching situation. We will also look at some special circumstances which may affect attitude, enthusiasm and progress.

The classroom

Often a tutor is required to conduct a literacy course in a school building belonging to the authority which operates the scheme. There are, of course, advantages in teaching in a school; blackboards, chalk, desks, chairs, equipment like projectors and tape recorders are more likely to be around. Your student may feel differently. School may for him be associated with failure and distress. He may feel worried about his friends and relatives finding out that he is going back to school. Well, considering our function as that of satisfying our student's demands, a little effort will be needed in order to turn this situation into one which he will find not only tolerable but also conducive to a positive learning attitude. A school building can be presented as a relaxed working environment if you try to make it as adult and informal as possible.

The selection of a room will probably be your first step. You may find that the library, cafeteria or music room will provide the type of atmosphere you feel your students require. Tables and chairs which can be arranged in small groups, circles or semi-circles will dispel the memory of rigidly set rows of desks. If you have to use a classroom try to ensure that the desks and chairs are comfortable for adults. Sitting in a third form desk with chins on knees is not the greatest boost for your students' egos. Nor will it allow them to work easily. Desks can be arranged in a semi-circle and the teacher's table can be set to one side to break from the established classroom setting.

Students' motivation

Students whose motivation is questionable, or lacking, can present you with particular difficulties. In such circumstances, two approaches are available:

- define and extend what incentive your student may have;
- provide an incentive which will excite and encourage your student.

It is not your function as a tutor to force reading and writing upon a student. Not only will the lack of success of such an attempt discourage *you*, it may well put the potential student off literacy for life.

In rare circumstances a student may be embarking on a literacy course in order to satisfy a referral agent (perhaps a probation officer, wife or employer) and feel absolutely no personal desire to acquire literacy skills. Murray may certainly present such a problem but at least he seems willing to have a go. The questions arise: 'How can I show Murray that reading and writing skills will be of some positive use to him?' and 'How can I convince him that he can acquire these skills?'

Using what we know about Murray there are a number of possible answers to these questions. Murray 'hated reading because he was not any good at it'. He may also have baulked at the particular kind of reading material, as, unfortunately, much of the remedial work in schools is still based on rather insipid, childish situations or on the tedious 'Pat the fat cat'. If this is the case, then you have some indication of the possible reading material to use:

- offer Murray material which is well within his level of competence;

- offer him material which will excite him and permit him to view himself as an adult.

Specific sensory difficulties

The processes involved in reading, spelling and writing are complex and involve the coordination of several senses and perceptions. In reading we see the word; the image is transmitted to the brain; the brain remembers or decodes the image and gives it meaning. Then the meaning of that word is put in context with the rest of the sentence, paragraph and passage. In writing and spelling we picture what the word looks like or we decode it using sounds; the brain transmits the message to our arms and fingers and the eye follows the message to confirm it. With so much going on in both processes, it is no wonder that when one of the factors is out of joint, the whole sequence suffers. However, so long as the specific difficulty is not too severe as in the case of deafness or blindness, for example, the problem may well be overcome with your help.

Visual memory

Someone who suffers from defects in visual memory and visual perception will have difficulties in short term memory span, or in other words, difficulty in remembering things that he sees. Work on a basic sight vocabulary previously outlined in this book will have to be reinforced by emphasising the phonic approach. The degree to which you will need to avoid *whole word* teaching and rely on *sound-symbol* association will depend on the severity of the problem involving visual memory. In particularly severe cases you may have to employ auditory, tactile and kinasthetic methods in order to reinforce the visual image.

- Auditory. The term auditory covers the functions of listening and saying and is best applied to the phonic approach. The student first listens to you say a word. He then repeats the word and spells it out either phonically – by letter, sound or syllable – ca-t, rab-bit, in-ter-est, or by naming the letters. The choice may be left to the preference of the student but generally speaking the approach involving blending the sounds has proved most successful. Variations on the auditory approach involve the use of a tape recorder (see the later section on resources) and repeating lists of words having similar phonic constructions – head, bread, dead and spelling them out loud. This method is, of course, most effective if your student has a good auditory memory. By looking at words and sounding them out he will be employing his asset (auditory memory) and assisting his deficiency (visual memory).
- Tactile. The term tactile refers to the function of feeling and in teaching can mean tracing letters on sandpaper or felt or using a fibre tip pen. Just as we use our tactile sense and memory when we select covers for our furniture, your student can reinforce his other senses through feeling the shapes of letters. By tracing an a on sandpaper while looking at the letter and saying the sound, he is applying several techniques in order to imprint the shape of the letter in his memory bank. Sandpaper or felt need only be used in severe cases, but the use of a fibre tip pen for writing is a good general tactile exercise. The fibre tip pen will transmit the feel of the letters and words through the comparatively rough contact it has with paper.
- Kinaesthetic. 'Write out that spelling mistake fifty times' is a phrase remembered with horror as we recall this punishment incurred for our spelling errors. As an adult, however, your student

should try and accept that writing out a word three or five times will reinforce the image and feel of the word. It is thought that children need to see, read and write a word about thirty or so times before they can reproduce it. With an adult it is difficult to be precise but clearly a lot of repetition will reinforce and consolidate learning. It should no longer symbolise a punishment as the method can be justified as a sound learning technique. Its value can be related to several abilities previously acquired by your student through repetition. He no longer has to remember the H formula in order to shift gears in his car. This apparently natural sequence of movement has been learned through kinaesthetic repetition. In severe cases your student may feel the need to exaggerate or expand the movement in order to reinforce the shape of a letter, syllable or word. Here, writing out the image in the air or on the wall or carpet may prove to be a useful exercise.

So far, in dealing with visual memory difficulties we have stressed the importance of relying upon the auditory, tactile and kinaesthetic approaches. Of course, using these systems will incorporate the visual aspect as well. In each exercise the student will be *looking* at the image he is dealing with as well as *saying* it, *feeling* it and *moving* with it. Thus, even though the object of the exercise is to find ways around his visual memory problems he will be exercising and using what visual memory he can call upon.

Visual perception
'I still get confused over b and d!' This comment *may* indicate difficulties in perceiving differences between similar shapes and symbols. Often the confusion between left and right is related to this problem, but again many of the exercises previously outlined in the book can be adapted to circumvent this difficulty. Reinforcement of specific patterns can be achieved through the concentrated use of auditory, tactile and kinaesthetic methods, and the introduction of visual mnemonics can prove to be of considerable value. A student having difficulty in distinguishing between b and d can for example be shown the image of these letters in the form of a bed with the bedposts at either end.

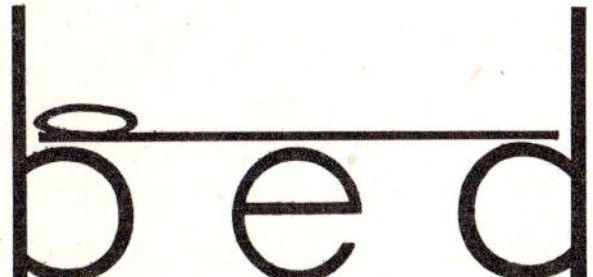

If your student is secure in his knowledge of the shape of the letter p, a mnemonic might evolve using the brand name BP.

A kinaesthetic approach can also be used to discriminate between these two similar symbols by encouraging your student to employ a cursive handwriting style. Thus *b* and *d* will become more easily distinguishable in shape and movement.

In dealing with visual perception problems, keep in mind that you are *working with an adult*. He has had years of experience in solving problems and once presented with the specific difficulty, e.g. b, d confusion, he may well present the appropriate solution. The BP mnemonic, use of a familiar word such as beer, the image of b as Bertha's bottom and other interesting ideas have all been offered by students on literacy courses.

If the difficulty is such that a mnemonic method is unsuccessful, the visual, auditory, tactile and kinaesthetic methods will have to be employed. Looking at a letter, sounding it out and writing it will reinforce the symbol and enable your student to feel at home with it. Perhaps the main point to remember with this system is to *isolate* the letter you are dealing with. Make certain that the shape and sound of the letter b is thoroughly established before attempting to introduce the letter d. By working on both these letters at once you may only increase the confusion.

Other symptoms of visual perception difficulties include the reversal of words (saw for was), the inversion of certain letters (m for w) and the omission or addition of letters to words. With children, such symptoms of the visual dyslexic – (a neurological term often used to describe visual perceptual difficulties in the process of decoding) require careful handling, accompanied by much skill and patience. The problems these symptoms cause to adults are diminished since the adult dyslexic has had the advantages of learning to cope with and compensate for the disability through intellect and maturity. You, as the tutor, can feel free to rely on these resources to circumvent the deficiencies and employ his assets.

Auditory memory
A student may have a poor auditory memory and suffer from defective auditory perception. Again it is the job of the tutor to work around the deficiency and exploit the student's abilities. Most of us can spell the word *thorough*, not from the sight of the word, but from the rhythm of the sound of the letters in *orough*. We can remember, with ease, a sequence of sounds which gives us the correct spelling combination. Some students will lack this facility and may have to rely on visual, tactile and kinaesthetic approaches to these awkward words. Reinforcement, using these alternative methods, will prove very effective. Keep in mind that the visual approach to spelling is, for the most part, reliable and rapid.

Auditory perception.
The term auditory perception covers the ability to discriminate between sounds. The student who writes pet for pit or free for three may be lacking in this perceptual skill. Exercises involving repetition of sounds either with a tape recorder or across a room may, to some degree, alleviate the problem. However, again you might consider working round the difficulty and rely on your student's visual memory and adaptability to a tactile and kinaesthetic approach. By arranging words in visual families, like bough, through, cough, and by writing them out a few times and using them in sentences, your student will store the image of the words in his visual memory bank.

Accent.
'A tinker is a philosopher. You know, someone who tinks.' With our diverse population we have several accents to deal with, each presenting particular peculiarities. The Irish and West Indian *tree* and the Cockney *free* are examples of differences in pronunciation of the word *three* which may lead you away from teaching this word using an auditory or phonic approach. It is not your function to change your student's pronunciation or accent and, indeed, lacking an English Academy, we really have no criterion for correction – to a man from Peckham an 'ouse' is definitely not a *home*. Certainly, it would make your job easier if your student produced a BBC World Service announcer's accent, but when we consider teaching words such as cough, night and through, the varieties of pronunciation of a few other words becomes less of a worry. The same methods used to teach irregular sight words can be employed with these words which may seem phonically accurate to you but bear no sound-symbol relationship to your student.

Intelligence
Intelligence is a term which covers a variety of mental abilities including such general items as alertness, quickness of mind, brightness, possession of intellect, thinking and reasoning powers. These faculties among students can range from brilliant to a degree of dimness. As you have seen in the section dealing with causes of illiteracy you have no reason to assume that your student will be very far off the average intelligence range in either direction. There may arise, however, the exceptional case in which the student's level of intelligence will have to be considered in the teaching situation.

● Superior intelligence. The student of superior intelligence may present problems when he becomes frustrated that he cannot progress as fast as he would like. Possibly he has no trouble grasping other skills, in say measuring, computing or coding, and feels that the same speedy technique can be applied to acquiring literacy skills. The fact that he has not as yet learned how to read, write and spell may indicate a specific problem – perceptual, blending, visual memory that will have to be handled in a methodical structured approach.

Perhaps the two most useless words in teaching are 'Slow down'. After all, why should your student? However, you must find ways by which you can limit your student's speed in order to give him a chance to absorb and consolidate the patterns being taught. The highly intelligent student can, no doubt, be approached on this subject and he will probably offer solutions to the problem of speed himself. At the same time, you can provide the type of atmosphere, lesson structure and material which will thoroughly reinforce learning patterns without offending your student's intellect. Perhaps the main items to keep in mind are his awareness that you recognise him as a highly intelligent adult and your treatment of him as such. With this attitude the sharing situation in the lesson is reinforced through mutual recognition of skills and talents.

● Low intelligence. The student whose intelligence has been diagnosed as being considerably below average will have to be taught using methods which do not incorporate a high degree of intensity or student initiative. Aside from the inability to cope with literacy skills the student's own self image will influence the lesson situation. His dealings with society have taught him two things: that he cannot grasp concepts and understand ideas at the same rate as most people; he cannot compensate for that deficiency as others might do by acquiring information through reading.

As a result of these impressions, he will have experienced many failures and may view himself as unteachable. The very fact that he has embarked on a course of literacy learning may be his first step in changing that self image. It is up to you to extend this step by proving to your student that he can learn.

It will certainly be necessary to counteract the history of failure with a series of successes. By aiming for short term realistic goals you can provide your student with recognisable rungs on his ladder of success. Each achievement must be pointed out to your student in order to diminish his sense of failure. To the average student, learning to write out his name and address after six concentrated lessons may not be the height of literary achievement; but to the student with limited ability the impact of this accomplishment must be made positive and exciting.

● Educationally sub-normal

ESN – educationally sub-normal – is a *general* term having, as yet, no specific definition but covering a multitude of learning difficulties, e.g. low intelligence, behavioural problems, mental blocks, etc. Your student may as a child, have been diagnosed as ESN due to his lack of success at school. This classification may no longer be applicable. Don't forget, at the age of sixteen you were classified as adolescent! The low intelligence factor may still remain but many of the other above mentioned problems may have disappeared. With adulthood comes experience in coping with difficulties, solving problems and adapting to learning situations, e.g. factory work, cooking, repairing one's car or using automatic ticket machines. These experiences, through maturity, will negate not only many of the symptoms of the classification, but their effects as well. Your student may, however, still view himself as ESN and again it is up to you to help him change this self image.

'Out of Bounds' cases

On occasions an individual with very difficult problems may slip through the screening process of a literacy scheme. Such individuals may have problems beyond the scope of the scheme and the tutors working in it. Specialist help is required for obvious disabilities such as deafness, gross speech defects and most cases of brain damage.

However, other problems may arise which you may not be able to cope with in your teaching situation. You are not only entitled to, but obliged to, refer these cases back to the scheme or to the appropriate referral agency. Obviously your student is entitled to know why you are doing this.

Several emotional problems may hamper the lessons to such an extent that progress becomes discouragingly slow or non-existant. Learning disabilities may be so severe that none of the methods within your experience, outlined in this book or from your training have any effect on the literacy problem. Resistance to learning may be so strong that you are unable to break it down. For each of these cases you must be prepared to recognise your limitations and offer the student an alternative solution to his difficulty. Many of these problems will have to be solved before your student can be ready to embark on a course in literacy. Remember, your role is that of technician, not that of amateur psychologist, social worker or educational therapist. Referrals can be made, with your student's permission, to the local social services, the local education authority, the local Citizens' Advice Bureau and the local dyslexia association. Each of these services should be able to provide specific specialist help to your student and relieve you of the burden of trying to conquer a problem beyond your capabilities. Seek help from your scheme or your local authority on these matters.

● Personality conflict. One problem that is difficult to acknowledge is the situation involving a personality conflict. The last thing a second form school teacher would say is that she 'can't stand Johnny Smith'. If a conflict does arise between a teacher and one of her pupils, she generally has to grin and bear it.

As a tutor in adult literacy you can acknowledge personality conflict and need feel no reluctance in dealing with it. The second form teacher feels that as an adult, she should be expected to adjust to the personality of an eight year old child. You, on the other hand, are dealing with an adult and the task of adjustment may prove difficult if not impossible. You, therefore, have the choice, either you grin and bear it – so long as the conflict does not interfere with literacy progress – or you transfer your student to another tutor.

Tactful means will have to be employed in order to make the transfer as smooth as possible. Of course the situation may arise whereby your student finds it difficult to work with *you*. You will soon sense negative vibrations from your student and, as he may be unaware of the options available to him it is up to you to initiate the change.

● Other factors. The student who misses lessons may be expressing his dislike for you but may feel unable to express himself. Of course, there are a variety of possible reasons for students skipping lessons and you may, at some time or other, have to deal with this problem.

● External factors: the student may well find that the programmed times for the lessons conflict with job or family commitments or a particular TV programme; illness; or the student may feel discouraged through apparent lack of achievement with his lessons. These difficulties will all have to be sorted out keeping in mind that the lessons are sharing situations. Times must be convenient for both you and your student. It may have been decided at the first meeting to meet every Tuesday night at seven o'clock without having checked to see that other commitments would not interfere. Now is the time to sit down with your student and work out the best possible schedule.

● Illness is, of course, a factor beyond your control. If it is a recurring problem a solution could be found whereby your student is taught at his home. If you cannot manage this, then perhaps another tutor could help.

Discouragement over failing to reach preconceived goals is a factor which generally crops up periodically. This feeling can be countered in several ways. Certainly, it is up to the student to establish his goals; but it is up to you to help him reconcile them in terms of time, effort and rate of success. Record-keeping shows its value at this stage when you present your student with the work he was doing four weeks ago and contrast it with the results of the last lesson. A short quiz covering items that have been thoroughly reinforced will further encourage your student. Finally, emphasising the fact that by maintaining consistency in attendance your student will progress step by step to his established goals will secure the need for a regular learning pattern.

Failures

'My student's child was taken to hospital last night with appendicitis, his wife ran off with the milkman this morning and this afternoon his dog got run over. This evening we had a terrible lesson. What did I do wrong?' From time to time you may experience what might be termed a 'dud' lesson. Whether the dud lesson is a result of your hangover or your student's is not important, so long as your student does not feel guilty or discouraged by it. In the same way plateaus may be reached when no outstanding progress seems to be made for two or three lessons. You need then to maintain your student's enthusiasm and try new methods: face the problem with your student and explain that just as we all have good and bad days socially, at work and at home, we can't expect that every lesson will be outstanding; have contingency arrangements available in the form of games (see the section on resources) and reinforcement material; put acquired literacy skills into practice by going out for a walk and reading roadsigns, advertisements and labels in a shop or pub.

By maintaining a positive attitude you will be able to put the difficulties in perspective and steer your student back on the upward track.

4. Planning and evaluation

The plans that you are able to make for your first lesson with your student will be limited by the amount and type of information you receive from your literacy scheme organiser. Practice varies in different parts of the country. Some organised literacy schemes subject potential pupils to a battery of achievement and diagnostic tests, the rationale being that the information derived from these helps the organiser to match students with tutors. Other schemes operate a more ad hoc system of assessment and leave it to the volunteer tutor to find out what assets and deficiencies the student possesses. Whatever the system, it is obviously essential to gather as much *relevant* information as possible about a student *before* attempting to plan a course for him, so that you can clarify both his and your objectives.

Reading tests

The most common method of assessing a student's current level of achievement is to give him one or more of a readily available series of published tests, usually one which purports to assess reading achievement. Probably the most well known and frequently used of these is the Holborn Reading Scale. This test of mechanical reading achievement was first published in 1948 and was standardised on children. It is a simple test to give: the student is required to read aloud a series of 33 sentences which become increasingly more difficult. He continues until he has made four consecutive errors. At the end of each sentence a reading age is given. A student's reading age on this test is the figure given at the end of the sentence in which he makes his fourth error. Thus 506 means a reading achievement age equivalent to that of an average child aged 5 years 6 months; 903 means a reading achievement age equivalent to that of an average child aged 9 years and 3 months. The same series of sentences can also be used to yield a comprehension age.

The usefulness of tests

Although superior to some tests in that it requires the reading of words in context, and not in isolation, the value of the Holborn Reading Scale, or any reading test designed for children, is dubious when it is administered to adults. The format of the test is unattractive, the content of the sentences progresses from the infantile to the ludicrous and totally unreal, far removed from what ordinary reading is about. The test is not worthy of an adult's effort to comprehend it, and any potential student faced with it might be excused for thinking: 'if this is what reading is about, why should I bother with it?'

HOLBORN READING SCALE	
1. The dog got wet and Tom had to rub him dry.	509
2. He was a very good boy to give you some of his sweets.	600
3. My sister likes me to open my book and read to her.	603
4. Go away and hide behind that door where we found you just now.	606
5. Please don't let anyone spoil these nice fresh flowers.	609
6. The string had eight knots in it which I had to untie.	700
7. Wine is made from the juice of grapes which grow in warm countries.	703
8. Mary went to the grocer's and bought some sugar and some syrup.	706
9. Quench your thirst by drinking a glass of our sparkling ginger ale.	709
10. The people could scarcely obtain enough food to remain healthy.	800
11. Elizabeth had her hair thoroughly combed and her fringe cut.	803
12. By stretching up, George just managed to touch the garage ceiling.	806
13. Father had a brief telephone conversation with my cousin Philip.	809
14. This coupon entitles you to a specimen piece of our delicious toffee.	900
15. The chemist could not suggest a satisfactory remedy for my headache.	903
16. Nobody recognized Roger in his disguise as a police official.	906
17. Leonard was engaged by the Irish Linen Association to act as their London agent.	909

The same limitations apply, to a greater or lesser degree, to most other published tests of reading achievement. There are some which involve merely the recognition of single words in isolation, e.g. *The Burt word recognition test*; the *Carver word recognition test* and the *Schonell graded word reading test*. These tests, and others of comparable format, all test *something* but usually it is only one of the many skills which in combination can make an efficient reader.

How useful is the concept of a reading age?

Two students can obtain identical scores on a test such as the Holborn, yet their achievements and problems in reading may differ widely. A reading age score tells you that a student performs at a *certain level* on the *particular* test used; it does not tell you *why* he performs at that level, *what* you should do to improve his performance or *how* to set about the improvement. Moreover, how valid is it to describe an adult's achievement in terms of the expectations we apply to children? We have already established that adults as learners present a totally different set of demands from children as learners, so why attempt comparison between them?

Surely the criterion for using any test must be: how well does the information it elicits help you to do your job of teaching this student better? A test can only fulfil that criterion if it goes some way towards showing you, not merely that your student has some deficiencies in learning (which by definition, you know already), but exactly *what* these are, so that you have some idea of what the content of your lessons needs to cover. There are some published tests which attempt to analyse a student's performance in this way, e.g. the *Neale analysis of reading ability* which attempts to measure reading comprehension, accuracy and speed and which includes a diagnostic form on which the tester can record the types of mistakes made (the content of the test was designed for children and was not intended to be used with adults).

The standard test of reading skill comprises phonically regular questions to be read and answered orally by the testee, with very infantile vocabulary and illustrations. Other diagnostic tests which pinpoint specific weaknesses include a phonic skills test with an accompanying handbook of practical suggestions for teachers.

The limitations of all the tests so far mentioned as far as their use with adults is concerned are:
- they were designed for, and *standardised* upon, children;
- they yield only a partial picture of an individual's current reading achievement;
- they emphasise weaknesses and failures in reading skills rather than strengths, and adult learners have had plenty of evidence of their failure in reading skills already;
- different tests investigate different reading skills; therefore, their scores in terms of reading ages, are often not comparable;
- their language, subject content and format is child-oriented and therefore unlikely to appeal to adults, who in any case may resist or resent formal testing, particularly on a children's test;
- they give either no, little, or very limited guidance as to the teaching procedures you might need to adopt to help a student improve his performance, on the test itself, or in real reading situations, which are most relevant to his situation.

The importance of diagnosis

These criticisms of tests often administered to adults when they apply to literacy schemes are not intended to imply that diagnostic procedures are either unimportant or unnecessary. Diagnosis of your student's current achievements and deficiencies is the vital link between what you will plan to teach him and hope that he will learn. You have to look at your student as an *individual*. Which skills has he already mastered and when and how did he do so? In which skills is he deficient and can you find out reasons for his failure? Has he failed through lack of schooling (e.g. like Michael Wells); unsuccessful schooling (like Murray Johnson); or as a result of social or emotional problems which prevented him from benefiting from his schooling.

There are a number of procedures you can adopt for ascertaining what and how your student needs to be taught. Admittedly, it may take rather longer for you to acquire some of the information you need this way than if you use a series of published standardised tests, but on the other hand, you will be able to be sensitive to your student's attitudes and expectations, and you will be giving him the chance to show what he can do in a real reading situation, without his necessarily being aware that he is being assessed.

What do you need to know?

The answer to this question lies in your own notions of what literacy means, broken down into its component skills and functions of *listening*, *talking*, *reading* and *writing* and what sub-skills lead to competence in these areas. It is upon these sub-skills that you will be concentrating in your direct teaching aiming to equip your student with sufficient adequacy in each so that he can *practice* literate activities. You need to consider each aspect of language activity, analyse it into learning components, and find out at which level your student is operating in each.

● *Listening and talking*.

You will be able to find out how well your student listens and talks during your first meeting. Does he listen to your explanations and respond in such a way that you know he has mentally recorded and comprehended what you have said? Does he ask questions? Are they related to your conversation or are they inconsequential, as if his mind is on other things, or several steps ahead, while you are talking? How does he respond to questions? Does he attempt to answer the question you ask or does he make a response not really related to the question? What kind of vocabulary and language structures does he use in talking? Does he talk in monosyllables? Jerkily? (like Sean O'Reilly) or does he talk confidently and fluently (like Jackie Baker)?

● *Reading*.

Type out in double spacing a passage from a book which you think your student may be able to cope with. Make two copies, one for your student to read, the other for you to note his responses upon. Explain to your student *why* you are asking him to read to you; that his doing so will help you ascertain what you need to teach him and what his special difficulties seem to be. As he reads, record his responses as suggested below: e.g.   flower

1. Tick if read correctly .... flower √
2. Underline if only attempted after encouragement .... <u>flower</u>
3. Cross through if no attempt made...................... ~~flower~~
4. Write above any misreading or substitution   floor / flower ⎫
5. If an attempt at phonic analysis is made, put stops after the letters (or digraphs if noted) ...... f.l.ow.e.r.
   If finally blended correctly add a tick.................... f.l.ow.e.r. √
6. If letter names are given write capitals .... FLOWER / flower ⎫
7. If pupil is able to blend sounds after you have given them, put 'T' .... fl.ow.er (T) / flower ⎬

(Adapted from the format suggested by Mrs E. M. Hawkins, ILEA.)

If you follow the pattern suggested above as a checklist, you will afterwards be able to pick out the particular *types* of error and deficiencies in knowledge your student is displaying by considering the following questions:
- does he know any common sight words?
- is he attempting phonic analysis? are they silent or voiced?
- does he know phonic sounds? Single letters? Digraphs, etc?
- can he read regular words comprised of known phonic sounds (i.e. can he blend sounds)?
- if phonic sounds are not known, can he blend voiced sounds to form regular words?
- is there confusion through attempted use of letter names?
- is there evidence of reversals?
- can he recognise and blend syllables?
- is there evidence of ability to use contextual clues (prose reading only), i.e. does he read so that the passage makes sense, even if some words are read inaccurately?
- does he show awareness of punctuation?
- does he read haltingly/fluently/with expression?
- does he indicate by his reading, and in response to subsequent questions, that he has understood the passage?

If you feel that you want to assess your student's current achievement in terms of a reading age (possibly so that you have some criteria by which to select reading books at a suitable level), the following guide compiled by Mary Arnold for the Cambridge House Literacy Scheme in London may be of assistance:

Reading ages – a rough guide to standards
R.A. in years

5 –5½ Can the student read a few words here and there – possibly a sentence like 'Is the sun wet?' Is he beginning to understand that letters represent sounds? Are there a few words he can recognise at sight?

5½–6 Does the student know all the simple sound-letter relationships? Alphabetical names of letters? Several sight words?

6 –6½ Can the student read words ending with <u>ing</u>, <u>ed</u>, and plurals made by adding <u>s</u>? Is he able to analyse and blend simple three-letter phonic words, e.g. mad, yet, act? Has he started to recognise the digraphs (th), (sh), (ch)? Has he begun to use context clues plus first sound in order to read new words?

(up to this point reversals may occur, but need not be worried about – e.g. <u>b</u> for <u>d</u>, saw for was, on for no.)

6½–7 Does the student know (ch), (sh), (st), (th), (wh) and words ending with (er) and (ly)? Is he managing longer sentences?

7 –7½ Does the student know ee, oo, ea, and the long vowel sounds? Add the long <u>y</u> as in my and the silent <u>e</u> rule?

7½–8 Can the student manage these phonics:
(ai) (ay) (ie) (oa) (ar)
(er) (or) (ur)
(bl) (br) (pl) (pr), etc. ?
Is he reading compound words like postman, handbag, lipstick?

8 –9 Is the student managing these phonics:
(str) (scr) (au) (aw)
(ou) (ow) (oi) ?
Is he remembering what he's reading? Can he manage fairly complex grammar? Is he tending to see words more and more as a whole and less as individual sounds?

● *Writing and spelling*

As far as your student's writing abilities are concerned, there are various spelling tests which can be given, e.g. the Schonell Tests 1A and 1B, but again their value is questionable, particularly as most such tests require the writing of words in isolation, which is an unreal activity. If you ask your student to write *something*, even if he is able to attempt only his own name and address, you will acquire the information you need, e.g.

> T Bown
>
> on my way to the colhery in the morning i was ginley and i theede it was becorsd i hadti not being to a cacrat in sinch class yanad. I was thing of my days in school and my teachers. I remade one teacher onhen was the one i hengen the monecen of a remade he wathe not gonds me to wsteche he wathe meont me to wratte. I en soerex the tength he was my teachers. The nencan of the teacher i won six in cacsst and the langa war onfor my health

This student's writing indicates that although he has something he wishes to communicate, his grasp of spelling is so poor that the reader has difficulty in comprehending the message. Indeed, after a lapse of an hour, he could not read it back himself. Notice that he has spelled his own name Bown instead of Brown.

This sample gives some useful evidence about his current abilities. He can spell some simple words, e.g. on, my, way, was, of, days, sit, and; also longer words: morning, teacher. In the words he misspells, the first consonant is usually correct, e.g. <u>c</u>othent (college), <u>f</u>integ (frightened), <u>th</u>iede (think), <u>b</u>ecorned (because), <u>c</u>acest (class). It would seem that he is able to recall some sight words and is just beginning to make some phonic generalisations. Note thing (thinking), with two parts of the word spelled correctly and a syllable omitted. This student needs to build up a more extensive sight vocabulary and then to do plenty of phonic activities to build up his knowledge of sounds and their combination into syllables. He shows some knowledge of sentence structure, using full stops and capital letters but is inconsistent in his writing of I, sometimes writing <u>i</u>, so this would be an early learning topic. His handwriting is quite good, joined cursive, and this asset will be a valuable aid in teaching him spelling patterns. Look at this next piece of writing.

> When I went to Finton two summumer ago I went with my muther becuase she need a rest and this was it Just the place. we went there for one week and it seamed like two week all we ded evry day was to go for long works ether along the top or along the pech in the afternoon when the see see sea was in you could wrim [swim] about 100 yard aut to a diving borad board and there were not many people who went ont there so sometimes me and my mum would sunbathe there it was very nice in the evning we would ether go for a wodk after supper or go for a little drink.

What would be the teaching/learning implications you would draw from this passage? Compare your notes with what follows.

This student, a girl, is more competent than Mr Brown, and her writing reveals fairly specific deficiencies, e.g. Finton (Frinton), muther (mother), evry (every), works (walks), sumumer (summer), ether (either), pech (beach), evning (evening). She has reached the stage of being able to recognise and correct some of her mistakes, e.g. sea, swim, showing that she is approaching a level of automatic recall of spelling patterns. Her handwriting is quite clear. She needs some help with sentence structure, tenses and punctuation, in addition to specific teaching of the sound patterns and spellings she has not yet grasped and sight words, e.g. either.

> It's been a long time sencer [since] I've witen anything. about four mouthes and even then. there were breif maintenance reports. but just thinking about this easier. has brougth about a remarkable changes in me. in what way. just by thinking about what I have to do. thinking is the key to my problem. ocur is it consintration. stopping covering to think about what I want to say. stopping thinkeng how it sounds. remembering how it looks witen down on paper. Charlie Gilllett once wrote in. my report that I was still not very good at my reading writing and spelling. but that is not True. I can read anything. and the only thing [evening] [ALMOST] that noulds me back in my writing in not being sure haw to spelling the words. I feel if I spend more time writing I my pick up or wakeyp something in my head.

Check list of basic sounds Name________ Group ______

This list (developed during four years of work at the Word Blind Research Centre for Dyslexic Children, Coram Fields, London WC1) is intended for diagnosing individual or group errors in spelling, and for recording what has been specifically taught.

X for not known   **√ for known**   **△ for taught**
N.B. If these marks are used other teachers can interpret the check sheet.

Single letters
a, b, c, d, e, f, g, h, i, j, k, l, m, n, o, p, q, r, s, t, u, v, w, x, y, z

Double consonant blends
br, -ck, cl, cr, -ct, dr, dw, fl, fr, -ft, gl, gr, -mp, -nch, -nd, -ng, -nk, -nt, pl, pr, sc (sk), sk, sl, sm, sn, sp, st, sw, tr, tw

ch, sh, th, wh, bl

Triple consonants
scr, shr, sph, spl, spr, squ, str, thr

Silent 'e'

Vowel groups
ai, air, alk, ar, -are, au, aw, -ay, ea(e), ēa, ear (er), ee, er, ew, -ie, igh, ir, -ire, oa, -oe, oi, oo, or, -ore

ou, -ould, -ound, ow, ōw, -oy, -ue, -ur, -ȳ

Whole words for word building
ace, act, age, ale, all, ape, arch, ark, arm, art, ask, ass, each, ear, east, eat, ice, ill, oak, oar, oil, old, other

Endings
-ed, -er, -est, -ing, -ly, -ble, -dle, -gle, -kle, -ple, -tle

Whole word prefixes
over +, head +, under +, snow +, sun +

Early rules
qu always together
No word ends in 'v'
No word ends in 'j'
'll' at end of short words
'ff' at end of short words
'ss' at end of short words
'l' or 'ee' sound at end is 'y'
Regular plural adds 's'
Hissing plural adds 'es'
'all'—one 'l' at beginning
'full'—one 'l' at end
'till'—one 'l' at end
Drop 'e' before 'ing'
'ck' follows short vowels
'dge' (R) fol. short vowels
'tch' follows short vowels
Doubling rule
'f' changes to 'v'
'y' stays before 'ing'
'y' changes to 'i'

Beginnings
ab, acc, acq, ad, aff, all, ann, ante, anti, app, aqua, arr, ass, att, auto, be, bi, circum, coll, comm, con, de, dis, eff, em, en, ex, exc, epi, fore

geo, ill, imm, in, inter, imp, irr, mis, mono, ob, occ, octo, opp, per, pre, pro, quad, re, sub, succ, supp, sur, tele, terr, trans, tri

un, uni, sym/syn, syll/sys

Endings
ain, ate (ut), ant, able, age, al-ly, ance, ary, cial, cious, eer, eigh, ence, ent, ere, ery, ess, graph, ian, ible, ic, ice (is), ier, ily

ine, ion, ious, ise, ism, ist, ite (ut), ity, ive, less, ment, ness, ology, ory, ough, ought, our, ous, sion, ssion, tial, tion, tious, tude, ture, ual, ure, wards

Hard sounds
augh, -ch (k), gn, gu, -gue, silent 'h', silent 'l', pn, ps, pt, -que, -re, rh, sc (soft), silent 't', ui, y for i

o sounds ŭ, ou sounds ŭ, a sounds ŏ

Roots
tract, port, form, serv-, press, gest, struck, tain, use

Harder rules
ce, ci, cy (soft c)
ge, gi, gy (soft g)
o + es (plural)
ci, ti, si, say 'sh'
wor (were)
i before e
When to double 'l'
When to double 't'
able/ible
ery/ary
er/or
ance/ence
ise, ize, yse
ify, efy
cede, ceed, sede

The last example, written by a man of 22, yields more helpful information to you as a tutor than any test possibly could. Not only has he written enough to give a very clear picture of where his weaknesses in writing lie, but the excited style of writing and the content of what he says tell you a great deal about his motivation and what he hopes to gain from the learning situation. It is an excellent example of self-diagnosis, of which, of course, adults are much more capable than children. It is worth asking your student what he feels his specific problem to be: he may cite difficulties with, for example, b, p, d, which it might otherwise take you some time to discover. This student approaches spelling syllabically, but his visual memory lets him down. Note the words he has spelled using all the correct letters but in the wrong sequence, e.g. brough (brought), wirting (writing), breif (brief). Where he cannot recall the visual pattern of a word, he probably writes it as he pronounces it, e.g. consintration (concentration). He is self-correcting, notice his alterations to thinking, remembering, wake up, or. He writes confidently and himself says that he feels he will improve with practice. He needs specific teaching of those word patterns of which he's unsure, and possibly some help with handwriting, with which he needs to slow down so that he becomes more aware of what he is writing as he writes.

The *Check list of basic sounds* by Gill C. Cotterell above provides a useful structure for checking and recording students' areas of competence and deficiency, both at the beginning of his work with you and later when you want to check progress. Keep in mind, however, that this is a *general check list* and is not necessarily intended to indicate the *sequence* of basic sounds which you should teach. I have discussed this on an earlier page.

Record keeping

If you adopt a systematic approach towards teaching your student, diagnosis of his current achievements and deficiencies will be a constant feature of your activities. You will need to keep records of *what* he has learned, what is still a problem to him and, as time goes on, *how* he appears to learn most successfully, i.e. the kind of activity which seems particularly effective with him. Is it emphasis upon the *visual* patterns of words which appears to help him most, or emphasis upon *sound* patterns? Can he learn and remember spelling generalisations through a logical approach which he tries to apply to new, unfamiliar words, or does he learn them more easily if they are grouped into patterns without much explanation of structure? This kind of knowledge will be increasingly valuable to you in your teaching as you will then be able to exploit your student's strengths to the full. These are also important for your student, to provide evidence that he's made progress over a period of time.

Record keeping is very important too in connexion with the organisation from which your student was referred to you. It could happen that for some reason you or your student cannot continue with your lessons and that a new tutor has to be found. Any detailed information you can supply will be extremely valuable to your literacy organiser in selecting a new tutor, and to that tutor, who will then be more able to continue where you have left off. Teaching records enable you to keep note of successful techniques and materials which can be used again with other students, recommended to fellow-tutors or passed on to people concerned with researching methods of teaching literacy to adults.

There are various ways of keeping records and you may choose to invent your own system, or your literacy scheme organiser may give you some directives. Here are some examples.

Recording an individual lesson plan and comments
● this style of record keeping may be suitable:

Friday, 16 March
1. Put into alphabetical order: strip, strong, strap, stroke √
2. Reading *Banana boy* (Frank Norman) p. 24–26.
Check 'austere', 'chronological', 'arduous' = understood √
3. Spelling – revise final *ck*. √
Dictation – Bill gave his *son* a stick of rock. √
      Let's go to the dog track tonight. √
*talked about 'chronological'. Found some other words in dictionary – chronometer, chronicle, chronic. Not clear about apostrophes yet (go over again next time). Son/sun – talked about *son* being a b*O*y.

● a briefer format for recording individual lessons may help.

date	reading	writing/spelling	comments
16.3.74	Dictionary skills *Banana boy* p.24–26	*ck* rule	Still weak on apostrophe.

In planning the next lesson, you can refer to this record and may well decide to concentrate on the use of the apostrophe.

● progress report sheet:

	tutor's comments
letters and sounds sight sounds phonic combinations comprehension use of context clues free writing work related exercises	

A useful technique for keeping an on-going objective record of your student's progress is the *cloze* test, sometimes called context cueing, a test which you can construct yourself by using the following procedure:
● select a passage of prose of about 300–500 words from your student's current reading material;
● delete every fifth word;
● re-write leaving blanks;
● student completes;
● score wrong/incomplete responses.
● total correct responses.

Score: If 40%–60% of the responses are correct – your student has no comprehension problems.
If less than 30% are correct – your student is having problems and you may be using material which is as yet too difficult for him.

This is a context cueing exercise used by Tom MacFarlane on his tutors' training courses. Try and fill in the words in the blank spaces. When you've completed the exercise look up the missing words that follow.

Context cueing passage 1

It was .... the advent .... Kaiser Wilhelm .... caused men .... speak with .... breath or .... the colour .... the lips .... their womenfolk. .... was not .... prospect of ...., distant in ...., that caused .... to imagine .... they could .... blood from .... The horror .... ran through .... land and .... cranks to .... of a .... of Cain .... inspired by .... series of .... quite without .... in the .... of crime. .... autumn of .... was the .... when a .... killer was .... in the .... of London's .... End, striking .... his victims .... warning, slitting .... throats, mutilating .... bodies in .... fashion, and .... through police .... to murder ....

Tom Cullen *Jack the Ripper* Fontana, p.9.
answers

not	of	that	to
bated	drained	from	of
it	the	war	1888
some	that	smell	afar
which	the	caused	speak
revisitation	was	a	murders
parallel	annals	the	1888
period	mysterious	abroad	streets
East	down	without	their
their	hideous	escaping	cordons
again			

Context cueing : 1

Context cueing passage 2

Normally, you should drive .... in to the left. .... does not mean that .... should drive in the ...., but simply that you .... not drive on the .... of the road. Just .... far out from the .... of the road you .... to drive will depend .... the road and the .... on it. For instance, ... driving in a town .... where cars are parked .... intervals along the kerb, ... in and out between .... cars is unnecessary and .... to other drivers. It .... therefore wrong.

Ministry of Transport *Driving* HMSO, p. 53.
answers

well	this	you	gutter
should	crown	how	side
need	on	traffic	when
street	at	weaving	stationary
confusing	is		

Context cueing : 2

The value of a context cueing exercise like this is found in the questions about how a reader behaves when filling in the missing words. How did your lack of background knowledge affect your performance? How would it affect a student's performance? Did you need to scan backwards and forwards for clues? Did the author's choice of words differ with your own? Did it alter the sense?

The rationale for careful and consistent planning, evaluation and record keeping can be summed up as follows:

● if you know *what* you are aiming to do, *when* and *why* you are going to do it, and *how* you are going to do it, you will feel much more secure in your role of tutor. This includes what might, out of context of the real face-to-face situation, seem trivialities, e.g. the ea spelling of (ĕ); it is advisable to consider the words you intend to present to your student *before* the lesson. If not, you are liable either not to be able to think of any, or to introduce a complication, or exception, you'd rather avoid for the present – which can cause you and your student to feel inadequate and embarrassed.

● your student needs to feel that you know what you are doing. If you fail to plan your lessons and thus present him with confusing information, his confidence in you is likely to diminish and, subsequently, his confidence in himself and his developing capabilities. He needs to be able to see that he is making progress, and you will be able to show him this evidence only if you can produce records of the work you have been doing together – even if you show him only your check list duly annotated.

● records of your teaching provide a means of ensuring continuity in what you do with your student. You will then be able to check when you need to revise a point you have covered during earlier weeks, any special learning problems and what activities you have already covered and need to vary. You will also be able to refer to these records when you have opportunities to ask for advice from more experienced tutors, or to give advice to less experienced tutors in the case of transfer to another tutor or for research purposes.

Bibliography

1 TANSLEY A. E., *Reading and remedial reading*.
   Routledge and Kegan Paul, 1967; 2nd edn. paperback 1972.
2 HEILMAN A. W. & HOLMES E. A. *Smuggling language into the teaching of reading*,
   Ohio: Charles E. Merrill Publishing Co, 1972.
3 HANNA P. R., and others *Spelling: structures and strategies*,
   Boston: Houghton Mifflin, 1972.
4 HUGHES J.M. *Phonics and the teaching of reading*, Evans Bros, 1972.
5 FERNALD G. M. *Remedial techniques on basic school subjects*,
   McGraw-Hill, 1943.
6 HUGHES J. M. *Reading with phonics* Evans Bros, 1973.
7 COX A. R. *Situation spelling*,
   Cambridge, Mass.: Educators Publishing Service, 1971.
8 COX A.R. *Structures and techniques/remedial language training*,
   Cambridge, Mass.: Educators Publishing Service, second edition, 1974.
9 DEAN J. and NICHOLAS R. *Framework for reading*, Evans Bros, 1974.
10 VALLINS G. H. *Spelling*, Andre Deutsch.
11 BOWEN C. *Angling for words*, Educators Publishers, 1972.

5.Resources

❛A lorry driver goes into a transport cafe and orders eggs, bacon and chips. Three Hell's Angels roar up on their motor bikes. The first one comes in and eats the man's bacon, the second eats the man's eggs and the third the man's chips. The lorry driver leaves. One motorcyclist says to the cashier: 'He's not much of a man is he?' The cashier replies: 'No, and he's not much of a lorry driver either. He's just run over three motor bikes'.❜

Moral: use your resources appropriately.
(adapted from a story told by Paul Forgoch, Trainer-Consultant, Tucson, Arizona, USA).

Making your own materials

Although some students and tutors may be able to beg, borrow or steal the odd commercially produced teaching aid, many of you will not be able to do this; nor will most of you want to spend money on heavily advertised materials, which may in any case be of only short-term value. Furthermore, most of the commercially produced teaching aids are geared towards children, and require so much adaptation for use with adults, that you will probably find it both easier and quicker to make your own. You may not possess artistic talents – but don't worry. Whatever your home-materials lack in professional finish, they gain in their design for a specific purpose, and for a particular individual or group. Your students will appreciate the efforts you have made. Your drawings might make an amusing point – and one of your students may be moved to use his own talents to do your illustrations for you, not only boosting his morale but enabling him to feel that he is contributing in an active way towards your joint task.

Workcards

The workcard is probably the most common kind of home-made aids. As its name suggests, it is usually a piece of card showing a task of some sort on which your student is expected to work and complete. The design of the card and the nature of the task will vary according to the level your student has reached. In the early stages it may be an exercise of matching words to pictures; later it may be labelling pictures; later still it may be sentence completion, comprehension or spelling exercises, or even a combination of activities involving looking, reading and writing. The possibilities are endless.

The workcard, and variations upon it, can provide valuable experiences for your students in a number of ways:

Practice and reinforcement
When you have studied a particular skill or concept with your student, you can give him opportunities to practise and reinforce his learning by providing a series of workcards which require plenty of *repetition* of the specific skill. Remember, the more often your student makes a correct response, the more likely he is to recall it in future. An additional advantage is that your student can work at his own pace, e.g.:

the student copies the words

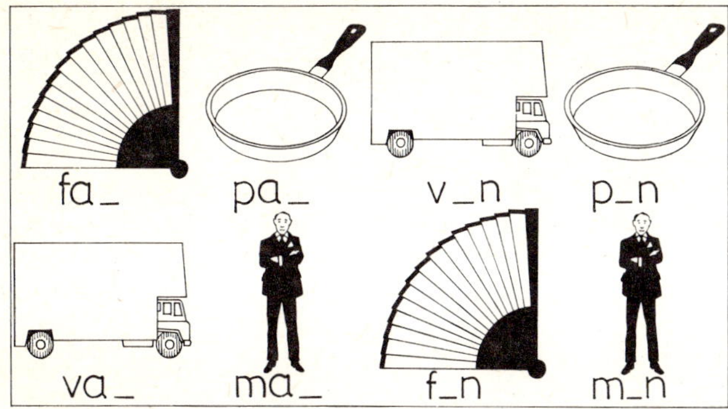

the student completes the words

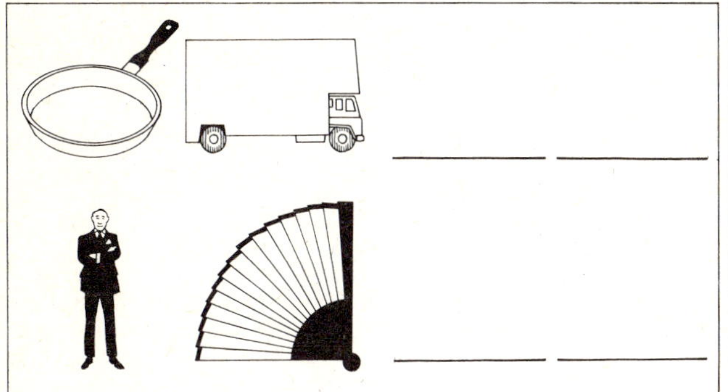

the student fills in the missing words.

Exercises like those shown above can provide practice material for your student at all levels of his learning of writing and spelling.

Progress and extension

Workcards can be graded so that they become progressively more difficult, perhaps by gradually providing fewer helpful clues for your student, so that he has to draw more and more upon his own powers of recall. If the cards are numbered, or colour-coded, in some way, he will be able to mark his own progress and is likely to feel motivated to move through the series. He may like to take some home to work through and this will be fine *provided* that you are sure that he will be able to cope successfully: you don't want him to reinforce bad habits.

Interest, independence and objectivity

Workcards can be geared to your students own *interests*. He can practise basic skills, e.g. of looking up information, using the alphabet sequence, A–Z etc. within the context of a real situation, e.g. with a dictionary or with a street guide. He will then feel that not only is he gaining from the process of *practising* his skills but that he has achieved a worthwhile objective at the end, in terms of increased information about or insight into his chosen subject. The literate adult *chooses* what he wants to read and to learn about; the illiterate has experienced no such choice. The workcard also enables him to work independently, in an adult manner, proving to him that he can use his skills. This will give your student the confidence to apply his new learning in other situations. His responses, which should be at least 85 per cent correct if the task is within his capabilities, will provide him with objective evidence of his success and progress.

Sharing the burden

Just as your student needs to learn to work unaided, you may wish to leave him, either to attend to other students if you are teaching a group, to make some coffee or to go to the lavatory. Teaching an individual for an hour at a time can be exhausting and you may need a few minutes to renew your energy. Your student may feel the same, but may not like to say so. He can be given his workcard for a period and complete it at his own speed.

Making workcards

You can buy card from most stationers which you can cut to a suitable size. Alternatively much of modern packaging is a good, cheap source of card and paper – the boxes in which shirts, handkerchiefs, shoes are packed or the thin cardboard often placed between the folds of linen, tights, etc. Backs of birthday cards or calendars can also be used. Cards can be made more durable with transparent plastic film. Your student can then write on the card with a water-based felt tip pen and his writing can later be erased with a damp cloth and the card re-used with other students. Shirt and shoe boxes provide good storage for these materials and you may find a local shop willing to supply you with these and other paper materials which would otherwise be wasted.

Planning the content of workcards

If the best use is to be made of workcards, so that they are valuable in at least some of the above mentioned ways, you need to decide:
- what you want your student to practice and to have achieved *when he has completed* the exercise.
- how this is related to his past and his future language activities.
- you need to ensure that he can cope with the level of the material which you are offering him so that he does not become confused or discouraged.

This obviously requires some planning in advance, especially when you are starting with a student. As you go along you will gradually build up a stock of such materials which can be used with other students too.

Levels of practice

Work cards can be used to provide practice in the two main aspects of literacy learning:
- the skills aspect at which your student is pre-occupied with learning a vocabulary of sight words, and basic phonic relationships. Word completion and labelling exercises, as already shown, are worthwhile activities at this stage and give your student an opportunity for independent work from the beginning, even before he is able to cope with whole sentences. You could make up such exercises from the material you collect during your language experience activities (see page 25), so that he ends up literally writing his own book. Similar activities can be used in the later stages of your teaching, when you are practising spelling patterns, as already suggested for Michael Wells (see page 41).
- the comprehension aspect. Your student is learning to read so that he can absorb and understand information and ideas, and use his knowledge in everyday situations. It is important that you give him opportunities to show that he comprehends the content and meaning of what he reads: learning to put together the letters and sounds of words are a *means* to this end, not an end in themselves. Of course, you will gain some idea of how much your student understands what he reads just by listening to the fluency of his reading and by asking him questions afterwards. However, oral reading is an artificial activity, in that it is not often required in real situations, and you want your student to be able to work independently.

You can begin activities involving comprehension skills while your student is still learning the basic mechanics of reading, e.g. give him a series of pictures which make up a story and ask him to put them into the correct sequence:

He can then relate the story to you and you might write his version down and use it as reading matter. Similar exercises can be done using instructions for performing a task, e.g. boiling an egg.

An alternative is to show the first three parts of a sequence and to ask your student to supply the fourth. Such activities are useful if you are teaching a group of students – they can compare and discuss their results. When your student is able to read simple prose you can construct similar exercises in written form, e.g.

Turn on the oven grill.
Put a slice of bread in the grill pan.
When bread is browned, turn it over.
When the other side is browned, butter it and eat it.

Further comprehension exercises could comprise a piece of simple prose followed by a series of questions.

Linda works in a school kitchen. She helps the cook get lunch for the children in the school every day. Her work begins at 10 a.m. when she lays the tables in the canteen. That takes her an hour. Then she has some coffee before helping the cook to put the food on to the plates. The plates of food are kept warm in a special heater.

1. Where does Linda work?
2. What time does she begin work?
3. What does she have to do first?
4. At what time does she have her coffee break?
5. What does she do after her coffee break?
6. How is the food kept warm?

In the early stages you may need to provide your student with a structure for answering questions, e.g.

Linda works in a ....
She begins work at ....
First she ....
She has her coffee break at ....
After her coffee break she ....
The food is kept warm ....

As your student progresses you will need to provide fewer clues.

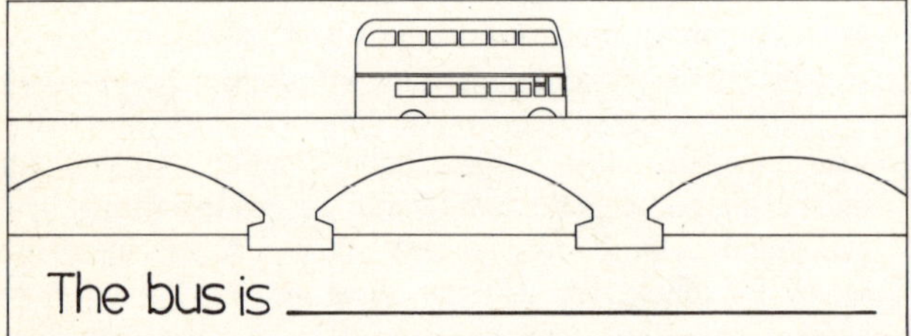

There are many other patterns for developing and checking your student's comprehension skills using work cards, and you will be able to think up your own exercises based on the kind of reading materials you are using with your student, e.g. time-tables, do-it-yourself instructions, maps and street plans, recipes, dress patterns, or whatever subject appeals to your student and which gives him opportunities to apply his skills. You will be able to increase the level of difficulty of the tasks as your student's experiences of different *kinds* of reading matter increase – prose, time-tables, instructions, advertisements, letters, forms, etc. diagrams; diagrams with written instructions or written instructions only.

Non-book material

Collect and keep samples of all the general literature available to the general public – forms, DHSS pamphlets, advertisements, notices, catalogues, free magazines, etc. They will provide useful reading matter, illustrations and diagrams which you can use in making your own workcards and books.

Many commercial firms offer free literature, with a definite educational intent. An invaluable source of information about such enterprises is the British Trades alphabet, available free on applica-tion from the British Trades Alphabet Ltd, Alpha House, Main Street, East Ardsley, Wakefield, Yorks, and published yearly. Each year it presents a different theme. The theme for 1974 was 'Discovery' and each firm or association featured offered materials for both teachers and pupils. Subjects covered included the nationalised industries, social organisations, building societies, the Stock Exchange and food manufacturers. Children's weekly magazines such as *Knowledge* are useful sources, as are many of the short items in the colour supplements.

Making your own books

You and your student can create your own reading materials right from the start – indeed, you will need to do so, since there is very little suitable published material for adults in the early stages of learning to read. You will also want to use material which is relevant to your student's interests and, of course, which is of minimal cost.

All you need to begin with are: a scrap book or plain exercise book, a felt tip pen or HB pencil, scissors and glue, a collection of magazines or colour supplements, etc.

Ask your student to select a picture which interests him and to cut it out and stick it on the first double page of his book. You can then ask him to name objects in the picture and you can label these for him. Next, ask him to say something about the picture – write these down for him, and read them aloud, pointing to each word as you read. Then ask him to repeat each line while you point to each word as he says it. Finally, ask him to copy what you have written.

You can make individual flash cards of some of the words and test him upon these. These can be kept in an envelope stuck into the back of the book, added to each time he has selected a new picture and practised at regular intervals.

By the time your student has filled the book, he will have a mass of material which he is able to read, material which has a high interest level for him because he has selected it. You will be able to use that material subsequently to point out and reinforce his developing knowledge of phonic relationships. If you are teaching a group, the members will be able to share their books, even teaching one another.

If you feel your student may reject the idea of choosing pictures on the grounds that he sees it as a childish activity, you can try another strategy. As indicated in the section on page 25, one of your early activities will be teaching a social sight vocabulary. One idea is to take a few of these words, preferably a group which can be associated in some way, e.g.

PUSH PULL DANGER SLOW STOP EXIT

First of all, write these on separate pieces of card or paper and teach your student to read them by one or more of the methods already described. Then suggest that he arranges them in various ways to see what different effects can be achieved. He will have more scope if you write each word several times. You can join in this activity too, it will help your student to appreciate that the activity is worth-while. Here are two examples:

PUSH PUSH PUSH
DANGER PULL STOP
SLOW PUSH SLOW PUSH
SLOW PUSH EXIT
DANGER DANGER EXIT
STOP
PULL PULL PULL STOP
DANGER PUSH
PUSH SLOW PUSH
DANGER PUSH PUSH EXIT

When he has decided upon his arrangement you can read it with him, copy it into his book or encourage him to do so – he will then have a permanent record of his creative effort.

In doing this kind of activity your student will not only practice and reinforce his learning; he will also become aware of a very important concept about language – that the position of a word, whether by itself on a line, in a phrase or in a sentence, affects its meaning. You can also introduce the idea that intonation and speed of reading can affect meaning. Hitherto, he has had no control over the written language; now he will begin to realise the power that literacy can give him.

Another variation on the same exercise is to play a word association game. For example, give your student the word *work* and ask him what words come into his mind. Record these and do the exercise described above. You may get some result like these examples:

    WORK
    HARD SWEAT MONEY
    HARD MONEY
    TIRED
    SWEAT
    WORK HARD SWEAT TIRED MONEY
    MONEY MONEY MONEY
    WORK HARD
    MONEY
    HARD SWEAT WORK
    TIRED HARD WORK
    MONEY MONEY MONEY
    WORK HARD
    WORK HARD SWEAT TIRED MONEY

As time goes on and your student's grasp of written language develops, you can extend this pattern to include short phrases, sentences and short paragraphs. Here is an example of a poem dictated by a nineteen-year-old girl which became part of her reading material:

    Sad
    I wonder why
    I can't read
    I think to myself
    Where have I gone wrong?
    Sometimes I think I'll never be able to read
    Other times, if I try, I can really do it.

In addition to creating books from your student's personal language, you may find it necessary to produce material for practising specific skills, particularly once your student is launched into phonics. There are a number of publications designed to give practice in phonics but most of them are designed for children. You may find it valuable to have a few of such books to hand for your own reference and to provide you with a structure and sequence for presenting new concepts. For actual teaching purposes, it will be both cheaper and more effective to write your own practice material as the need arises, writing in an exercise book or using a loose leaf folder. It is important not to include too much material on one page and not to clutter the arrangement. You can emphasise common patterns in words by using different colours. At later stages you can make booklets to illustrate words of similar meaning, words of opposite meaning, words relating to particular themes, etc. You can paste into a book examples of the various kinds of forms your student may need to fill in – driving licence application, premium bonds, post office deposit or withdrawal forms, cheques, telegrams, etc. He can fill them in and keep the book for permanent reference. A similar book can be made of sample letters – answering advertisements, job applications, enquiring for information, etc. All these will be of much more value to your student than childish reading books which he dutifully plods through and then puts away, and forgets for ever. Furthermore, you will be linking reading and writing activities and each will help to reinforce the other. Most important, you are allowing your student the choice that is the right of the literate person; he can *choose* what he wants to read.

Which books will you choose?

Open any paper or magazine connected with education and you will find lots of advertisements for reading schemes, supplementary books, games and apparatus. These are usually accompanied by a few details and claims of what the material can help to achieve. Treat all this with caution; publishers have to make a living and naturally they'll work hard to sell their products. Before you rush to buy, ask yourself what you want your reading materials for. Is it

● to use the book or scheme as a *teaching* medium?

● to provide *practice* in particular mechanical reading skills which you have already taught or for developing powers of comprehension of the written word?

● to *motivate* your student's interest in reading by providing texts which give him information, excitement, pleasure or insight into a situation?

Having decided upon your main objective, you then need to apply some critical judgements to the books you think may serve the purpose you have in mind. Ask yourself the following questions:

● do *you* like the book? Does it appeal to you as a tutor? It is important that you feel happy with the materials you are using. If you are really irritated or bored by them, it is likely that your student will be too.

● will *your student* like the book? (You could give him the opportunity to select it with you.) Look at the format, particularly any illustrations, carefully. If it is infantile, and if the language is childlike or unnatural, he is likely to reject it. Look at the tone of the content – is it pious, patronising or puerile? Is it worth the effort *he* is having to make to read it?

● who was the book written for? This is linked to the previous question. Think about your student's age, interests and the reading level he has reached. Is the book intended for use by small children, older children, adolescents, backward readers?

● how is the book intended to be used? Is it part of a graded reading scheme and meant to be used as a *teaching* medium? Is it a supplementary reader, a book designed to complement a reading scheme, to give additional practice in certain skills? Is it a book independent of any particular scheme, designed to occupy, provide information or interest to a particular age group and/or level of reading achievement?

● does it fit in with your ideas about teaching? Is it a book containing a structured phonic approach? Or does it attempt to build up a look and say vocabulary? Is it a mixture of both methods or does it employ an entirely different approach, for example, using colour coding or a modified symbol system. If so, will these additional features help or hinder your student? Can you see a pattern in the way the material is presented throughout the book or is it difficult to work out what the author is trying to do? How are you teaching your student, will the ideas about teaching implicit in this book conflict with your practice?

● does it do its job well? Look at the claims made in respect of the book or scheme and ask yourself whether these are justified. If it is claimed to be a book containing 'a systematic phonic approach' *is* it carefully graded, do you agree with the sequence of presentation of new sounds, is enough opportunity for practise and reinforcement included in the text? Is the presentation clear or is it confusing? If it is a book with a look and say approach, is new vocabulary presented systematically or in an arbitrary fashion? Is there sufficient repetition of each word as it is introduced to reinforce and consolidate learning? Is there too much repetition, so that the sentence structure is babyish or unnatural? Look at the size of the print and the amount on each page. Is it arranged with a phrase or sentence on each line, or as continuous text? Which best suits your student?

● what do you want your student to have achieved when he's read the book? Do you want him to be able to read a new group of words? To have consolidated some of his learning so that he is reading at an automatic level? Do you want to boost his confidence by showing him that he can read a whole book unaided, using all he has learned to date? Do you want him to have had an enjoyable, interesting, exciting or sensitive reading experience? Do you want him to have become interested in or have absorbed some information about a particular topic which will be of use to him? Do you want to have whetted his appetite to read more? You may have several of these objectives in mind.

● is the book worth the money it costs? Is it a valuable aid to your teaching? Will you be able to use it with other students? Would it be better to borrow it from the library?

● what will your student go on to read when he has finished that book? If you are fairly systematic about your teaching you will have both short term and long term goals. Does this book fit into the scheme you have worked out or will it interfere with your plans?

These may seem to be a lot of questions to ask about a book which may cost only 20p. *But*, your aim is to teach your student to read as well as he wishes to, and you don't want to make your job more difficult by giving him experiences which bore him or confuse him.

Bibliography
Reading – which approach by Vera Southgate and C.R. Roberts, published by ULP 1970, suggests useful criteria for evaluating published schemes.

A list of selected resources
The following selected lists of commercially produced books and teaching aids are intended to give you an indication of the type of material which is available, and which tutors have used with success with *some* adult students. The lists are not definitive, and many of the books and items mentioned may not be suitable for *your* student. You may choose to adapt some of the materials, or to adapt the teaching structures they suggest when making your own materials.

Structured schemes

Title	Author	Publisher	R. Age	Comments
Sound sense books 1–7	A. E. Tansley	Leeds: E. J. Arnold, 1960–61, n.e. 1971	6.6–9.0	Systematic phonic approach. Teacher's book.
Teenage twelve	S. Richardson et al	Glasgow: Robert Gibson, 1966–67	6.0–10.0	Laboured phonic approach but useful for practice if student's problem persists. Comprehension exercises. Teacher's manual.
Sounds & words books 1–6	V. Southgate and J. Havenhand	ULP, 1960	8.6	Systematic phonics with writing exercises. Teacher's book.
Royal road readers books 1–9	J. C. Daniels and H. Diack	Chatto & Windus Educational, 1954–1961.	6.0–9.0	V. childish but systematic phonic approach, some exercises and comprehension activities. Very gradual progression of steps. Teacher's book.
Clumsy Charlie books 1–4	H. C. Gunzburg	SEFA 2nd edn 1975	5.0–6.6	A 3-part scheme, progressing from social sight to interest vocabulary with some phonic analysis and exercises. Rather static, dated illustrations but tolerable.
Out with Tom (Remedial readers) books 1–18	ed: E. Brownsword	Methuen 1967–8 o.p. SEFA 1974	6.0–8.6	
Spotlight on trouble books 1–8	ed. H. C. Gunzburg and R. Londt	Methuen, 1964–7 o.p. SEFA 2nd edn due 1976.	9.0–10.0	Stories about school leavers constantly in hot water.
Step up & read books A–F	W. R. Jones	ULP, 1965		A phonic scheme comprising sets of cards, reading books and exercises and Teachers' Book. Rather dull format but has been used with all ages for many years. Cassette also available.

Reading series

Title	Author	Publisher	R. Age	Comments
Inner ring books	Various	Ernest Benn, cased and paperback 1972–73.	7.6–8.6	Adolescent interests, idiomatic style. Good size print.
The jet books 12 titles	ed. M. Kamm	Jonathan Cape, paperback, 1963–66	8.0–12.0	Adult format, paperback style. Well written stories despite limited vocabulary.
The look out gang books 1–6	M. B. Chaplin	Glasgow: Robert Gibson, 1968.	5+–8.6	Sight vocabulary, large print. Stories about detective activities of groups of adolescents. Phonic bias.
The Ann & Jenny books – books 1–6	B. Boyers	Ginn, 1966–67.	8.6–9+	About 2 girl school-leavers – 'magazine' tone. Notes for teachers.
Adventures in space 12 titles	S. K. McCullagh	Hart-Davis, 1968–70.	7.0–8.6	Short, lively books with controlled vocabulary.
The Joan Tate books – 18 titles	J. Tate	Heinemann Educational 1964–70.	9.0–12.0	Adult-looking paperbacks. Very well written stories.
Booster books with 5 workbooks 10 titles	W. C. H. Chalk	Heinemann Educational, 1967.	8.0–10.0	Male interest subjects. Workbooks give phonic practice – use *before* reader they accompany.
Instant reading and readers 1–10	W. C. H. Chalk	Heinemann Educational, 1971.	6.0–10.0	Short books with 'action' photographs and captions. Sentence method, plenty of repetition. Some childish but *real* situations treated. Teacher's book.
What happens when? 8 titles	G. Bell	Oliver & Boyd, 1970–71.	9+	About civil engineering projects. Stimulating.
Far west readers books 1–6	K. Rudge	Pergamon Press, 1969.	6.0–9.0	Attractive format.

Title	Author	Publisher	R. Age	Comments
Inswinger books 6 titles	G. T. Gregory and R. Ward	Hulton Educational, 1973–4.		Written for young adults. Football-centred. Workbooks available but not recommended.
Trend books 32 tit's	eds. B. Bird and A. L. Scanlon	Ginn, 1969–71.	7.0–11.0	Originated in Australia. Adult format, stories about teenagers. Useful teachers' handbook accompanies series.
Reading skill builders	Various	Reader's Digest, n.d.	9 graded reading levels	American. Available from The Reader's Digest Assoc. Inc., P.O. Box 235, Pleasantville, New York. 10570.
Adult readers	Various	Reader's Digest, n.d.	6.6–8.6	In 3 stages, 4 books each stage. Available from the Reader's Digest Assoc. Ltd., 25 Berkeley Square, London W1X 6AB.
The Manxman books 1–6	C. Edwards	Dent, paperback, 1972.	6.0–8.0	Clear print, illustrations with speech balloons; puzzles; word games.
Topliners 44 titles	Various	Macmillan, 1968–74.	8.6–9.6	Adult format paperback range of stories, most well written and engaging.
Nippers 57 titles	Various	Macmillan, 1968–74.	6.0–7.0	Finding a key; Lesley's story; Jimmy's story. For children, but acceptable to adults.
Data books books 1–18	P. Young	Schofield & Sims, 1966–70.	8.0–10.0 +	Variety of subjects – stories and factual, and six accompanying workbooks.
Crown Street kings 9 titles	A. Oates	Macmillan Educational, 1972.	7.6–8.6	Short stories on adolescent themes.
Trigger books 8 titles	ed. C. Parfitt	Collins Educational, 1974.	8.0–9.0	Adult format paperback. Stories about young people.
Can you solve it? books 1–6	S. Belmont and B. A. Akhurst	Ginn, 1956.	7.6–8.6	Each story poses a problem in deduction and exercises.
Challenge books 27 titles	A. E. Smith	Holmes McDougall, 1965.	7.0–9.0	Adventure stories written using controlled vocabulary.
Easy reading	Various	Ladybird Books, to date.	9.0	More adult format than key words scheme. Plenty of illustrations.
Longman simplified English series 68 titles	Various	Longman, to date.		Include classics and popular stories. Intended for English as a foreign language (EFL) students, so language structure is simple though some vocabulary is quite advanced.
Simon and Dorothy books – 4 titles	P. Emmens	Blond Educational, 1963. o.p.	8.0–9.0	Stories, in country setting, of adolescent love/hate relationships. Simple vocabulary and sentence structure.
Tempo books books 1–10	P. Groves and L. Stratta	Longman, 1965–67.	6.0–9.0	Modern format. Stories about teenagers in urban setting. Good illustrations.
Spotlight on Mystery	H. C. Gunzburg	SEFA, 1971.	10.0–11 +	Similar in format to 'Spotlight on Trouble'. Junior version of Agatha Christie style.
The adventure road to reading – 4 titles	V. S. Petheram	Hulton Educational, 1960. o.p.		Lively stories, controlled vocabulary with irregular words presented for study beginning of each story.
Teens		University of London Press.		Forthcoming.
Sounds right books 1–3	J. A. Willsdon	Robert Gibson, 1968	5.0–6.0	Phonic families: lists and illustrations.
Sounding and blending – 5 titles	J. A. Willsdon	Robert Gibson, 1967.	5.0–6.0	Introduces short vowels. Vowel practice pads available.
Stories without words		Remedial Supply Co., n.d.	Beginners	12 books in series – recommended – 1. Building a House; 5. In the Garage; 12. The Motorway.
The marriage scene books 1–8	C. Parfitt	Collins Educational, 1974.	6.0–9.0	Simple stories on adolescent themes. Slides and cassettes also available.
Oxford graded readers, 1000 headwords, junior level 3 titles		OUP, 1973-4.	9.0–11.0	
Stories for today books 1–6	P. Abbs	Heinemann Educational, 1972.		Teacher's notes.
Modern reading for modern times books 1–4	ed. J. Kennet	Blackie, 1965–66.	Sec	Include 'Cockleshell Heroes', 'Diary of Anne Frank', 'Lillian' (about Lillian Board).
Breakthrough to literacy	D. Mackay and others	Longman, for Schools Council, 1970–72.	Beginners	Designed for Primary level but well illustrated; about real family situations. Good for beginners. Sentence maker can be useful.

Title	Author	Publisher	R. Age	Comments
Oxford progressive English readers grades 1–3		OUP, 1974.	EFL	Series of retold stories.
Longman structural readers; stages 1–6	Various	Longman, 1900. to date.	EFL	Series of retold stories – including James Bond; plus specially commissioned tales. Controlled sentence patterns and vocabulary.
Bull's-Eye books 3 titles	Various	Hutchinson, n.e. 1973.		'Dr. No'; 'The Triffids'; 'Red in the Morning'.

Information books

Title	Author	Publisher	R. Age	Comments
Learning library 76 titles	eds. J. Cutforth and J. C. Gagg	B. Blackwell, to date.	8.6 +	Useful for early practice in using reference books. Large numbers of titles, wide range of subjects.
Junior reference library 70 titles	Various	Macdonald Educational, to date	9.0 +	Attractively presented. Wide range of subjects.
Inside & outside books – books 1–11	Various	OUP, 1969–72.	7.0–9.0	Range of subjects. Clear illustrations, good sized print.
How it works 14 titles	Various	Ladybird Books, to date.	9.0–10.0	Range of subjects. Written for children but useful vocabulary.
Understanding maps	N. Scott	Ladybird Books, 1967.	11.0	Clear illustrations and explanations.
Recognition	D. Carey	Ladybird Books, 1972	11.0	Cars, aircraft, vehicles, flags, etc. Clear illustrations.
Matter of fact books 12 titles	N. Geddes	Methuen, 1968–69.	6.0–7.0	Range of subjects. Useful vocabulary on each topic.
The Post Office books 3 titles	L. Sealey	Macmillan, 1971.	9.0–12.0	Colourful, modern layout.
What happens 6 titles	D. Smith and D. Newton	Hart-Davis, 1969–70.		Factual text, some vocabulary rather advanced. Plenty of photographs.
As we were books 1–24	H. Grant Scarfe	Longman, 1962–68.	8.0–9.0	Small booklets about history. Colour illustrations; large print; simple sentences.
Inner ring sports 6 titles	D. Clark	Ernest Benn, cased and paperback, 1972–73.	7.0–8.6	Teenage sports themes.
Services we use books 1–2	K. Nuttall	Longman, 1964–66.	7.0–9.0	Small booklets, coloured illustrations, good print.
The way to work 10 titles	J. W. Hodgson and K. Charlesworth	Macmillan, 1971.	7.0–8.0	Amusing approach; simple, well spaced sentences. Covers a variety of occupations. Work cards available. Teacher's book.
What do they do? 22 titles	ed. J. Blackie	Macmillan, 1971–74.	7.0–9.0	Simple paperbacks about range of occupations. Photographs, diagrams, sight vocabulary. Easy reference and index sections. Excellent for beginners.
Communications signs & signals	P. Harverson	Penguin Books, 1972.		Intended for Primary level but an excellent and attractive introduction to different kinds of language material.
Read about it Books: 1–24 geography 25–48 history 49–72 nature study and science 73–96 scripture topics 97–108 birds	O. B. Gregory	Wheaton, 1963–73.		
Communication (wonderful world)	L. Hogben	Macdonald Educational, 1969		
How our alphabet grew	W. Duggan	New York: Golden Press, 1972.		
First interest books 42 titles	Various	Ginn, 1966–72.	8.0–9.0	6 sets with workbooks.
Starters	Various	Macdonald Educational, to date.	8.0–9.0	Dogs; mountains; bread; bees; the sea; roads; apples; magnets; spiders; homes.
Stand & stare books 33 titles	Various	Methuen, 1964–71.	9 +	Lorries; cars.
They were first books 1–12	D. Smith and D. Newton	Oliver & Boyd, 1967–9.	7.0–8.0	12 biographies.

Title	Author	Publisher	R. Age	Comments
Clue books 8 titles	G. Allen and J. Denslow	OUP, 1968–73.	9 +	Range of titles on native topics.
Key words easy readers 6 titles	W. Murray	Ladybird Books, 1970–72.	8.6–9.6	Range of topics.
The beginning of words	C. Pickles and L. Meynell	Blond Educational, 1970.	Jnr/Sec	A readable, well organised and entertaining account of our hybrid language. Excellent source book for tutors.
Data Stage 1. Book 1 Told by an arrow	P. Young	Schofield and Sims, 1966.	Jnr/Sec	Very simply written. Explains functions of a particular symbol and traces its usage through history and in the modern Highway Code.
Books (open gate library)	S. Bartlett	Chatto & Windus, 1970.	Sec	Readable account of history of book printing.
The Puffin book of football	B. Glanville	Penguin Books, 1973.		About the history of football with photographs, diagrams and pictures.

Books (miscellaneous)

Title	Author	Publisher	R. Age	Comments
The case of Kate Webster (Ranger books)	K. Hounsel-Roberts	Macmillan, 1973.		One-act plays based on facts of C19 murder.
Our world (atlas)	C. Thornford	Schofield and Sims, 1975	Jnr	
The Data book of 'Joe Miller' jokes (Data 13)	P. Young	Schofield and Sims, paperback, 1969.		
Hackney half-term adventure	K. Worpole and J. Boier	Centerprise, paperback, 1973.		
Flashback 3 titles	A. Jackson	ILEA Media Resources Centre, 1974.	7.0–8 +	Stories of the supernatural, specially written for adults.
Listening and reading	Various	BBC, to date		Stories accompanying broadcast series.

Reading, comprehension, writing practice books

Title	Author	Publisher	R. Age	Comments
Judge for yourself books 1–4	S. H. Irving	Chatto & Windus, 1964.	8 +	Interesting, informative short prose passages and exercises. Adults enjoy the content of the passages.
Six phonic workbooks	E. H. Grassam	Ginn, 1966.		Childish format but good phonic practice for absolute beginners.
Progressive picture compositions	D. Byrne	Longman, 1967.		Written for EFL students but useful vocabulary and structures for any adult group.
Book builder books 3 titles	G. R. Crosher	Methuen, 1955	7.0–9.0	Comprehension and composition activities at end of each chapter.
Comprehension and study cards – 4 sets	O. B. Gregory	Wheaton, 1969.		
Once a week books 1–3	H. Perry	Ginn, 1960.	lower sec	Short reading passages followed by comprehension and word study exercises. Excellent for homework.
Pictorial and practical English book 1	J. Trevaskis and P. Pringle	Evans Bros., 1963.	sec	Systematic, progressive course in reading, composition, language study, spelling and dictionary skills. Interesting content.
Correct English	D. A. McLennan	Robert Gibson, 1973.	Sec	15 diagnostic tests and remedial pupils' book.
Sounds and words books 1–6	V. Southgate and J. Havenhand	ULP, 1960.	Jnr Sec	Systematic phonic reading and writing activities. Dull format but useful practice.
Domain phonic workshops (test kit) 32 sheets	J. Mcleod and J. Atkinson	Oliver and Boyd, n.d.	Jnr	Accompanies set of tests. Childish format but excellent practice material.
Read, write and remember books 1–8	C. Milburn	Blackie, 1971–2.		
Exercises in punctuation	J. Trevaskis	Evans Bros., paperback, 1950.		
Programmed punctuation books 1–3	F. Hughes	Hart-Davis, 1965.		3 books: 1. The full stop; 2. Using commas; 3. Apostrophes and punctuation of speech.
Remedial reading sheets		Robert Gibson, n.d.		Each sheet is designed to remedy a specific error. 16 topics covered.

Title	Author	Publisher	R. Age	Comments
IRMA scheme & associated materials	Programmed Learning Centre, St. Albans CFE, St. Albans, Herts.		Beginners on	Expendable work sheets; systematic phonic approach.
Suzie and the supershopper	ILEA Media Resources Centre, in collaboration with the BSI, 1974.			Designed to teach consumer skills – story information sheets; work sheets and teachers' notes.

Spelling

Title	Author	Publisher	R. Age	Comments
Alphabetic spelling list	G. L. Arvidson	Wheaton, 1963.	3 graded lists	Modern format. Helpful teacher's guide.
Spelling books 1–5	J. Smith	Cassell, 1973		Practice in spelling phonic families of words.
My books of word families books 1–3, and 2 work books	N. Taverner	Philip & Tacey, 1962–65.	Basic	Simple exercises. Sound shown in isolation; then in words; then incorporated into sentences. Rather childish format.
Working with words (Word and meaning books)	J. Trevaskis and R. Hyman	Evans Bros., 1967.		50 exercises and puzzles.
Systematic spelling for juniors (to be used with)	W. H. Richards	Evans Bros., paperback, 1960.	Jnr	Graded lists of words.
Systematic crosswords for juniors books 1–2	G. Lawrence	Evans Bros., 1960.	Jnr	Explains how a crossword works. Solutions to crosswords at end.
Scientific spelling books 1–4	W. S. Fowler	Holmes McDougall, 1962.		More advanced 10 + spelling. Systematic spelling rules.
The essential spelling list	F. J. Schonell	Macmillan, 1932	7.0–12.0	3,000 keywords from children's vocabulary.
Basic word list	F. J. and F. E. Schonell	1965	7.0–12.0	Word families showing root word above its derivatives.
Senior speller	H. P. Schoenheimer	Mills and Boon, 1965.	Sec	Rules systematically presented + exercises.
Spellaway books 1–2	S. A. Stagg	Schofield and Sims, 1972–73.		Mixed approach. Intended for children, but various activities; word completion exercises, etc. Good for homework once student knows all sounds.
Six phonic workbooks	E. H. Grassam	Ginn, 1966.		Primary level format, but useful for absolute beginners.
Find the word	E. G. Bailey	Robert Gibson, 1950.		4 sets of workcards.
Classified spelling	W. J. Leonard	Schofield and Sims, 1940.		
Spelling book	J. B. Marshall and A. Gibson	E. J. Arnold, n.e. 1972.	Sec adult	Useful lists of words classified according to 1. subject, 2. rules, 3. word history and homonyms, etc.
Key words for easy spelling	T. J. Fitikides	Longman, 1965	Sec	Well presented rules and examples. Not many exercises but useful ideas to be imitated and extended.
Debden suffix-changing cards	K. Hadley	Philip and Tacey, n.d.	Junior/sec	6 sets of boards and suffix cards illustrating rules plus reading exercises showing words in context. Good for introducing rules.
Word perfect books 1–8	R. Ridout	Ginn, 1957–60.	1–5 primary 6–8 sec	Exercises showing word usage as well as structure. Teacher's book and introductory book.

Word lists, dictionaries + dictionary and vocabulary exercises

Title	Author	Publisher	R. Age	Comments
Chambers essential English dictionary	ed. A. M. Macdonald	Chambers, 1968; Pan, n.e. 1973.		Good for students for whom auditory aspects need emphasising.
A simplified dictionary	ed. C. W. Airne	Schofield and Sims, 1958.		With exercises.
An easy dictionary	ed. W. L. Darley	Schofield and Sims, 1961.		
A first dictionary and a first English companion	W. D. Wright	Welwyn: Nisbet, 1959.		Excellent for developing reference skills and extending vocabulary. Exercises. Teacher's manual and exercises.
Exercises in using your dictionary	J. Trevaskis	Evans Bros., 1964.		
First spelling dictionary	P. S. Freyberg	Macmillan, paperback, 1972.	1000 words	Simple definitions provided.
Use your dictionary	E. E. Willton	Wheaton, paperback, 1954; 2nd edn. 1955.	Advanced	Exercises in dictionary skills and word usage. Useful source for constructing exercises.

Title	Author	Publisher	Level	Comments
When I write	D. J. Jerstice	Macmillan, 1968.		A book of commonly used words listed according to subject.
Young student's dictionary		Wheaton, 1963.		9,000 words defined in simple language, with 'sound picture' guides to pronunciation.
A first practice dictionary	O. B. Gregory	Wheaton, 1965		A simple dictionary with short exercises.
Contextualized vocabulary tests books 1–4	L. A. Hill	OUP, 1970.	EFL	Systematic and clearly illustrated vocabulary completion exercises.
Increase your vocabulary	W. Hadyn Richards	Philip & Tacey, n.d.		Book and exercise sheets.

Spelling and Word Dictionary   Collins. [handwritten]

Handwriting

Title	Author	Publisher	Level	Comments
The teaching of handwriting	A. Inglis et al	Nelson, 1961–64.		Writing patterns lead to practice of letter forms and joined letters. Advice included about left-handers. Teacher's book.
Handwriting	T. Gourdie	Ladybird Books, 1968.		Specifically for teaching cursive writing.
Basic modern hand 48 work cards	C. Jarman	Osmiroid Educational (S. Perry Ltd.), 1975.		
Everyday writing books 1–5	R. Fagg	ULP, 1962–64.		Teacher's book.
Semi-vertical copy books	T. Gourdie	Holmes McDougall, n.d.		
Beacon writing books 1–6	ed. A. Fairbank	Ginn, 1957.		
Writing and writing patterns	M. E. Richardson	ULP, 1935.		5 pupils' books + teachers' book.

Reading and spelling games, puzzles and aids

Title	Author	Publisher	Level	Comments
Phonic sets & phonic pairs + several other phonic games	B. Root	Hart-Davis, 1968.	5 +	Simple phonic card games based on 'Happy Families' idea.
Programmed reading kit	D. H. Stott	Holmes McDougall, 1962.		Sets of apparatus designed to teach phonic skills through games. Very useful. Each item can be bought separately.
More or less?	ed. K. A. Dougall	Oliver & Boyd, 1969.	6.0–6.6	Presents comparison adjectives in an attractive and amusing format.
Systematic crosswords books 1–2	G. Lawrence	Evans Bros., 1949.		Answers to crosswords follow phonic progression. Clues may need to be read aloud and explained to student.
A first crossword puzzle book	L. A. Hill and P. R. Popkin	OUP, 1968.	EFL	
First knight book of crosswords	M. Raybould	Brockhampton Press, 1974.		Simple crosswords.
The 1st armada book of picture crosswords	D. and C. Power	Collins, 1974.		Excellent for beginners.
The 1st armada book of picture puzzles	D. and C. Power	Collins, 1974.		Excellent for beginners.
A book of picture crosswords	R. Ridout	Purnell, 1974.	Jnr	Excellent for beginners.
Cartoons for students of English books 1–5	L. A. Hill and D. Mallet	OUP, 1972.		In the first few cartoons humour is entirely visual; in later cartoons there are simple captions. Fun for 'relaxation points' in lessons.
Piccolo picture puzzles books 29 titles	M. M. Mays and L. W. Webb	Pan Books, to date.		
Essential notices flash cards	P. B. Radnor	Philip and Tacey, n.d.		Useful signs, white on blue laminated cards.
Word games books 1–6	B. D. Saint	Robert Gibson, n.d.	Infants	
Lexicon crosswords	D. F. Stapleton	James Nisbet, 1951.	Junior & Middle	Designed to accompany 'A first dictionary' by W. D. Wright, 1951.

Title	Author	Publisher	Level	Comments
Lexi word building dice	A. G. Wolff	available from: 44 Cleveland Walk, Bath BA2 6JT.		Box of 9 word building dice with clear instructions plus lists of phonic units.
Back you go		James Galt		Dice game with board designed to reinforce and check spelling of common words. It's possible for the tutor to lose this game of chance.
Cluedo		Waddington		'Detective game' which provides useful practice in deduction thinking and can lead to written activities.
Wordmaster major	M. Hardiment and others	Macdonald Educational	primary	Accompanied by booklet suggesting reading games, including Bingo – good with groups.
Happy words	Devised by J. Hicks and T. Kremer	Macdonald Educational	primary	A group learning aid for phonics.
Spill and spell		Parker Bros.		
Goal		Pepys		Soccer card game.
'Victory' map jigsaws		Spears		
Road pairs		James Galt		Matching game with Highway Code signs.
Epsilon		Invicta Plastics		Game involving categorising pictures into sets on the basis of a chosen selected feature.
Plan-a-jig map of London		Waddington		
The London game		7 Towns Ltd., Axtell House, 23 Warwick Street, London W.1.		A dice game which helps to familiarise people with London Underground system.
Lexicon		Hope Educational Suppliers		Capital letters.
Shakewords		E. J. Arnold		
Early stages: book 1. Silent letter cards; book 2. Sentence building word cards		James Galt		This firm produces many excellent phonic aids plus an exceptionally well illustrated catalogue.
Spell-it		James Galt		3 solid cubes with letters on four sides, can make 70 different words.
Change the word		Spears		Word building game using letters and syllables, designed for children and adults.
Kan-U-Go		Jarvis-Porter		Crossword card game.

Readability Guide

In selecting material for use with your student you will need some guide to its readability level. The following is adapted from *Fry's Readability Graph*, an American formula.

Method

1. Select three separate 100 word passages, preferably at the beginning, middle and end of the material.

2. In each passage find:

● the total number of syllables. The easiest pattern to adopt is to start with one hundred (one syllable for each of the 100 words) and go through the passage adding on all the syllables in addition to the first syllable in each word.

● the total number of sentences.

3. Average out the number of syllables and sentences for all three passages.

4. Read off on the graph opposite. The nearer the black line, the more accurate the figure.

The first hundred words of the following single passage have been worked using this formula. Reading age 10.5 approximately.

Book sings the praises of Liverpool

By MIKE ELLIS

Liverpool 4, Man. C. 1

LIVERPOOL, the title favourites, are back to their best and top of the League again — at long last !

It's not the Anfield camp blowing their own trumpet —the compliment comes from a stunned Manchester City boss, Tony Book.

He said: "Liverpool were right back to their best today and when they are on song there is no-one to touch them."

Poor Tony must dread going to Liverpool. Last season City crashed 4-0 and it would have been the same score this time but for a last-minute goal from Colin Bell.

It was the "Old Guard" who delivered the goods.

Brian Hall, reclaiming his place from £170,000 signing Terry McDermott, celebrated with two goals and John Toshack, who is keeping £200,000 Ray Kennedy on the sidelines, maintained his goal-a-game average since his move to Leicester broke down.

Steve Heighway, showing a welcome return to form, scored the other.

Creaky

City did not know what hit them and their creaky defence was in danger of total collapse. Only the industrious D o y l e and Corrigan spared them from a worse thrashing.

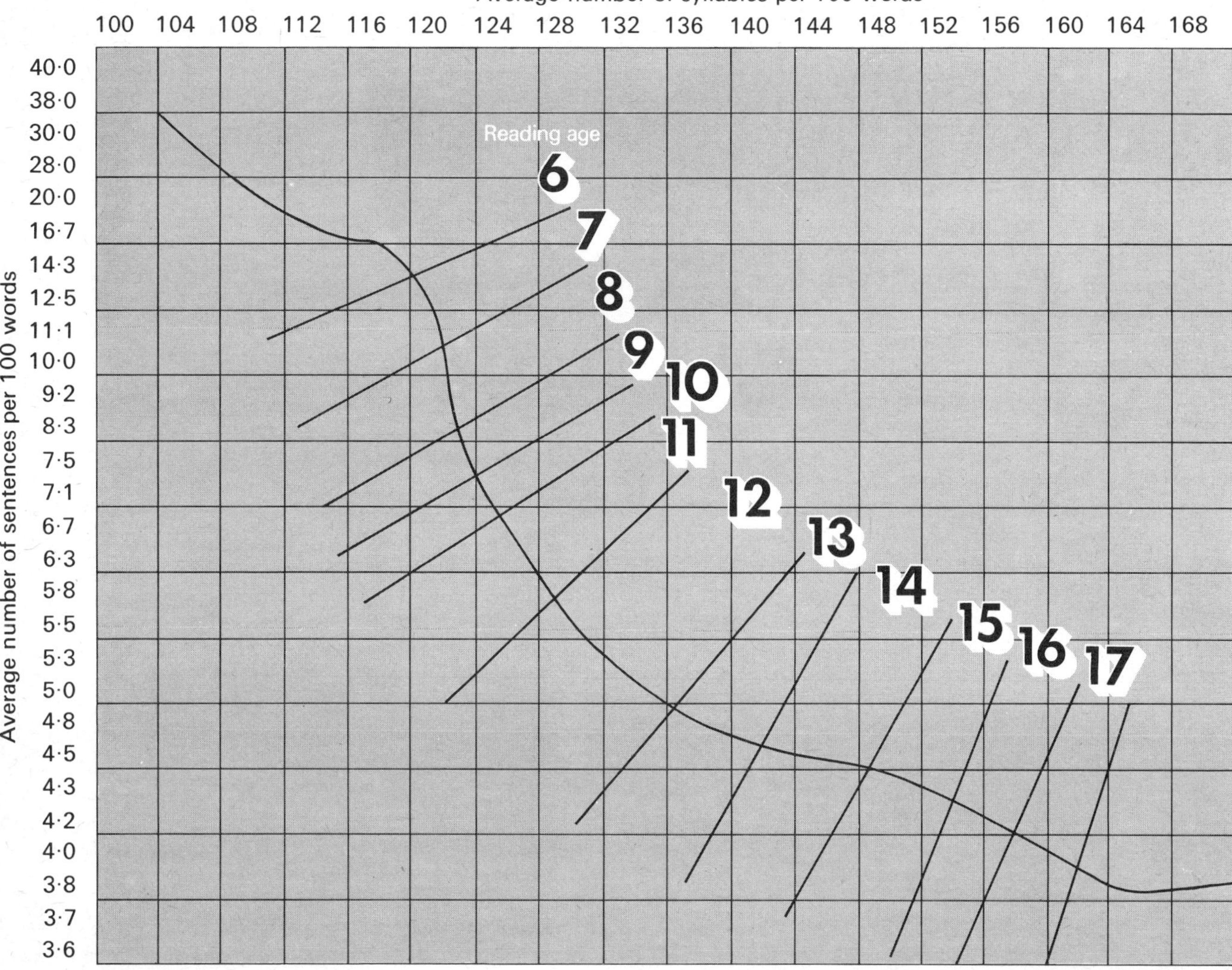

The cassette tape recorder

Cassette tape recorders can be bought fairly cheaply these days, but if you don't possess one, you will almost certainly be able to borrow one from someone in the family, a friend or a neighbour. A tape recorder isn't essential to your work but it can be a great help. As has been emphasised before, in helping your student to learn and remember, you need, as often as possible to use all *the ways* in which he can learn *together* – his eyes, his ears, his voice and his writing hand.

The same maxim applies to using a tape recorder as to using a computer – rubbish in: rubbish out! To get the best from your tape recorder as a teaching aid, you have to decide:

- what you want to achieve by using it,
- when would be the best time to do it,
- how are you going to use it.

Once again, that means some hard thinking and some time spent in actually making your programme. The question to bear in mind all the time when you are planning a tape is: 'What will my student be *doing* when he reaches this point on the tape?' Will he be:

- listening,
- talking,
- listening and following a list or a text,
- listening and responding to questions, recording his answer on the tape,
- listening and responding to questions in writing.

Developing listening skills are an important part of literacy teaching. Your student has to learn to *receive* and mentally *record* verbal instructions or information so that he can then *recall* and *respond* to them correctly. The advantage of a tape recorder here, particularly if you can provide him with earphones or an ear piece, is that it will focus his attention and cut out distracting noises and movements. A further advantage, is that he can have power over the machine, controlling its output and his input, switching it off for a moment if he needs more time to think or a short rest. In this way he will be able to work at *his* own rate, which is the optimum rate for his learning. By observing him you will be able to find out something about his learning characteristics which will be useful in helping you to plan other activities. Also, he will be working *independently* of you, which is an important feature of his progress.

In the initial lessons with your student, you will be trying to find out about his interests and his general level of language competence at an oral level. You need this information to help you plan your teaching scheme. Your student may be shy or nervous and he may find it easier to talk about something which interests him, or to describe an object or how something works, into a machine rather than directly to you. This will enable him to pause without feeling embarrassed, to have time to sort out his ideas or to correct himself. Then you can listen to his recording together and either just talk more about the subject he has chosen or you can write down what he has said and use this as a basis for his reading material. He may also enjoy using the tape recorder as a means of sending 'letters' to his friends or family.

Alternatively, if your student has reached a sufficient level of writing competence, he may be able to write down what he has said. Students with literacy problems usually find writing difficult; they are so anxious about trying to put words on paper correctly that they lose track of their ideas. You can encourage him to record his ideas on the tape recorder before trying to write them down so that the two activities are separated, enabling him to concentrate on one thing at a time.

A tape recorder may be useful in providing your student with various kinds of reading activity. Initially, you may just want to give him the pleasure of listening to a story or a recording of a pop song

– remember, anyone with limited literacy has been deprived, not only of the information, but the sheer pleasure that books can give. Your student may feel impatient to reach a level where he can read for information or pleasure without struggling over the process of reading itself. You know, and will have to convince him, that this cannot be achieved overnight, but meanwhile he can enjoy stories and you can help him to follow a text while he listens if the recording reads at a sufficiently low speed. Various agencies supply 'talking books' (some of these are listed later) and you may be able to borrow some from your local library, or of course you can record yourself, your family or friends reading.

To whet your student's appetite for reading, play fairly short sections at a time, if possible finishing each at an exciting or intriguing part of the story; he will then look forward to his next session when he will find out what will happen. You will find plenty of opportunities for talk arising from this routine; you can encourage your student to speculate about possible developments in the story, to anticipate events, to talk about the characters involved. Through such activities he will become aware of some important features of written language – that there is usually a structure; that successive chapters are linked in some way, and that our knowledge of the characters involved is built up gradually. You can talk about his feelings as he listens to a suspense story, what there is about the story that makes him feel this way. The ideas he develops from such discussions will be useful to him when he wants to structure his own writing and to use words effectively.

The tape recorder can be a useful aid towards teaching specific skills at each level of literacy learning.

Basic mechanical level
- give him a pack of social sight word cards arranged in order and let him work at each one as it is read on the tape.
- jumble the cards so that he has to find the card which matches the word he hears.
- make up some sentences or a short story which include the social sight words he has learned. Leave them out when you read the story on to the tape and either ask him to fill them in verbally or to point to the appropriate card. Later he can write the word in the gap shown in the text you provide for him to read while he is listening, e.g.

As the thief grabbed the woman's handbag she yelled out

The same ideas can be used for teaching the most important words in learning to read which do not fit into your phonic scheme, e.g. said, come, any, etc. You will be able to think up many more. For example, if you are teaching the names of colours or numbers, you can use rhyme to elicit the correct response from your student prior to showing him the spelling of each, e.g.

Purple grass I've never *seen*
The grass I've seen is mostly (*green*).

Robert was a handsome *fellow*
He wore a shirt that was bright (*yellow*).

This number rhymes with *late* and *gate*,
There's only one, it must be (*eight*).

If I say the colour *blue*
The rhyming number must be (*two*)

Words like *be* and *tree* and *see*
Rhyme with good old number (*three*)   *

*from *Smuggling Language Into The Teaching of Reading*.

The tape recorder is useful for early phonic drills, particularly if your student finds it difficult to discriminate between particular sounds, e.g. (d) and (t) or (ĕ) and (ĭ). You can:
- provide three sheets of pictures of objects whose names include one of the two sounds causing confusion; on the first sheet the sound should be at the beginning of the word, on the second sheet at the end of the word, and on the third sheet in the middle of the word.

- ask your student to listen to the name of each object read on the tape, listen for one of the two sounds in a particular position and then write the letter representing that sound beside the picture. If he does this successfully, you can then ask him to do a similar exercise without the tape so that he has to say the word himself and listen for the particular sound.
- this can be extended to using the letter shapes themselves, e.g.

b   d   b   b   d   b   d   b

Your student looks at the letter on the left, listens to its sound and names it. He then listens to the sound of the letters in the line and circles each one with the same sound as the first letter.

Comprehension and Spelling Level
Once your student has mastered the most basic mechanics of reading, the tape recorder can be used in conjunction with work cards. These can involve completing a written task, such as using a particular spelling rule.

The tape recorder can be particularly useful as a means of reinforcing the visual learning of irregular words which can be placed into a pattern, e.g. night, might, sight, fight, light, tight, etc. Encourage your student to repeat the letter names until the sequence is secure in his mind and he can recall and reproduce the pattern accurately. You may construct a comprehension exercise, either involving listening to a piece and answering questions on it, or following a written text while listening prior to answering questions. You may want your student to complete a practical task, such as wiring an electric plug or making a paper model, which require the following of verbal instructions supplemented by a printed text and diagrams.

Writing
The tape recorder may be a means of helping a student who writes fairly fluently but has not grasped the conventions of punctuation. You can record sentences requiring the use of commas, speech marks and question marks, pausing where these are required to give your student a cue that some kind of punctuation is necessary. For more advanced students, the tape recorder can act as a self-checking device. Your student can read a piece on to tape, then listen to himself, checking the text as he listens and marking any mistakes he has made. He can then aim towards producing a 'perfect' recording.

Many of the ideas suggested here can be used with, or adapted for, two students working together or small groups. Or you can use most of these ideas without recourse to a tape recorder but, if possible, have a go; it will give your throat a rest and provide your student with some variety and the chance to work independently.

Taped material
The Remedial Supply Co produces tape cassettes on various aspects of phonics – sound discrimination, blending, spelling, etc. The spelling tapes are particularly useful as they incorporate both visual and auditory approaches and show the student how to check his own response (there are 40 lessons covering 400–500 words).

E. J. Arnold & Co produce tapes as part of a revision programme linked to Tansley's *Sound Sense* series. They also manufacture a system called the *Synchrofax Audio Page* which gives scope for longer pieces of writing and recording prepared by you for your student. The student can read each page while listening to the recording.

ILEA Media Resources Centre produces *Hands; Faces; Voices* – packs of slides, cards and cassette tapes providing a reading of the printed material on the cards.

The Language Master produced by Bell & Howell is an audio-visual aid using cards, each with a strip of tape at the bottom. The tutor can supply her own illustrations and writing and record what is written so that the card is 'read' to the student as it passes through the machine. The student can also record his responses and listen to them. Very useful for early sight vocabulary and phonic work.

Libraries as a resource in literacy teaching

Only 25 per cent of the population use local lending libraries and those who do are of course, literate people. Although attention has been paid to the contribution libraries can make towards children in the process of acquiring literacy, it is only recently that libraries have begun to turn their attentions towards adults going through the same process. This is understandable: your student is unlikely to have visited a library, because he has felt that it had nothing to offer him. As he cannot read, or can read only a little, he is probably unaware that libraries can offer a good deal more than books to read, that they tend to be centres of information, that they frequently mount or house exhibitions, and that as *public* libraries they are there to provide a service to the community as a whole.

Obviously, you will want to introduce your student to his local library as soon as possible, but if he is to become a library user, and as an adult he probably pays his share of rates and taxes like everyone else, so has the same right of access, you will not stop there. Your student will see 20,000, 40,000 or even more books about him; he will see people roaming from shelf to shelf, looking purposeful, confidently asking questions of the assistants, checking out their books in an almost automatic way. And if he looks at the books on the shelves, he will not be able to read most of the titles and he certainly will not appreciate the numbers on the base of the spine of each book – the Dewey system can confound even the literate.

Therefore, once again you will need to do some careful thinking and planning before you embark on this venture. There are two good reasons why you should try to involve your local library in your work. They exist to serve the community, old and young, literate, semi-literate and illiterate and at present they are serving only an exclusive section of the community; secondly, most literacy schemes are short of funds and are able to supply only a limited selection of materials for the use of volunteers and students. Your library may be able to help you to extend the range of reading material you wish to offer to your student, at no cost to you and to the benefit of other volunteer tutors and their students. You can help your library to provide the service that your student wants by:

● informing the library staff of your work, the extent of the problem in your area and the range of provision offered, so that they can make this information available to other people. You may even persuade them to mount an exhibition, or to allow you to do so, which will inform the public of what is going on. If you are working as a member of a volunteer group, it would be a good idea to make these initial overtures jointly;

● you can provide your librarian with details of published materials suitable for use with adults, including reading books, word games, tapes, slides and filmstrips and ask if some of these can be acquired. Details of these materials could then catalogued and made available to everyone involved in the work;

● your librarian may welcome suggestions about how to arrange and display materials so that students can find them easily and without embarrassment. It may be possible to organise displays on subjects of particular interest to students showing them in the range of material available on a topic ranging from non-print picture books through simple readers, stories, articles, collection of newspapers to reference books. Since the whole continuum of reading ages would be represented, your students need not feel self-conscious about browsing through the display;

● some of the library staff may be interested to hear you talk in detail about your work and how you use the materials they provide. You will be able to explain to them how they can approach and assist in an unobtrusive way people who may have literacy problems. For example, rather than giving someone like your student an application form to fill in, they could, if at all in doubt, offer to fill it in for him at his dictation. Such a person may also want help to find a book but be too embarrassed to ask. You could suggest that if he wishes to borrow a book, the date upon which it is due back could be mentioned aloud in case he is unable to read it;

your local library may have some rooms available which could be used for teaching purposes during the day and evening. It is worth asking, as you may have a student who prefers to have his lessons on neutral ground – and what better place than a library?

All the suggestions listed here are being practised in various parts of the country. Are you making the best use of your library, are you helping it to serve both you and your student?

Books for tutors

Title	Author	Publisher	Comments
Smuggling language into the teaching of reading	A. W. Heilman and E. A. Holmes	Charles E. Merrill: Prentice-Hall International, 1972.	American. Excellent practical suggestions and examples of presenting language in context.
Diagnosis in the classroom	G. C. Cotterell	Centre for Teaching of Reading, University of Reading, 1973	Includes check list of basic sounds and pointers towards diagnosis of specific problems.
Spelling: caught or taught	M. L. Peters	Routledge & Kegan Paul, cased and paperback, 1967.	A lucid account of attitudes towards teaching spelling.
Reading and remedial reading	A. E. Tansley	Routledge & Kegan Paul, 1967; paperback, 1972.	Detailed account of basic difficulties in learning to read and practical teaching suggestions.
Breakthrough to literacy – Teacher's manual	D. Mackay and others	Longman, for the Schools Council, 1970.	Accompanies the children's reading scheme. Useful background and teaching information.
Reading: which approach?	V. Southgate and G. R. Roberts	ULP, cased and paperback, 1970.	An appraisal of nine popular reading schemes.
Aids to reading	J. M. Hughes	Evans Bros., 1970.	Extremely useful books of practical suggestions.
Phonics and the teaching of reading	J. M. Hughes	Evans Bros., 1972.	
Success and failure in learning to read	R. Morris	Oldbourne, 1963; Penguin Books, n.e. 1973.	

Title	Author	Publisher	Comments
Towards literacy	K. Gardner	B. Blackwell, 1966.	A short, readable book about teaching reading to children, but with implications about our approach to adults.
The teaching of reading	D. Moyle	Ward Lock Educational, 3rd edn., cased and paperback, 1972.	Account of basic difficulties in learning to read and practical teaching suggestions.
Roads to literacy	D. H. Stott	Holmes McDougall, 1965.	
Practical reading	J. Webster	Evans Bros., 1965.	
Learning to read: a guide for teachers and parents	B. Thompson	Sidgwick and Jackson, 1971.	
Imprisoned tongues	R. Roberts	Manchester University Press, 1969.	
Backwardness and educational failure	R. Gulliford	NFER, paperback, 1970.	
Books for the retarded reader	J. A. Hart and J. A. Richardson	Benn, cased and paperback, 1971.	Useful paperback catalogue of books to use in teaching reading – gives no. of paper, reading age, price, print, illustrations, vocabulary and evaluation.
Key words to literacy and the teaching of reading	J. McNally and W. Murray	Schoolmaster Publishing Co., 1969.	Philosophy behind Ladybird schemes.
Reading and related skills	ed. M. M. Clark	Ward Lock Educational, 1973.	Proceedings of the ninth Annual Study Conference of the UKRA, Hamilton, 1972.
Reading and the curriculum	ed. J. Merritt	Ward Lock Educational, paperback, 1971.	Proceedings of the seventh Annual Study Conference of the UKRA, Durham, 1970.
Learning to read	R. Morris	Penguin Books, 1974.	
Dimensions of reading difficulties	A. T. Ravenette	Pergamon Press, cased and paperback, 1968.	
Adults learning	ed. J. Rogers	Penguin Books, 1971.	
Adults in education	ed. J. Rogers	BBC, 1973.	
The standard reading tests	J. C. Daniels and H. Diack	Chatto and Windus Educational, 1958.	Very useful manual of diagnostic tests.
Games to develop reading skills	McNicholas & McEntee	NARE	
Reading, how to	H. Kohl	Penguin Books, 1974.	A lively book, designed to give the tutor confidence. Plenty of practical suggestions but rather confusing at times.
Overcoming learning difficulties	ed. B. Crouch	Benn, 1972.	A series of articles by experts in various fields. Useful contributions by Betty Boot on 'Reading' and 'Mathematics for the Slow Learner' by James Irving.
Success in spelling	M. L. Peters	Cambridge Institute of Education, 1970.	An ideological and theoretical consideration of spelling. Contains a useful graded spelling test, spelling ages 0–15.
The foundations of language: talking and reading in young children	A. M. Wilkinson	OUP, paperback, 1971.	A comprehensive approach to language structure; language levels; their developmental sequences orally, reading, writing. An excellent introduction to the theme of communication.
Reading: teaching and learning	R. Lansdown	Pitman, 1974.	A brief paperback covering most of the topics involved in considerations of literacy and illiteracy.
Teacher	S. Ashton-Warner	Secker and Warburg, 1963; Penguin Books, 1966.	An inspired account of experiences teaching Maori children to read.
The development of reading	A. Evans	Remedial Supply Co., n.d.	
A basic vocabulary of reading terms		UKRA (United Kingdom Reading Association)	
Assessment of reading skills		UKRA	

Acknowledgments

Thanks are due to teachers, volunteers and students at the following institutions for help in providing suggestions and examples:
Bethnal Green Adult Education Institute; Brixton College for Further Education; Cambridge House Literacy Scheme; Camden Adult Education Institute; Dulwich Adult Education Institute; Islington Elfrida Rathbone Literacy Scheme; Lambeth Libraries (Special Services); The Lee Centre, Lewisham; Liverpool University Settlement Literacy Scheme.

Bibliography

SOUTHGATE, V. and ROBERTS, C. R. *Reading: which approach?* published by ULP 1970, suggests useful criteria for evaluating published schemes.

For a list of publishers see page 94.

6. The BBC Adult Literacy Project

Broadcasting can reach people in the privacy of their own homes. It can lessen the sense of isolation which many illiterate adults feel, and it can publicise the sources of help. The first and burning need is to make it less difficult for people to come forward. We believe that broadcasting can be effective in this. We believe, too, that it has a responsibility to educate society about illiteracy and to encourage those of us who are literate to help those of us who are not. Broadcasting allows us to share the experience and insights of that small number of people who have already taught non-readers.

In trying to use radio and television to help illiterate adults in the United Kingdom we are working with little experience to guide us. Broadcasting has been used in literacy campaigns in rural societies, but these were situations in which illiteracy was normal, and bore no stigma. They were situations in which groups came together to view the one set in the village, and followed the viewing with discussion with a teacher. Nobody really knows how far television can help a totally isolated individual to learn to read. In broadcasting to those many people who hide their problem we cannot know their present skills, or their particular difficulties. We can only guess as to their aspirations – what it is they want to read, and why. We know little of what sort of instruction or encouragement a home viewer is likely to react well to, and what he will find childish, offensive or patronising. Such little evidence as we have comes from the tiny proportion of people who have already come forward for help. How far are they typical of the larger, hidden number? We can't know.

So in planning the BBC Adult Literacy Project we must recognise these limitations in our knowledge and understanding, As we get feedback, so we must be prepared to modify, to remake, and above all to rethink.

Programmes for the learner

We have planned two 'levels' of programmes – the first designed mainly to motivate and encourage, with a modest teaching content, the second designed for more committed learners.

The first level consists of fifty weekly ten-minute television programmes on BBC-1. Why fifty? Because that allows a year-long provision, excluding Christmas and Easter weeks. We can't rely on our audience watching conveniently from the beginning of the series – the programmes should be on the air for as many weeks as possible, so that there is chance for non-readers to discover them, and for their images to work recurringly upon inhibition and anxiety.

Why ten-minute programmes? Because we want the programmes to have at least one peak viewing time, so that people can come across the programmes by chance, and can subsequently watch in a casual way. Ten-minutes is a guess at the time suitable for both the attention-span of the illiterate not yet committed to learning, and the interest-span of those of us who can already read and write. Besides this peak viewing we must also arrange two further showings within the week, which enable people with varying domestic and work commitments to watch without embarrassment or difficulty. The programmes contain these elements:

- film of adults who have (or had) reading and writing difficulties talking freely about them;
- strategies for finding information without embarrassment;
- a continuing attempt to give the viewer a successful reading experience – to create in him the sense that he *can* learn and that the process can be pleasurable;
- a continuing attempt to encourage the viewer to practice writing;
- an invitation to telephone a referral service.

Our basic aim is to encourage people to seek individualised help, perhaps by ringing the telephone referral service. But we feel we shouldn't simply rely on exhortation. We should try to give the viewer an enjoyable taste of starting to learn again. And here our difficulties begin. What can we assume our viewers already know? As Ann Risman has written earlier in this book, there are probably more people with a little knowledge than with no knowledge at all. But what common knowledge can we safely assume? We have decided that the best course is to assume zero knowledge and to begin by teaching letter recognition and formation and the earliest word-building skills together with a very basic social sight vocabulary. We hope that some people will draw encouragement from the realisation that others have even more extreme difficulties. Of course we can have no guarantee that it will have that psychological effect. As in every aspect of the project we must stand ready to learn.

The level 1 programmes are scheduled to run for a year from October 1975, then to be repeated starting in October 1976 and October 1977. The level 2 programmes will begin transmission in October 1976. This series will comprise twenty twenty-five-minute programmes, and are intended for the more committed learner. They will develop the skills acquired in Level 1 and will be reinforced by a radio series of readings from the accompanying print material. In October 1977 this level 2 series will be repeated.

Throughout the period in which the Adult Literacy Project is running, BBC Schools Television and Radio will, of course, continue to provide learning materials suitable for reading ages of 7 and above. We hope that class organisers will look seriously at the potential of this 'Schools' material for adult learners. Perhaps particularly relevant here is 'The Electric Company', a television series produced by the Children's Television Workshop in New York, to be broadcast on an experimental basis by the BBC in the summers of 1975 and 1976. It will be accompanied by student's booklets. It is designed to help reading in secondary schools and it will be broadcast in daytime 'Schools' placings. It is clearly not ideal for adult use, but it is recognised in the USA to be attractive and of value to some adult learners.

The aim of the television series is basically to help the illiterate to seek individualised help. The programmes in level 1 are not designed for use by a tutor with an individual or a group although the later series could well be useful in that context. However, you may find that your students are following the programmes regularly and that useful work may develop exploiting the social sight vocabulary, the interview material and the activities shown on television. Whatever approach you use with your student the programmes can be used as revision or reinforcement.

Print material

We are trying to create students' workbooks and readers to accompany the Adult Literacy Project. At the first level this presents a particularly acute design difficulty – how do you make something self-explanatory to an isolated illiterate (assuming zero knowledge)?

At both levels there are distribution problems. How do you get the print materials to the learner without exposing him to embarrassment and the risk of disclosure of his problem? One approach is to make some material copyright-free. We would like to encourage local and national groups to duplicate the first ten units of the first workbook, and to distribute them free in places where non-readers might be expected to come across them. We'd like to tap local goodwill and local knowledge in this difficult task of getting the material to the embarrassed learner.

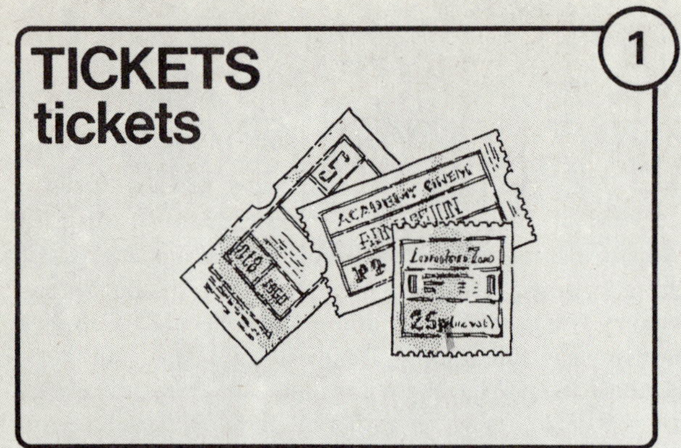

This is the kind of material the students' workbook will contain.

Student referral service

A telephone service for viewers seeking help will operate as a central part of the project. The student referral service will start during late September 1975. We envisage displaying regional telephone numbers on the screen during the period until Christmas 1975 and perhaps a single national number after that.

We will also cater for a postal referral service for those who are reluctant or unable to telephone. This might involve the would-be learner or friend completing a simple form printed in, for instance, the *Radio Times*.

We see the function of the telephone service as:
- to take details of the caller's name and address and of the sort of help he or she seeks;
- to forward these details to the appropriate Local Education Authority referral point.

Broadcasting and the tutor

As the demand for help and provision increases so the need to mobilise and train tutors will increase. This book together with a radio series for tutors are designed to make some contribution towards training and organisation. In Autumn 1975, alongside the television series, eight programmes on radio will be broadcast for those who would like to start teaching an adult illiterate. A postal referral service will be available for would-be tutors who wish to be put in touch with their local literacy scheme. The address is at the end of this section. It is also hoped that the series will be of interest to those already engaged in teaching. Notes on the programmes will be available for organisers who wish to make use of the radio material in training schemes.

The programme for tutors

The series will explore the following themes:
- defining objectives for teaching and learning: students' needs and expectations; tutors' expectations and attitudes.
- motivation and the nature of adult learning: self image – confidence/competence; interpersonal skills; implications for teaching and learning.
- diagnosis: what a tutor needs to know about the student at the beginning: formal testing; evaluation as part of the teaching/ learning process; individualised lesson planning short term and long-term; keeping records.
- basic approaches to reading and writing: language experience – social literacy, phonic/whole word approach, word attack skills – context and comprehension, reading for a purpose, spelling and writing, writing and creativity, choice and use of materials.

Wherever possible the programmes will explore and develop these themes through material recorded in teaching/learning situations.

Further information

The broadcasts could stimulate a massive student demand which must, of course, be properly prepared for. We've started an information dissemination service providing details about the broadcasts, to help people concerned with the organisation of tuition to make adequate plans. The address to write for these details is:

Adult Literacy Project, BBC Television, London W12 8QT.

Organisation

This section is written by Margaret Bentovim, Director of the Liverpool Adult Literacy Project and Dr. Susan Shrapnel, Organiser of the adult literacy programme for the Metropolitan Borough of Knowsley. The section offers information, advice and suggestions on: the extent of provision; training and co-ordinating staff, objectives and organisation.

1. Extent of provision

With the 1870 Education Act it became public policy to work for mass literacy through elementary education. With the 1975 government grant of one million pounds to be spent on adult literacy provision, it can be said to have become public policy to work for mass adult literacy through adult education. There has been a growing recognition in the last ten years that elementary education is failing to provide a significant number of people with basic literacy skills. This recognition can be seen in the groundswell of adult literacy provision during the 1970s. This can best be illustrated by a comparison of the findings of two surveys of provision: Haviland in 1972 and National Association for Remedial Education (NARE) in 1974.

	Recorded provision		
	Voluntary	LEA	Prisons, etc.
1972	12	119	81
1974	21	420	No information

Haviland lists 119 'programmes', NARE lists 420 'entries'. Even allowing that one 'programme' covering more than one centre will have several entries, this seems to indicate a greater spread and growth of work. But that provision is still acutely small can be seen in a closer look at the implication of these figures. In the 119 'programmes recorded by Haviland 'approximately 5,170 adults received literacy instruction'. In the BAS Right to Read report, it is agreed that at least two million adults in Britain are functionally illiterate. If we accept this figure then in 1972 no more than one quarter of one per cent of the people in need received literacy tuition. If we look at the NARE figures we can say, very optimistically, that provision has quadrupled since 1972. Even if this is so, in 1974 still no more than one per cent of the people needing tuition received it.

To date studies into adult illiteracy have concentrated on finding out the amount of provision that exists rather than on attempting to assess the quality of any provision. Recently it has been very encouraging to see the DES inspectorate surveying the work of adult literacy programmes in a way that will reveal a much more detailed picture of the practice and quality of provision than normally emerges from surveys. It will be interesting to see what develops from this for it is clear that although provision varies from authority to authority, a considerable proportion of that provision is inadequate. Certainly if we are to aim seriously at reducing the number of illiterate adults in Britain provision must continue to expand, but it also becomes crucial to begin to define the areas of development necessary in what and how we teach.

2. Organising literacy provision

In this section we are not going to offer you a master-plan. The comments that follow are drawn from our own experience – not all of it successful – and we hope that it will help you to see and question what you are doing, to make the most of whatever resources you have got and to make a case for more, and to try to work your practice into closer conformity with what you think it should be. We have tried to be practical, but we have also tried to expand beyond the practical where this seems necessary to indicate the dimensions of the issue. We hope that bursts of rhetoric as well as handy hints will have their uses, and perhaps make it possible for us to widen the basis for discussion in future. We are not thinking here so much of 'management by objectives' as of intellectual consistency. It seems to us one of the more curious features of the current scene that similar *practice* is adopted by a number of different providers, and yet when they come to expose the *rationale* for what they are doing, they reveal quite different understandings of basic points. We ourselves hold, for example, that illiteracy is an acute result of the general working class experience of education, and that this experience cannot be changed in the educational field alone. The economic prospects of the early school leaver as he begins to perceive them during his schooling, and the perception he has of the school's own response to these prospects, are facts as important in our decisions about literacy provision as the newest piece of work on the teaching of phonics. We hope that our practice and the activities given in these pages is in conformity with these positions. But we are aware that many colleagues disagree with them, and hold perhaps that the problem of adult illiteracy is adequately explained by the individual case histories of various students, rather than by being part of a class predicament. This is one of several areas of argument which must surely be developed, though as yet the debate has hardly begun. What we are writing in this section is only incidentally a contribution to it. We would ask you as readers, however, to think, particularly when you disagree with us, about *why* one kind of practice is preferable, as well as about *what* you prefer.

The student's progress

Our aim in this section is to look at the organisation of adult literacy tuition through the eyes of the person for whom it is being organised – the adult with reading and writing difficulties. Too often provision and practice are looked at purely from the viewpoint of the administrator, organiser or tutor, seldom from the viewpoint of the student.

We have decided to imagine the experiences of three adults with literacy problems who came forward for tuition. These experiences are of course a composite picture and have been exaggerated especially to make our points. But although no organisation probably has *all* the characteristics of any of our imaginary ones, every feature of them, taken singly, has parallels in reality. What we have of course left out is the experience of the vast majority of non-readers: they never become aware that they could be taught, and so don't even go through experiences like these.

Mr Jones received a brochure for the local Further Education College's evening classes through his letter box. He threw it away, as he did all printed material. Fortunately his friend, who knew he had wanted to learn to read for years, noticed in the small print that there were classes for basic reading. The only way to join, apparently, was to go to the college on enrolment night. As this drew near Mr Jones began to feel very nervous. He did not know what to expect. On enrolment night Mr Jones arrived at the college along with 200 other students wanting a variety of different courses. A large sheet of written instructions was pinned up on the notice board in the college foyer giving information about enrolment procedure. Mr Jones unfortunately could not read these instructions. He steeled himself to ask the receptionist what he should do, but she knew nothing about literacy classes, was very busy and could not wait for him to make himself clear.

That Mr Jones did not turn round and walk out of the college was due to pure chance. On his way to the door he met his friend who had come to enrol for a Car Maintenance class. His friend found the right table for him to go to, waited for him while he queued, helped him to fill in his form, return it and pay his fee. He also helped Mr Jones to gather the information he needed; when the class started, which room it would be held in, and the name of the teacher. He gave him the support necessary to cope with the bustle, confusion and public nature of the situation.

The chaotic scene at enrolment night.

● there are several ways in which this history could develop . . .

Mr Jones attended the class at the appointed time and found it to consist of seventeen people. Five of these did not seem to speak English at all; four were very obviously mentally handicapped; four seemed to be under the misapprehension that they were attending a pre 'O' level English course; and four, like Mr Jones, had problems with basic literacy. Mr Jones attended the class regularly, but he found the varied nature of the people's problems and the lack of time the teacher could give to his particular needs extremely frustrating. He felt that he was getting nowhere and so he did not return after the Christmas Break.

or it could develop in this way . . .

Mr Jones attended the class at the appointed time and found it to consist of five people. The class ran for a month and Mr Jones began to think that he was making progress. On the fifth meeting the college administrator closed the class because the numbers were too low.

or alternatively . . .

Mr Jones attended the class at the appointed time and found it to consist of ten people. All had come to improve their literacy, but some were fluent readers with spelling problems, while others had severe reading problems. The teacher taught a 4th year Junior school class during the day. He had very little experience of teaching reading and none of teaching adults. He felt somewhat overwhelmed. No one had told him anything about his students. He had no materials, books or audio-visual aids to use. Eventually after a few lessons he brought to the literacy class the books he used with his junior class at school. Mr Jones was disappointed. He felt that the teacher did not really know how to tackle his particular problem. He also found the situation in the classroom somewhat disturbing. The desks were in rows and the whole atmosphere brought back unpleasant memories of school. The college seemed to him to be continually closing for holidays and after each break Mr Jones found it harder to settle into the class routine. In May the college closed for the summer and was not due to re-open until the following October. After a break of 5 months Mr Jones did not enrol for the literacy class again.

Poor practice can be found elsewhere in independent schemes . . .

Mr Jacobs went along to the Citizens Advice Bureau to ask if they knew where he could go to improve his reading and writing. The CAB telephoned the Education Authority and eventually got the number of the local voluntary literacy scheme which took Mr Jacobs name and address and telephone number and asked the CAB to tell him that they would be in touch in a few days. Three weeks later Mr Jacobs

received a letter, which his wife read for him, asking him to telephone the scheme for an appointment. Mr Jacobs telephoned that evening but got no reply. The next day in his lunch hour he telephoned again. He was nervous telephoning from the works canteen, but he made an appointment to go to the scheme for an interview.

Mr Jacobs arrived five minutes early for his interview. No one answered his knock and he waited on the doorstep. Half an hour later the interviewer arrived rather flustered and breathless. Mr Jacobs felt a little depressed, he was cold and tired after a day's work, a long journey and a 35-minute wait, and the rushed atmosphere made him rather nervous. The interviewer took Mr Jacobs into a small uncomfortable room. She spent some time gathering papers together. Mr Jacobs felt that he was in the way. The interviewer then started to ask him some questions. She had a form in front of her which she was filling in. The questions seemed a little pointless to Mr Jacobs and the interviewer herself did not seem quite sure exactly what she wanted to know. Mr Jacobs was puzzled by the fact that she didn't ask him to read or write at all. After about half an hour the interviewer thanked Mr Jacobs for coming and said she would be in touch with him shortly. Mr Jacobs was very unclear about how the scheme actually worked and he did not know what was going to happen next, he was not sure what she would be getting in touch with him about, but he did not like to ask her and so he left.

Now show me something you can't do.

Eight weeks later after he had given up hope of any further contact Mr Jacobs received a letter, which his wife read for him, asking him to get in touch with a Mrs Davies who was to become his tutor. Mr Jacobs felt a little nervous about contacting Mrs Davies but he did so. Mrs Davies also felt nervous about teaching Mr Jacobs. She knew she had been matched with him because she was the only tutor in his area. She was not a trained teacher and her only contact with the scheme was her initial interview. She had asked the scheme for guidance and been told to drop in on the day the voluntary organiser was regularly at work. Unfortunately Mrs Davies was always busy on that particular day of the week. Mr Jacobs and Mrs Davies met several times but neither of them felt they really knew what they were doing. Mr Jacobs wanted to telephone the scheme organiser to ask for help but he did not like to bother her and so he stopped his lessons. Mrs Davies felt so demoralised with the whole process that when six months later she received a letter from the scheme asking her how tuition was progressing, she sent back a rather sharp reply. On the other hand a student may receive excellent advice and help...

Mr Jeffries. Everything seemed to conspire to make Mr Jeffries do something about his reading and writing difficulties. His wife had read an article on adult illiteracy in the local paper. He had seen a notice about help for adults with literacy problems on his union notice board and the local radio station had run a series of programmes on adult literacy. With each piece of publicity the same name and telephone number was given out, and people who needed help were urged to make contact.

Mr Jeffries rang the number. The receptionist seemed to know just why he'd telephoned and asked him to make an appointment to come for an interview. He made an appointment for the following week which fitted in well with his shift time. The woman on the telephone explained exactly where he was to come, whom he was going to meet and what was going to happen. She took his name and address and asked him if anyone could read his letters for him. Two days later a letter arrived confirming the time and place of his appointment.

Mr Jeffries arrived for his interview and was met by a friendly receptionist. She seemed to expect him, and took him into a small comfortable room where he was immediately joined by the interviewer. The interviewer began by explaining that the building they were in was a special adult literacy centre run by the Local Education Authority. This centre co-ordinated all the adult literacy work going on in the City, both statutory and voluntary, and because of this she would be able to offer Mr Jeffries a large choice of teaching situations. She explained that she was going to ask Mr Jeffries a lot of questions, but that he wasn't obliged to talk about anything he didn't want to. As the conversation progressed, far from feeling unwilling to talk, Mr Jeffries felt that discussing the history of his reading problems was helping him to believe something could be done about them.

He was nervous about doing some reading and writing, but the interviewer talked to him about his mistakes and about how a teacher might use this information to help him. The interviewer spent some time explaining exactly what was available to Mr Jeffries:

- individual tuition in his own home, the tutor's home or the centre;
- a group in the local community centre;
- a group in his factory which would operate on a day-release basis;
- a group at a literacy centre;
- a class at the local College of Further Education.

All the groups were small with six or less students and no one in the group would be very much better or worse than him. Groups could start at any time of the year and stopped only for the normal public holidays. Mr Jeffries was also told that the DEP (Department of Employment) at certain times throughout the year organised full-time paid courses for unemployed people. After much discussion he and the interviewer both agreed that individual tuition in the literacy centre would be the best thing for him. The interviewer explained the next steps, said there might be a short delay in finding the right tutor and told Mr Jeffries to come straight back if he wasn't happy with the arrangement. Before he left Mr Jeffries was shown the centre library. Its contents were explained to him and he was encouraged to use it as soon as he felt it appropriate.

Two weeks later Mr Jeffries received a letter (he is not on the telephone) asking him to contact the literacy centre. He came in, arranged a meeting with his tutor and decided he would get on well with her. They met regularly every week for two months; he saw the interviewer from time to time at coffee breaks and told her how well he thought he was getting on. After two months his tutor suggested that he might have some slight sight problem. The centre arranged an appointment with a local optician. It was discovered that he needed glasses.

After about six months of regular tuition Mr Jeffries was asked to come to the centre for another interview so that some assessment could be made of his progress. He was met by the same interviewer as before. Mr Jeffries was pleased when she confirmed his own opinion that he had made excellent progress in his reading and writing. The interviewer suggested that maybe Mr Jeffries would now like to attend a group at the centre. Mr Jeffries agreed but decided to carry on with his individual tuition as well.

From the student's point of view it is possible to identify six main stages at which the operation and organisation of the adult literacy provision can be crucial:

- publicity
- initial contact with the organisation
- first meeting with the organiser or tutor
- beginning lessons
- progress of lessons
- conclusion of lessons

What do the three imaginary cases suggest about practice to be avoided and practice to be encouraged?
How do you manage at these essential points?

We have taken these six stages of the student's progress as the headings for the detailed discussion which follows. If you've set down your ideas you will be able to compare your notes with ours.

The organiser's response

The question we will have in mind throughout our discussion of these six stages is what kind of organisation, staff and other resources go to make the student's experience a good one at all these points? It may be worth considering this question for a moment as our economic masters are likely to consider it. Why should we spend more money on this than on other kinds of adult education? After all, the student enrolling for a normal class also needs consideration and efficiency; diffidence and embarrassment can affect someone enrolling for 'O' level Spanish; and the need to avoid well-meaning amateurishness applies as much to a Workers' Educational Association (WEA) 'Travel Abroad' class as it does to voluntary literacy provision.

The overwhelming answer is, of course, that success or failure in this area matters more to the student than in most other kinds of adult education. Literacy is still a fundamental power in this society, and its unequal sharing is as basic to life chances as the distribution of other kinds of power. The public education system may be said to undertake to share this power equally: for our students it has failed. An education authority must surely give the highest priority to redressing this position at whatever age, and by whatever means this can best be done.

The other reason why this kind of adult education needs more manpower and care is exactly that all our students in this field have come to see themselves as failures at education, in a society which uses education to mark degrees of success. There is a great deal we do not know about this experience, but we do know from the testimony of our students, that it tends to put people beyond the self

It says if you want to know about literacy classes would you write to the director of education.

respect they might be able to draw from their skills, capacities and achievements in other areas of life. In our own country it is not easy for them, less easy even than among racial minorities in America, to adopt a 'counter culture' position that exempts them from the standards of the majority. Irrationally, but overpoweringly, it affects them with shame. This syndrome, usually referred to as the 'embarrassment' of the illiterate, makes particular demands on the organiser and tutor. A momentary brusqueness or an unnecessary delay can drive someone away from something which may have been a 'last chance', as our imaginary Jackie Baker sees it, or a way to preserve a livelihood, as it is for Michael Wells. These are not people who readily present themselves as students; many are deeply inclined to believe they cannot learn. Failure this time may be a final discouragement. It is clear that the approach of consumer demand and provider's response is inappropriate. (If you need a caution against adopting a missionary approach instead, look at Paulo Freire's *Cultural Action for Freedom*.) A practical demonstration of your conviction of the student's needs and rights cannot be created quickly or mechanically. However we can make a start, in terms of the organiser's response, by returning to those six stages of a student's progress. We shall suggest minimum and optimum resources for that job to be done well.

Most of us started with well below the minimum. But considering how much more is now known and said about the state of literacy in the nation, and considering that it is therefore less possible for an authority to regard literacy as a marginal, temporary or localized problem, we would like to suggest that if the minimum is not available it is better not to start at all. It's difficult because it is hard to walk away from even one student who wants to learn. But isn't it time we stopped offering provision which in fact betrays the needs of the students constantly by understaffing and under-equipping? By accepting an impossible task, you effectively walk away from many more students than just one.

A prior question, which is often not raised at all, is who you will accept as a student? Are you going to exclude those who have been to ESN or special schools? Are you going to regard anyone as too literate for your provision? Are you going to take 15-year-olds still at school? This must depend on your own resources (of skill and experience as well as of mere size), but it's better to make a decision before the hard case comes up for consideration.

Publicity
Publicity used traditionally by adult education centres seems to emphasise the constructive use of leisure, and it informs those who

are *already* thinking of coming to a class about *what* they can choose from. Clearly neither of these approaches will do in our case. Many of our students are like Sean O'Reilly and don't know evening classes exist at all. Many are unaware that anyone offers teaching for them. In no case is it a simple question of a use of spare time. If you add to this the fact that most of them put aside written and printed material, then we need new approaches.

The easier problem to solve is publicity directed at those to whom students turn first for help. This will cover everyone from the wife or best friend to the shop steward, priest, and the official and voluntary problem-solving bodies. The following list may be useful:

the education office; social services department; libraries; trade unions; political parties, clubs, etc.; churches; doctors; hospitals and hospital social workers, community councils, local action groups; probation service; prisons and borstals; Citizens' Advice Bureaux; Department of Health and Social Security; local industry.

(Incidentally many firms give a sight test, which is often a reading test, done on admission by the factory's nurse. She may in fact turn down people for employment because of this. It would be useful if she knew of your existence.)

Posters in some of these places – notably social security and employment offices, factory notice boards, and waiting rooms – will be seen directly by potential students. In addition you can try handbills in shops and pubs, articles in the community, local and national press, and discussions (and now possibly advertising) on BBC Local Radio and Commercial Radio Stations. Many American commercial stations have a free community spot where announcements of public interest can be made. If your Community Council or local politicians can be persuaded to press the new Local Commercial Stations for this, you may benefit from it.

Publicity on the national media is very useful in giving an airing to the problem and the possibility of solution, and in helping the long business of changing attitudes. It does act as part of the process persuading a student to come forward – which is often slow and cumulative. Remember that our students say the first decision is the hardest thing of all. When the BBC launches its Adult Literacy Project you may find that the national publicity makes it easier for you to get recognition and put on publicity locally. There is now a national literacy campaign logo which can be developed and exploited as you will.

Without something like this it is hard to devise publicity that doesn't demand the reading of a few words. There have been attempts but they are not often clear or arresting. Meanwhile, a short verbal message and a telephone number are bringing in plenty of people; but it may be partly due to the nature of our publicity that we attract relatively few students who can't read at all.

One last aspect of advertising for students seems to us the hardest of all. Most of the publicity we have seen is genteel and negative: 'Let us help you solve your problem' is the prevailing tone. It is true that it is easier to take a tone of positive recommendation when it is clearer what kind of change literacy will bring – for example, when it is part of a general social change, or part of a breakthrough into a new mode of production. Neither of those is the case in this country now, and we would be lying if we suggested that the newly literate man would walk into a job, solve his personal problems, and gener-

ally shed all the disagreeable characteristics of his present life. But can we move away from the inconveniences of illiteracy to the benefits of literacy? Is it just that they don't lend themselves to visual representation, or that we think them self evident, or that we aren't too sure what they are? The best I have seen is a poster from the West Indies whose slogan was: 'It *dread* when book and brain meet' – it's formidable when book and brain meet.

A warning: Don't overdo the publicity. You can to some extent and more in the early stages than later, control the flow of students by your action or inaction in this respect. If you can't cope with more – then don't put the story out, or issue the posters.

If you are using volunteer tutors, or if you want to enrol qualified and paid tutors on a large scale, then you will need publicity on this side too. It can be useful to make all your handbills dual-purpose: put a rider on the student publicity saying 'Could you help?' and on the tutor publicity saying 'Do you know anyone who needs help?' This will help to check the tendency to draw tutors from different parts of town with different social realities from those of your students.

When you are advertising for students, your objectives will affect the content of your publicity and where you direct it. Advertising for tutors is the nearest you may get to a public statement of what your objectives are. Make it good: you'll probably get who you ask for. Do you want people like Murray Johnson's previous tutor from the remedial centre, the 'vastly experienced lady in her early 60's'? Do you want a social service voluntary worker, branching out into something new? Do you want tutors whose educational, industrial and social experience has been closest to that of the students? In the first case, you may have trouble persuading them to take on overtime (or you may have trouble when you say you want to train them); in the last case, you may have trouble persuading them they have the capacity to teach.

Resources

minimum
● time, local knowledge, legwork on the part of organiser or teacher;
● borrowed photocopier, electronic stencil maker or silk-screen and some design flair;
● budget for press advertisements;
● paper, stamps, telephone.

optimum
● printing budget;
● commissioned design for the purpose;
● access to a resources centre;
● organiser's time;
● positive initiatives by local press and radio, local authority publicity service, and related agencies.

First contact

When you have advertised your name and telephone number, you will need to see there is someone answering the telephone, and that they know what is going on. There is no room for the justifiable impatience of the college secretary when the caller appears not to know what he wants. She must be well informed so that she quickly passes the call on, makes an appointment, or collects a name and address – whatever system you settle on. And she should know what you are offering as well. You will also need to think about the times the telephone needs to be manned. Most people at work can't reach you by telephone between 9 and 5, except possibly at lunchtime when you may be off duty too. To overcome this, some schemes advertise an evening.

The same considerations apply to the first visit to the college or centre for an interview. As the student sees it, everybody knows what he is there for, and most of them have cast him as a 'thickie'; or else it is just an experience like so many others of frustration and being unable to respond to signals. Whether it is the caretaker or the principal he bumps into, brief them and keep them concerned to make it easy for the student.

Your working hours may normally be a 9–5 day or a 10-session week, some of it in the evenings. If you want to make sure there's an informed person present at all times you are likely to need extra help. You may not even work in the centre at all. If you are a part-time tutor coming in from home or from another job, and you're also expected to deal with initial contact with new students, you are dropping below minimum workable conditions. You need extra pay for attending to this, or you need someone else's ungrudging time allocated to it. This is one of the pressures that builds up towards a demand for paid organising time. Modest advertising can bring enquirers at a rate of two students a week: if you interview and assess before putting them in a class, it takes an hour or two each. If you have no appointments system and have had to go hunting the student out, that is another hour here and there, plus travel costs.

Resources

minimum
- well briefed and concerned staff, who may not be working directly for you, but who won't say 'that's not my job';
- good telephone access, day and at least one evening;
- paid time for interviewer or willing and trained volunteers.

optimum
- enough staff with organising responsibility to cover day and evenings without strain;
- a secretary/receptionist.
- a building that can be open without the constraint of terms, half-terms, weekend and tea-time closure; preferably not one where potential students will have to wade through unconcerned and possibly curious strangers, such as school children;
- travel expenses.

First meeting with organiser or tutor

You will get a few people who will march up to your college or centre and enrol for a spelling class with as little fuss as if they were enrolling for a keep fit class. But the majority will not. Once they have identified a place where they can go to learn, you will still need to work through with them the choice between individual or group teaching or between one group and another in order for them to decide on the best choice for them. It goes without saying that it is not enough for the secretary to hand out an enrolment form. We are assuming that each student needs to be seen, and that the purpose of this meeting is to find out what his needs are.

So who does the student come to? The class teacher? The centre or department head? An organiser who will assign him to a class or a tutor? A volunteer? Whoever it is, they need to be prepared for the job, and to have a clear idea of what it is intended should take place. Not, surely, just a collecting of names and addresses and an 'O.K. start Tuesday week'.

There are disagreements about the use of a fixed interview schedule and even more disagreements about what should be on it. Clearly if a long schedule is to be mechanically applied in a way that discourages the student from talking about what he or she thinks is relevant, it is more harm than help. We use a long interview schedule that covers social circumstances as well as educational history and possible perception problems, and get students to do some reading and writing so we can watch the process and begin to see what extra skills are needed. In this way we can begin, with the student, to look at illiteracy as something with tangible causes and hopeful remedies; by talking about something which has often been kept in utter silence the student begins to work out the appalling shame and embarrassment; we find out enough to match intelligently with tutors; and we can begin to plan a teaching programme.

This programme will of course depend enormously on why it is the student has come and what his purposes are in wanting to improve his reading and writing. These purposes usually relate to the areas of distress and exploitation that have been discussed in the first section of the book. It is worth summarizing the most common *practical* purposes expressed by students are:

- to get a job or a better job;
- to help children with school work;
- to cope with bureaucratic demands, and what we might call social paperwork;
- to become an equal in social exchanges;
- to deal with leisure uses of print like newspapers, pools, betting, reading about other interests.

These are, we stress, practical purposes; they are also as far as you will find most analyses of 'functional literacy' carry you. But if we stop here, surely we are still talking about the uses of literacy as we might conceive them for others, not for ourselves – and for others whom we see as less complex and valuable people? We do not want to divert tutors and organisers from their attempts to satisfy tangible aims which have clear if limited advantages for the individual. But there is one area of aspiration beyond, which students often indicate by phrases like 'to get more self respect', 'to start a new life', and even 'to write the story of my life'. It's in responding to this that we need most sensitivity, and most clarity about the consequences of what we do. We can narrow motives here or widen them. We can act as if the only benefits someone can take from learning are those he can turn into private gain of a more or less exalted kind, or as if the natural use of a communication skill is to be communicable and to enter on shared understandings that may liberate others as the learner is liberating himself. If this sounds high-flown in relation to the things most students talk about, perhaps it is worth considering what motives to literacy have often driven people in the past, not to *be taught* but to teach themselves. We might begin this list with the desire to read the Bible, to read history and politics, to write to workers in a common cause, to seek, store and refine information, to feed an interest, to satisfy the soul. Are these motives dead, or just hard to talk about if you have been led to believe they are out of your reach? These may be some of the problems you will discover in trying to find out from your students what they see as their real needs.

After the interview you have to consider how you pass the information on to the tutor. What we have come to do is to write up a profile from the interview and impressions; not so full a document as the profiles that have been prepared for this book, *but covering similar areas* such as motivation, social and educational background, reading and writing performance, and expressed preferences for teaching (which may be modified by the interviewer's recommendation). These are impressionistic and are not intended to convey what diagnostic points have been learnt from the student's reading and writing.

The other thing you have to establish is that the information is confidential and not available to anyone else. The student must know this and everyone in the organisation, including the reception staff who take names and addresses, must respect it. We do know things about our students that they wouldn't want to come to the ears of their employers, or their neighbours. And while there is an argument to be had about whether we foster the sense of embarrassment by stressing the privacy of teaching, clearly the privacy of records is beyond dispute.

Whatever procedure you eventually adopt for this first meeting, it is important that those who meet the students should be well prepared, both to secure what information the working pattern requires you to know at this stage, and to ensure that the interview fosters and does not undermine the student's adulthood and autonomy. You may want to undertake specific training of interviewers. We shall discuss this later.

We ought to mention why we are not saying anything specific about tests. All the current reading and spelling tests in use were devised for children and have not been standardized with adults. It is important to test, but testing should mean exploring the limits of the student's performance and trying to find out the patterns of what he has learned so far. You need this information to plan his work sensibly. So what we need is diagnostic tests rather than attainment tests. Unfortunately there are no tests designed for adults that would be appropriate for use in this country, so anything you choose will be a compromise.

None of the available ones have a content that is related to the student's own reading experience or general experience, and the information they give us very limited. Would it be worth our attempting an adult version of the story with paragraphs of steadily increasing difficulty, like the one in Herbert Kohl's book *Reading, How to*? It would still be worth having a supply of casual reading – photographs of signs, leaflets, headlines, and the like – to add extra information.

1
The boy had a dog.
The dog's face was black.
The dog's body was brown.

2
Once the dog saw a rat.
It was a bad rat.
The dog did not like the rat on his place.
So he ran the rat into his hole.

3
After the rat got into his hole, he began to peek at the dog.
This drove the dog nearly mad.
He said: 'I like raw meat to eat. If you do not stop, I will eat you.'
Then he left the rat alone.

4
This talk only made the rat smile.
He could not stop smiling.
He stuck out his chin and cried:
'You are as dull as a donkey.
You are as silly as a monkey.
Let me give you a good tip.
You had better find a doctor now, before it is too late.
Maybe he can do something for your head.'

5
These remarks made the dog furious. He was so angry he could hardly control himself. He growled in dismay. He gnawed at the ground. Then he barked: 'I am the protector of this residence. I am the champion of this estate. I will have no nonsense here. If you value your life and freedom you will depart at once.'

Extract from Reading: How to *by Herbert Kohl.*

We are a bit more satisfied with our own practice on testing writing performance than reading. We ask for:
- name and address – which tests difficult words likely to have been learned;
- a dictated sentence – based on interview material, and so telling you about the writing of words commonly spoken;
- a freely chosen sentence – which can tell you whether the student avoids words he is not sure of;
- a graded spelling test – which can tell you about specific spelling rules and norms not mastered.

You will find more information on diagnosing students' difficulties in the earlier section on planning and evaluation. Just a note (obvious enough) about where you meet for the interview: in the hunt for privacy one of the writers was recently driven to interview in a partitioned off storeroom-cum-office, unheated and cramped. This just will not do!

Look at the four profiles of Sean, Jackie, Murray and Michael:
Would you like as much information as this when you start?
What information do you think you would prefer?
Would you like to be able to pass on as much to your tutors?
Even if you *want* to know all this, have you the *right* to know?
How and when would you amass it?
Is there any kind of information you think lacking in those profiles?

Resources
minimum
- time for briefing: training interviews and voluntary or engaged in other work;
- time for leisurely meeting with student;
- comfort and privacy.

optimum
- reception and organising staff who can be available at flexible hours, with a generous allowance of time for the job.
- comfort, privacy, immediate access to a wide range of reading that can be used diagnostically;

- time for briefing, revision of interview and test procedures, liaison with tutors to determine usefulness of information;
- access, as of right, to further help of the kind available to schools educational service.

Beginning lessons
What happens here clearly depends on the structure within which you work. You may have several choices to offer the student or you may have none but the choice of a tutor, or none at all if you have a single group. You may be handing the student on to a tutor experienced in adapting teaching to a particular person's needs and stage of progress, or you may be handing the student on to a tutor who has not taught before and who is uncertain how to use a student's successes and mistakes to decide on the next step in teaching. In other words you may need to give more or less advice and spend more or less time discussing objectives, methods and starting points with the tutor. What seems unlikely is that you will need to spend no time at all; unless the first contact is made by the person who also teaches. (It is hard, by the way, to think of a system by which this can always be so, once provision starts expanding.)

If you have a training course, it is helpful to allocate students to tutors before the course is over, or at least to have a first follow-up meeting very shortly after. This makes it practical for teaching to be jointly planned, and gives you a chance of finding out whether the first contact has gone well.

It seems to be most people's experience that what happens to the student first has a strong binding power, and if he is at all satisfied he is likely to resent subsequent changes. This makes it all the more important that the first choice – as between individual or group tuition, and as between one group and another – is made advisedly. If he isn't satisfied, of course, there must be easy ways for a change to be made and it must be clear to both tutor and student that a change may be made. 'Easy ways' is easily said; it probably involves an initiative on the part of the organiser or at the very least, a specific invitation to the student to telephone in if he has any problems.

When it comes to choices between one kind of teaching and another, you'll probably need policies and guidelines as well as responsiveness to individuals. We don't know of any evidence yet that one system of allocation works better than another; so your policies are likely to be based on your objectives and beliefs, and on the preferences and capacities of your tutors. It has become common practice to assume that where individual and group tuition are both available, the less confident and outgoing students go to individual tutors and the more socially at ease to groups, perhaps with the intention of moving the individual learners into groups later. Bear it in mind, though, that often people don't want to change, and bear in mind that you may meet students, as we have, who are too nervous for individual tuition. We met one woman who couldn't bear the idea that she would be under the scrutiny of her tutor for the whole of the lesson.

How do you group your groups? Do you favour mixing them, deliberately taking them as they come, or sorting them by age, sex, social or national origins, probable speed of progress, common interests? There may be some advantages but there are clearly strong arguments against streaming as such, particularly if it is carried out in such a way that a student knows the grade of a group to which he may be assigned or moved. If you don't stream, you need to take great care not to reproduce the situation in which those with the most to learn get demoralised. But this should be possible to achieve within a small group. It will mean encouraging some unlearning: we heard of a group on a full-time DEP course where some students resented the idea that they should help each other: 'He's stealing his knowledge', one of them complained, when two of his fellows started working together. Is the following account of co-operative learning a fanciful alternative? It comes from an account written by the pupils of a rural school in Italy.

The favourite. *Life was hard up there. Discipline and squabbles until you didn't feel like coming back. But there was a boy who had no background, who was slow or lazy, he was made to feel like the favourite. He would be treated the way you teachers treat the best student in the class. It seemed as if the school was meant just for him. Until he could be made to understand, the others would not continue.* Children as teachers. *The next year I was a teacher; that is, three half days a week. I taught geography, mathematics and French to the first intermediate year.*

You don't need a degree to look through an atlas or explain fractions. If I made some mistakes, that wasn't so bad. It was a relief for the boys. We would work them out together. The hours would go by quickly, without worry and without fear. You don't know how to run a class the way I do. Politics or stinginess. *Then, too, I was learning so many things while I taught. For instance, that others' problems are like mine. To come out of them together is good politics. To come out alone is stinginess.*

I was not vaccinated against stinginess myself. During exams I felt like sending the little ones to hell and studying on my own. I was a boy like your boys, but up at Barbiana, I couldn't admit it to myself or others. I had to be generous even when I didn't feel it.

To you this may seem a small thing. But for your students you do even less. You don't ask anything of them. You just encourage them to push ahead on their own. (Letter to a Teacher).

It may unfortunately be fanciful as long as we have only two hours a week to teach in. Which brings us to the further point that, of all the known variants of teaching reading to adults, the one clear advantage lies with those who spend more time on it. It is obvious enough; but how much of our attention is on extending the teaching hours for each student? It is part of the policy of the Association of Teachers in Technical Institutions to press for universal day-release for all under 18s.

Here are some questions you should ask yourself about the beginning of teaching:

- is the tuition programme planned?
- have materials and resources been secured?
- where and when is the first meeting?
- what did the student think of it?
- what did the tutor think of it?
- does the student know what other choices there are?
- do they both know what support you can give in future?
- is the group working well together?
- is it able to run for as many weeks of the year as it wants?

Resources

minimum

- part-time professional or voluntary staff trained to teach illiterate students;
- paid help to organise training programmes;
- continued access to refresher meetings;
- low tutor–student ratios (1 : 6 maximum?)
- costing on the basis of no student fees.

optimum

- all staff paid, regardless of the number of students they teach;
- training of such a kind that a tutor who is not a trained teacher becomes as much worth paying as a teacher trained in another field. (Lest this be misunderstood, we state it as a conviction that they often already are as much worth paying.);
- paid time available to tutors to participate in discussions and workshops;
- full-time staff also involved in teaching;
- support from organising secretarial and library staff.

Materials

minimum

- paper, card, felt tips, letrasets, etc.
- own stock of books plus generous loan from library, and other teaching outfits;
- papers, magazines, leaflets and forms;
- storage space for all of these.

optimum

- as above, but much more;
- plus: cassettes, recorders, teaching equipment; copying equipment;
- a paid curriculum development worker on your staff;
- television, video, cameras, projectors, etc.

Premises

minimum

- adult furniture;
- refreshments;
- reasonable privacy;
- reasonable accessibility.

optimum

- a centre with teaching rooms open all day all year if necessary;
- library, kitchen, creche, lounge could be shared with other adult education provision;
- rooms elsewhere in the district and/or a van as a mobile classroom;
- beyond that, it depends on your orientation and alliances in the neighbourhood.

Progress

Probably the first thing to suffer if you are under-staffed is your follow-up contact with students and tutors. The reason is simple. The priority is to get some teaching going, so you cannot avoid the earlier stages of this process. If you do nothing to check progress when you have got him working with a tutor, you will have literacy provision but you will know nothing about its nature and quality. This might appear preferable, but really it isn't. Any one of you who has been organising provision for some time must have your own horror stories of early days: inadequately briefed tutors, disappearing students, meetings that never took place, and none of it coming to light until months later.

It is essential that you keep in touch with what is happening mainly because we are all still exploring, and because of the student's sensitivity and your conviction that a great deal is at stake.

Your information should come from two sources: students and tutors. Your tutors' willingness to report may well depend on how you present the subject at your induction or training meetings. Paid class teachers are often not accustomed to reporting back, mainly because they work in the daytime in schools where any particular class is not so easy to lose touch with.

But information does not flow easily from the one-off evening class, and you will need to know from there as much as from individual tutors about who is getting on, who might be better in another situation, who hasn't attended lately, what they need next in the way of materials, and so on. You need a policy too about chasing up students who have missed classes. Of course it is their right to give it up; but you need to be sure it isn't for some avoidable reason – an unsuitable group; an enforced absence followed by nervousness at coming back; an accidental slight; too many familiar faces in the teaching centre; and so on. Even a strongly motivated student can be put off and can want to be *brought* back. Who is to do this – the organiser or the teacher?

Individual tutors, especially if it is their first time teaching, can be nervous and embarrassed themselves. To get accurate and prompt reports on breakdowns, you need to convince them, too, that it is not a question of 'their fault'. But let us hope that most of the reports will be of progress and not of breakdown. You will need a system to get them, perhaps a report form circulated at intervals.

```
                 ADULT LITERACY PROGRAMME
                           College of Further Education


Dear
        I hope the lessons are going well.  Please  do get in
touch with me if you are having difficulties or need advice
of any kind.   Could you also complete the  report form below
and return it to me straight away?  Thank you.


________________________________________________________________
The lessons are held at ...........BRANCH..LIBRARY
more than once a week/ once a week/ less often (please give
details ,

________________________________________________________________
When did you last see your student?
        4th November 1974

________________________________________________________________
What methods and materials are you using?
 1 Playing with words e.g. formation of words from 'stems' using prefixes & suffixes
                        building up word families.
              2 Identifying sounds with the way they are written (phonics)
                          3.  Using a dictionary
Materials (a) my own productions
          (b) newspaper articles/ language experience    (c) ideas from Smith's books.

Do you feel your student has made any progress?
        He feels he has - I think he has made some progress, but it is difficult
                                                   to measure how much.

Is there any aspect of teaching causing you particular
difficulty?
        Mr.B. has a particular problem with spelling and I feel lacking
 in the necessary range of techniques to develop ability in spelling. Is there
 a text which might give some clues about the kind of approaches which could be tried

Have you any bright ideas or particular successes to pass on?
     Is it possible that more resources should be put in with each student at the
beginning before the voluntary tutors get cracking? I mean 'resources' in the sense
of finding out more precisely what the problems are + suggesting to tutors more clearly how they
                                                   could be dealt with.

Is there anything else you would like to know or need help with?
This student makes a very positive effort and spends a lot of his own time working on his
reading + spelling. Ideally I think he needs 'diagnosis' of his difficulties by someone expert
                                                        in this field.
From:    Name
         Address

         Date.
            8. 11.1974
```

The report form will almost certainly need chasing. Expansion fairly quickly makes it impossible for one person to do this. An obvious expedient is to group tutors and students with a group adviser or contact who *can* chase the relatively small number of tutors – perhaps with students with like problems or like interests? A small group is also more likely to meet occasionally to grumble, exchange wisdom and perhaps make materials for common use. You should at least cover expenses for your group contacts.

You'll also need to suggest criteria for defining progress. Jackie Baker spent the time happily enough with her first tutor, but they did more chatting than learning. Have you made it clear you don't think this is what it's all about? Do you re-test students after an interval? Do you stress the value of simply keeping old work, so a student can *see* progress?

It is essential that you do find a way of making assessments. If progress is not being made then everybody's time is being wasted. What we do is to ask the student to come for a private meeting to discuss his progress or lack of it. This meeting must be carefully structured to determine how the student feels about his situation. Attention must be paid to the initial interview schedule, to the student's expressed motivation and needs, and to his original literacy level. Does the student himself feel he has progressed? Can he read or write anything he could not manage before? Does he feel more confident generally? Using the same reading and spelling tests as in the original interview, assess how much formal progress he has made. His development and progress *must* be frankly discussed both with the student and the tutor. His teaching situation must be discussed and altered where necessary and a new programme of work planned for him.

You may also find that you need specialist advice about some students. Sight, hearing, speech may all hamper a student's reading and writing, and if they haven't been diagnosed or treated already, you may have to suggest or arrange how they can be. It is very useful to establish contact with psychologists, speech therapists etc. who will help and advise in these areas.

Reports from students are very necessary. One splendid if extreme example illustrates the need for them. It is a story reported from Lancashire: a tutor was assigned to a student, arranged to meet him, and came back the next day saying, 'Well, there's one problem solved, how about another one?' What can the student have made of this instant tuition? Student reports are not easy to come by. So often the student will not want to bother you, or will defer to the judgement of the tutor even if things aren't going as he would want. And in the early stages, while you want to do everything you can to enable the student not to be passive about his learning, you can alarm him by putting too much of the initiative on him. But you needn't wait on the development of a particular student to make it clear that contribution and assessment by students is one of the things you regard as normal. If you are sincere about the contribution an adult can make to his own and his fellows' learning, and you show it by inviting him to lectures and policy-making meetings, and by providing him with a chance to comment and suggest, you will get surprising results. People are interested in how they are learning; and so are family and friends who will help them at home. We tend to write only to tutors because we know they can read. But why shouldn't a report form, for example, be sent to the student and jointly read, completed and signed?

This is what came back when one form went to a student by mistake.

```
           ADULT LITERACY PROJECT


                  REPORT    FORM

Name of Tutor:                        Name of student:

Address:   VICTORIA Rd.               Length of Tuition:  2 hours

1.   The lessons are held at....VICTORIA Rd............ once a week/
     once a fortnight/........................

2.   When did you last see your student?
        I have not see            For 3 month if you would
     like to find out if she is TEACHING me or not
3.   What methods are you using?
        we I read from books

4.   What progress is your student making?
        I have made very good progress in read
        I did have a very good tutor in
        but I have not see          for 3 month

5.   Are there any aspects of teaching which is causing you particular difficulty?
        NO

6.   Is there anything else you would like to know or need help with?
        SPELLING + READ.

                     Date...3 MAY 75........
                     Signature....................
```

We shouldn't suggest that the onus is all on the tutor to maintain and report progress, and that the organisation restricts itself to demanding news. Progress will be made and reported from your end, too; new resources discovered, links with other schemes, improvements in the service. Newsletters and refresher meetings are the obvious initiatives you can take, and again there is every reason why you should circulate students too. It is depressing, but true, that the main constraint on this will often be the cost of postage.

In the area of maintaining standards, of course, you aren't, or should not be, alone. If your authority has an in-service training budget for adult education, or if your local college of education can run such a course, you can enlist the interest and help of the inspectorate, then do bring them in. You may feel less like a puppet-master with too many strings. It is hard to make it a genuinely co-operative enterprise when most of the people who work in it only do so for an hour or two a week, but real progress will only come if we can work in that spirit.

Resources

minimum
- time;
- money for post and telephones.

optimum
- reproduction facilities, costs for a bulletin;
- team of paid, trained group contact workers;
- time and premises for refresher meetings; paid attendance;
- premises for students to meet in;
- access to specialist help.

Conclusion of lessons

We have heard of one old lady who wanted to learn to write her name and address on her pension book. When she'd done that, she had what she came for; as far as she was concerned the job was finished. Most students' needs, and the point at which they can be said to be satisfied, aren't so easily determined.

Here again you need to make some clear decisions about the scope of what you are doing before you start; and then to revise them in the light of what your students achieve and want. Do you intend to fill the gap between the student and the other educational provision in your area? Do you know what related or further courses there are that your students might move on to? Is it your business to know about job opportunities and job counselling? If you feel so pressed that you can only deal with *acute* literacy problems, what do you suggest for people who are too advanced for your kind of work? That is one area of decision that will affect what you see as completion of *your* labours. Another is what your student's aspirations are. We consider that as a general rule it is surely better to help them to pitch these high rather than low, and not to accept (if you can find out the reasons in time) the departure of a student who has stuck at one stage for a while and become convinced that that is all he can do; he may settle for the practical improvements he has made, but it is our job to urge him and help him to more.

So if we are talking about the students who sign off, we need to think of information about related resources in the area, information about what the student has achieved, and the relation of this to his original or later purposes in coming to learn. We've touched on what these might be in the section on interviews, and all we will do here is remind you that the functional literacy that students define covers functions of different and often subtle kinds.

Many students disappear, however, rather than sign off. One function of the growth of your organisation is to cut down the proportion of disappearances, and the proportion of tutor drop-outs too. But, as has been suggested in the previous section, you can't simply look on this as 'voting with their feet' in the time-honoured adult educator's phrase. Their presence has just as much need to be voluntary; but departures may be because of your mistakes, or changing work or family conditions, as much as because of a simple change of mind that it would be wrong to tamper with. And if changes can be made that can bring the student back – of tutor, lesson plan,

lesson time, working surroundings – of course they should be. Again, the heavy demand is on your time.

What would you like to see Murray, Jackie, Sean and Michael doing or able to cope with when they leave you? Here are some possibilities, far from exclusive, and cast for convenience in terms of institutions. Murray – some 'O' levels?
Sean – a bookkeeping class? (By the way – who's taught him to add?)
Jackie – subscription to Readers' Digest or book club?
Michael – secretaryship of a local recreational club?
Are these fanciful, patronizing, or restricted? Can you suggest alternatives?

Literacy provision must cost more!

This stage-by-stage approach has meant some overlap and some repetition in the lists of resources. We have chosen to approach it in this way, though, because we think it is important to be clear *why* you need time, money, or people; and the reasons lie in the kinds of job that need to be done. There's a danger with all causes that become prominent subjects of public concern, that when the concern dies down its only monument is a number of salaried jobs for professional people. We aren't advocating a model establishment; we are outlining tasks, which could be done by various combinations of paid and unpaid labour. But the current models of unpaid work or marginal part-time responsibility have had their day. It is clear that if you accept the need for the practice that we have described or something like it, then you need to move away from the costings, job-descriptions, work-loads and tutor-student ratios of normal further and adult education. You can't simply take over formulae arrived at for other kinds of work.

To deal with cost alone: the Russell Report stated that of the non-vocational adult education provided by local education authorities, universities and the Workers' Educational Association, the net cost per student was less than £10 in 1968–69. (Russell Report). This is clearly miserly for any kind of education and hopeless for literacy work. Even allowing a generous 50 per cent for expansion and inflation, a comparable rate would mean that a body teaching one hundred non-literate adults would do so on a budget of £1,500. In fact, even with unpaid volunteer teachers, that would be impossible – or impossible to do well. It is something like three-fifths of a salary, of a lecturer on the Burnham scale, with nothing over to spend on books, stamps or telephone calls. (Not that we are prescribing Burnham Scale L.1. as an appropriate rate, but we need some point of reference.) If on the other hand, all the money were to be spent on teaching it would give the students only 45 hours' teaching each during the year, if they were in groups of six. *Literacy provision must cost more* – if it is to be effective at all.

One thing we should make clear in passing. The figure from the Russell Report is a *net* cost. Net costs are of course reduced if the students pay fees. We have made a basic assumption that it is improper to charge a fee to an adult for teaching a skill which has not been imparted by ten years' compulsory education.

To be specific: if your working base is in a college governed by Burnham norms, what will probably happen is that a lecturer already on the staff, or one appointed to other duties as well, will be assigned the literacy scheme. But the balance between teaching time and organising time rapidly tilts towards organising, and the student-hours don't mount up as they would with any other staff member. So the literacy scheme is being carried by the rest of the department in terms both of distribution of teaching and of the grading of the department (on which depend the head of department's salary and the creation of new and senior jobs.) This is fine up to a point and with good will all round, but it risks straining good will, and straining the person doing the job, who still has several other teaching commitments. The logical move, if the scheme is to stay in the college, is towards an extra-departmental appointment with its own terms and conditions.

If your working base is in area-organised adult education and you are using adult centres as homes for your classes, you can run into a number of problems. The simplest, at which we have hinted in the story of Mr Jones (see p. 76), is: how long is the adult education year? How many evenings is the centre open? With many authorities economising and setting up a 24 or even a 22 week session, you are effortlessly approaching the 45 hours we glanced at before; and you are teaching your students during less than half of the calendar year. Can they be expected to make enough progress to tide them over the long summer break? At least get the questions asked. It may mean you have to accommodate the classes elsewhere during breaks, but in the experience of some authorities you'll have won a battle if you can establish that you should pay your tutors outside normal terms.

Again, the question of ratios comes up. If you get a ruling that your classes should have no minimum enrolment number, or a set but small ratio (we suggest no more than 1:6. Some authorities support 1:3 and some even pay tutors for individual tuition) then this will affect the overall ratio of the centre. The centre head may carry one or two classes on the strength of a heavy enrolment for Keep-Fit or Talking about Antiques; but again, if you succeed and expand you'll strain his charity. Why should he carry you? Again, what you surely need is to establish your own rules and work without reference to the usual economy.

3.Staffing the project

We are writing under the two headings of organising and teaching, although of course all forms of overlap of functions are possible.

Organising staff

If you accept the need for the practice we have been indicating, you will rapidly reach the point where there is too much work for an unpaid organiser. The demands on time, the need for acceptance as a professional by other professionals, the amount you will have to learn, discard and re-learn – these put the job beyond what most people would do as a voluntary activity. Behind that of course is the question of whether the job should be done voluntarily; it is our conviction that it is obviously and necessarily the responsibility of the local education authority. There are circumstances in which another organisation with educational purposes and special local contacts might be more favourably placed to do the job – an industrial branch of the WEA for example; but they shouldn't be protecting the authority from its duty.

If we have suggested more superstructure than other kinds of teaching carry, we hope we have also indicated that it is necessary. You can check yourself: go back to the three student experiences we detail on pages 76–78 and extrapolate the time and manpower employed in each of the patterns we have drawn. You will probably find that Mr Jones' history took least organising, that Mr Jacobs' was costly but wasteful of organisational time as well as his own, and that Mr Jeffries' took more organising, but that the time was more efficiently spent.

Again, let's specify. If you have two admissions a week, in four months you will have thirty students; if you match them individually, that means liaison with sixty people; if they run into trouble only once a year that means one crisis a week; not to mention the routine administration, ordering books and bookshelves, cutting stencils for bulletins or teaching material. What very easily happens is that, even if you are in a position to use voluntary or part-time paid help, you get too busy to delegate.

These are some areas in which you might consider calling in extra help, paid or unpaid.

Interviewing and reception
If you are seriously going to offer a presence in the evenings, then you should spread the load. The alternative is to become a twilight shift worker, but we've met no one yet who can stop himself using the daylight hours as well for the work that is bound to be there. An interviewer will be wholly tied up while he is interviewing, and shouldn't have to answer the telephone or deal with casual callers as well. So if business is booming, you'll need a team of two on the nights you are open; and it is worth sorting out clerical or library jobs for when the telephone doesn't ring. We are not specifying paid or unpaid workers; it is possible to rotate this job so it is not too much to ask of a volunteer.

Training
Here perhaps collaboration rather than delegation is the notion you need. It is such a vital area that it is not reasonable to chance tutors being prepared with an orientation to the work that is different from your own. If you have a good understanding with a colleague to whom you can pass on all or some of the training sessions, then again it will lighten the burden of evening work. But especially if you are using a large number of individual tutors, one of the main things they will be learning on the course is how you understand the task, what you expect of them, and how they will work in relation to you in future. An imported reading specialist who is not in any other way part of the organisation just can't do this. Here, as always, what you choose to do depends on your priorities for the scheme.

If you do wish to bring in other contributors to a training course, or to in-service meetings, or if you do them yourself in addition to the hours you are paid for, how are they to be financed? The authority's training budget is an obvious thought. In addition it is worth mentioning that the WEA and University Extra-Mural Depts. have found this to be one of the ways in which they can contribute to literacy work. We are not suggesting that they should take the course content out of your hands, only that they can give you access to funds in addition to those at your disposal. They may ask a fee for the course, but either your tutors may be willing to cover it (though it seems a bit much to ask them), or else it is cheaper for your scheme to pay the course fee than it would be for you to hire lecturers. It is worth trying to negotiate with the providers over this.

We discuss the nature and content of training later.

Library and resources
This is a vital area. It may also be the one you are most interested in and which drew you to the work in the first place: if so, hang on to this and delegate the pure administration. We have not dealt in detail with what your teaching materials need to be, you will find this in an earlier section devoted to resources. But what should be said is that of all the areas of the work where your wider understandings impinge on your practical decisions, the selection and use of materials is the most important. You will need to be ruthless with all booklists and library lists: apart from the ones on page 62, the most useful one is likely to be a critical list that Cambridge House is preparing. You may even decide that no published material will do at all, and that you want to spend your resources budget on developing material based on the students' own experiences and language, and on the tutor's solution to specific problems encountered with a student. This will shift the stress away from mechanical learning and on to the development of the learner's own powers to think and express thought, more even than the use of adult material of low reading ages extracted from magazines and the like. But it will throw different demands on your pattern of organisation and staffing. You may need to organise a regular series of workshop sessions for tutors, and

to think of your librarian as a developer and propagator of materials. In any case, an organiser will need to be vigilant, to build in time for investigation of new ideas, to develop good sources of information among colleagues in this and other fields of teaching and in libraries, and to innovate and help tutors to innovate and create material as they work.

You will also need a library procedure in the sense of purchasing, cataloguing and supervising loans. This can't afford to be routinized and divorced from the general purposes of the work. But again, it raises the question of evening attendance: when are tutors going to borrow what you have? One solution to the problem of security and availability is to house your own holdings in a public library, if their own hours are well adapted to access by working people. But this counteracts moves you may be making towards becoming a centre.

Secretarial help

Here are two extremes of difficulty:

> you are working in a college, whose secretarial staff does a small amount of work for the teaching staff, usually confined to running off duplicating. Suddenly they find you want more letters typed a month than most heads of department want in a year, you keep putting in stencils, you are constantly in demand on the telephone and monopolize one of the college lines for whole afternoons. There is a rebellion . . .

> you have got an independent base, but no staff, or you are working from home. Your own typing is atrocious and copying equipment is a mile away in someone else's office – or even in the next town. You are frequently out teaching or visiting, or off duty because you are working in the evening, and the telephone is unanswered. Communication slows down, tempers rise . . .

In other words, you will very soon need secretarial help at least part-time. Most LEA appointments are on lecturer scales, and lecturers don't command secretarial support, but you have to demonstrate exceptional need.

Teamwork

We have stressed throughout that the staff of a literacy scheme, and all the peripheral staff who may work for the major institution but who encounter students, need to work as a team, with common understandings of the purpose and nature of the work and what this entails in practice for each of them. This is an emphasis that will seem eccentric to some people. We know what we're doing, they argue; we're teaching people to read. What's the need for all this fiddle-faddle about objectives, attitudes, approaches, team discussions, contemplating one's navel? Given an efficient administration, a few books, and a skilful and sympathetic tutor we can do the job. What's more, we *have* been doing it for a few years before it got trendy and something to build a career on.

With the greatest respect, and in particular with respect to the amount of successful teaching that has been conducted on this basis, we have to disagree. The amount that is *known* about how an adult becomes literate is minute. No one can design an organisation that can simply *do* it, without reference to students' purposes, social possibilities, the effects of a stratifying educational system, and a vast range of other matters as yet not brought into adequately informed relationship with the mechanics of reading *as learned by children* – which is all we have to go on. What do we know about the cognitive effects of illiteracy in a literate world? Do you perceive yourself, the world, development over time, evidence, the possibility of learning, in different ways if you are illiterate? The best thing we can do, surely, is to set up an organisation with the greatest possibility of seeking further information as it works and revising its practice in the light of that information.

To return to a more mundane level; another aspect of the team approach and of delegation and collaboration is the managerial platitude that as soon as a system has to be run by more than one person, it has to *be* a system, not an idiosyncratic extension of the nerve-ends. I can lay my hands on that note about the student coming

in this evening (though it may take ten minutes): but can Mrs Griffiths, who will be interviewing him? I can remember the telephone message about the tutor who has suspended teaching for a while (although I may have forgotten it by tomorrow); but has Jane, who is sending out reminders about student reports, got it? No need to multiply examples, and we can't ensure that you avoid mistakes; but even if you learn the hard way, you'll have to learn some kind of method. We aren't claiming that we have finished learning ourselves.

The last aspect of organisation we want to touch on is your relations outside the scheme itself. Primarily these are relations with the parent institution, if there is one, with the education office and with the education committee. If you are involved in a voluntary scheme you still need to strike up relations with the major providers of education in your area; and aim high – aim for access to the Director and the Chairman. If you do work for the authority, then you may well need to resolve anomalies that follow from the novelty of this work. That is not to say you need to find yourself a niche in the hierarchy; it does mean you need to get your presence and your function known to a wide variety of people in the authority's employ, from the Director and the man who manages the budget through adult, remedial and secondary school advisers to resources services and teachers' centres. Don't neglect the councillors, who after all do decide the authority's policy; and you may find that a councillor who is on the shop floor, or is a building contractor, or who lives in a working-class area, is less likely to believe that the literacy problem is marginal than an education officer or a headmaster who believes in the efficiency of the schools.

Other external relations will depend on the kinds of help and associations you are seeking. The list we included in the discussion of publicity might serve as a range of options. Within that you will have to choose. If you're invited on the same day to the Local Advisory Council for Adult Education, to the Rotary Community Service Committee, and to a union branch meeting, which would you go to? It depends on who you think your real allies are.

Try completing this chart on the basis of what you have and do at present.

Tasks	Time per month	Resources	Staff
Publicity			
Admission			
Briefing teachers			
Teacher follow up			
Library			
Materials development			
General admin.			
External Relations			
Secretarial			
Extra: Janitorial domestic.			

Does this completed chart tell you anything about your organisation?

Teaching staff

Whether you work solely through paid teachers with groups, or solely through volunteers working with one student each, or any combination of these, you are faced with selecting tutors. Most of us are not yet in a position where we can be very choosy, but we do need criteria for selection and we need to think, as we have suggested before, about how well adapted our publicity for tutors is to the kind of tutor we would like to get.

One way you can pursue your thoughts on this is to study or invent profiles of the ideal adult basic education tutor. The drawback is that they tend to come out as highly-trained saints, and we don't know where to advertise for saints. Another seduction is to consider a seesaw of skills: attitudes – the stereotype being that the trained teacher may have the skills, the lay tutor may have more appropriate attitudes to teaching adults. Neither is necessarily exclusively true, or even necessarily true at all. Which skills are we talking about? We have known teachers quite unable to give a clear account of their student's progress, for example when another tutor took over. We have also known lay tutors whose notion of teaching came straight from the classroom, and sometimes the classroom of forty years ago. To be sure, you can try to do something about this in training, but you need to consider it at the stage of selection too.

Which of these possible characteristics of a tutor do you consider essential, desirable, less important? Any positively undesirable?
Previous training in teaching
Previous experience in remedial reading
Previous experience in teaching adults
Previous experience in social work
Patience
Persistence
Willingness to learn
Adaptability, innovativeness
Wide general reading
Good standard of spoken English
Sympathetic nature
Respect for students
Similar social background to student
Similar leisure interest to student
Understanding of social circumstances of student
Broad definition of tutor's task
Freedom from educational snobbery
Freedom from social snobbery

How do you find out if the tutor has these characteristics?

How does your list of essential characteristics affect the way you find and select tutors?

Is the list different according to whether you are considering class or individual tuition?

Is it different if you are considering any particular type of student?

When you have considered the kind of tutor you want, and what you want them to do – we deal with this below in the section on 'Training' – it is as well to consider the conditions of work you are offering them. These conditions may or may not include pay for the job; but while we can clearly *demand* more from someone who is paid to teach, we don't necessarily expect (or get) less from an unpaid tutor. Surely in the long run we must pay them all? More than one authority is already paying individual tutors. In the meantime, let us consider what kind of job we are offering.

We are brought back again first of all to the question of reception, diagnosis and briefing. Are we expecting the individual tutor to meet a student about whom we know almost nothing, decide what he needs to learn and work out a teaching programme for him without help or previous experience? Are we expecting the class teacher to find out about attainment and needs in a corner or in the next room while the other four (or twelve) get on with some work? Do we present her with an unsorted classful at the beginning of term? Are we then expecting her to bring in materials from her daytime place of work every time she comes? What are the surroundings like at the evening class base anyway? Can you get a cup of coffee, sit down quietly for ten minutes before the class? We won't go on, because what we are embarking on is the jeremiad of the part-time adult teacher of *anything*, and the relationships between teachers and organisers in that field in general. The committed part-time tutor is too often badly briefed, inadequately housed, hopelessly short of materials, out of contact with the organiser for months on end, never in contact at all with other tutors in the same kind of work, without any chance of developing the work through discussion and com-

parison. The result tends to be serious erosion of the original commitment. One thing we can do about this is get into communication with any groups in the locality that include among their aims improving conditions for part-time tutors. The organisations that accept membership from workers in this field are the Association of Teachers in Technical Institutions (ATTI), and the Association of Tutors in Adult Education (ATAE) which has recently become a section of the Association of Scientific, Technical and Managerial Staffs (ASTMS).

The other thing we can do as organisers is simply to be in the vanguard. With the kind of briefing, communication, resources, progress chasing, support over the problems of particular students, formation of development groups of tutors, and terminal reporting that we are suggesting, we should have the best organised part-time staff in adult education.

But it has to be recognized that where we use individual tutors, the problems of dispersal and isolation are even greater than usual, and so we need even more conscious efforts to overcome them.

What lies at the bottom of a lot of discomfort and strained relationships is that neither the volunteer nor the class tutor has an adequate description of the job when she starts. Some areas of anxiety for the volunteer and the organiser working with volunteers are likely to be recording, reporting, arranging follow-up meetings, re-assessment and progress checking. How far can these be considered *requirements* when the job is a voluntary one? And yet how far can an organiser tolerate their neglect? The volunteer may come to feel that the demands of the project go beyond the support it can offer. The class teacher, who signed on probably for a two-hour session once a week, may come into friction with you about following up absentees, about the students' not strictly educational needs, and about the time it takes to carry out the approach to methods and materials that you favour. In either case the problems may be eased, although not erased, if you can make the job description more specific and detailed at the outset. This is likely to make the job apparently more demanding; but we are suggesting that it simply makes the demands overt. It may also help to place the organiser on the same side as the tutors in letting it be understood what the job entails, and so what would be a proper return in payment and services.

Would tutors find it valuable to have specific terms of reference?
Could you write them for your own project?
Would a group of tutors find a contract worked out by them and their organisers a useful basis for negotiation over support and resources?

If we expect a lot from tutors (and we do), there remains the painful question of what we can do if we find they are not succeeding with a student or a group. The question is particularly delicate, of course, if the tutor is a volunteer and not an employee. But if we are seriously concerned with standards, must we not consider asking people to give up if they aren't coping? It involves an enormous amount of tact, probably willingness to lie, and ingenuity in diverting someone to making another kind of contribution to the scheme. But just as we must be able to say we can't accept people for teaching in the first place, we must be able to move them if the student's interests are suffering.

What would you do if Jackie Baker's first tutor (see page 6) presented herself to your scheme?

Most of what we have said about organisation and staffing has tended towards requests for more resources. We are aware that it is a bad time to press for more public expenditure; many education authorities already face budgetary cuts in 1975–76. But we can only recommend expansion for literacy work; if it must be at the cost of something else, all we would say is that it must *not* be at the cost of remedial work in schools.

4.Training

No one involved in adult literacy work in this country has yet been professionally trained in this field. We bring to the work a conglomeration of skills and prejudices acquired through other areas of professional training or general experience. If the high quality of provision that we all wish to see developed is to become a reality we must take very seriously the whole question of training, orientation and discussion for those organising provision and working within it. In saying this we would not like to surrender to the training mystique.

There is no finite body of knowledge about adult literacy to be passed reverentially from trainer to trainee. But there is a growing body of experience gained by those people who have been working consistently with adult illiterates and who have been involved in organising provision. We need to analyse this experience, work towards a point where it is more than an empirical accumulation, and subject it to wide and constant discussion. It is only in this way that changes will occur, that provision will be prevented from petrifying in the form in which our initial common sense and hunches set it up, and that dispersed work come together as a movement.

Organisers

There is a lot of extremely useful practical information that organisers need to gather together. Much of it we hope is contained in this book; much of the organisational detail has been dealt with in this section. Some of the practical skills you will need to acquire are not directly educational, or even directly related to the management and negotiation you will have embarked on as an organiser. You may have to learn about printing, press relations, audio-visual equipment, bookkeeping, office routine and a variety of other skills. (One organiser has suggested that what we need is a book called *String and glue literacy schemes*). But all this can be learned, and it doesn't particularly depend on overcoming the basic drawback of being a literacy organiser, which is isolation.

With a little effort we can collect the practical information we need to organise provision. What we cannot easily embark on alone is the intellectual process whereby we assess the intention and effectiveness of that provision. And here we do not mean primarily a discussion on the teaching of reading, but an opening up of the debate on why people have not learnt to read and an exploration of the relationship between the nature of the problem and the nature of the steps taken to eliminate the problem. If an illiterate adult is seen first of all as wasteful to the economy, and if literacy programmes are trying to ensure that labour power is not lost to the economy (and these are approaches we have heard offered in good faith), then we are working with motives not generated by the learners themselves and not necessarily coinciding with their own interests. In that case, we as teachers and as organisers will need a particular skill and determination to protect the interests of the student and to make it possible for him to protect his own interests. If, on the other hand, we are assured that what we are doing now is in the interests of the learners as they themselves conceive their interests, then this problem may disappear and the skills called on will be different. These are among the issues that need to be constantly brought up and discussed. The best 'training', therefore, for organisers, would be to meet regularly with other people in basic adult education, for mutual development rather than seeking (largely illusory) expertise.

Networks of contact and information centres are being set up throughout the country. They vary enormously and none of them will help you in all the ways we have outlined, but they are very well worth contacting:

National Institute for Adult Education,
Regional Advisory Councils for Adult Education,
Local and national groups of the United Kingdom Reading Association,
Local Authority Committees,
National Association for Remedial Education – Adult literacy sub-committee,
British Association of Settlements – Adult Literacy group,
National Right to Read Committee,
and various other groups of greater or lesser formality. One of the tasks the newly formed Adult Literacy Resource Agency has set itself is to develop more effective and fruitful channels of communication between literacy providers.

This kind of mutual development is the most appropriate, and probably the only form of preparation for those who have a major investment in time in running a scheme. Your orientation and definition of your own purposes must, as we've said before, be clear to all those who work for or in connection with your work, however marginally. But there are specific delegated jobs for which preparation is needed in a more directed form: where you will have to make it clear to those to whom you delegate what it is you want of them. This is particularly true when those who do the jobs come in for only a few hours a week and can't pick up your intentions and ways of working from general contact. We have singled out three such jobs:

- interviewing;
- the central job of teaching;
- the job of the group contact worker.

Interviewers

In previous sections we have outlined the content and aims of the initial interview situation. It is vital that whoever is involved in interviewing must have an extremely clear idea of why they are interviewing at all and must be skilled in the methods and techniques of interviewing. One project built up a small team of interviewers and the following training programme was designed for them. It is important to know that each course member had observed several tutor and student interviews before attending the course and was to carry out several observed interviews himself, after the course, before being given responsibility for interviewing on his own.

Interviewers' Training Course

Session 1
a. Discuss the overall aim of the interview.
b. Identify what information the project needs about potential tutors and students and why.
c. Analyse the existing interview schedules. Discuss their functions. Do they fulfil their function?
d. Identify what information the potential tutors and students need to enable them to exercise the maximum control over the situation.
e. Identify the feelings you wish to engender in the tutors and students.

Session 2
a. Methods of reconciling the needs of the students, tutors and project.
b. Interviewing techniques, i.e. non-directive questions, listening, observing non-verbal mannerisms, putting interviewees at their ease, etc.

Session 3
a. Discussion of testing – why? Advantages, disadvantages.
b. Importance of diagnostic testing.
c. Specific tests: Holborn Reading Scale;
   Daniels & Diack diagnostic tests;
   Diagnostic tests – Schonell;
   Swansea test of phonic skill;
   Schonell spelling test;
   Gunzburg Social Sight Vocabulary list;
   Phonic Skills tests.
Discuss function of the tests.
Discuss which are administered regularly.
Discuss it and when to administer others.
Instructions on how to administer tests.
d. How to judge whether it is appropriate to use tests at all.

Tutors

If you are teaching an adult with literacy difficulties to read, write and spell, you are involved in a complex and difficult job. You need to develop within yourself many areas of skill and understanding.

- an understanding of the importance of the relationship between tutor and student, and its ramifications;
- an appreciation of the social and political implications of working with an illiterate adult to improve his literacy;
- the basic processes involved in learning to read, write and spell;
- the basic methods involved in learning to teach reading, writing and spelling;
- the most effective ways of teaching an adult.

Since it is rare for any one person to be at ease with all these areas of knowledge and understanding, a course of orientation and training is necessary for everyone who is going to teach an adult illiterate, whether or not they are a trained reading teacher or an experienced adult educator.

We cannot come to the job confident that our goodwill, as obvious to our students as to ourselves, will carry us through.

The testimony of our students is often that our schools and our society have no use for their energies and talents. We may believe this to be distorted, and in particular to do no credit to the efforts of teachers. But what an adolescent sees of the world beyond school merges with what he sees of school. He may find that he is only offered different ways of being the instrument of the needs of others, in work, as a consumer, in his leisure and cultural life, or in not getting work at all. If people are to face the chance of humiliation, and labour again over the difficult ground of learning, it will have to be because they see the end of it as *having uses for themselves*, not as adapting more efficiently to the uses of others have for them. And, as we have stressed throughout, we as literacy tutors and organisers (and as human beings) reveal in everything we do whether or not we recognise that people may have uses for themselves. It is expressed by our organisations, by our tone of communication, our choice of teachers, our choice of what to teach; and it will be reflected in the response from the students themselves. To receive a letter like

this tells us a great deal about that student's experience of learning, and so about our own organisation.

If you are organising a training course for tutors it is essential for you to decide exactly what you are trying to achieve:

- who is the course designed for?
- do you want to train all tutors together?
- in what ways do you wish to affect the course members' consciousness and understanding?
- what specific skills do you wish members to acquire?
- what specific information do you wish course members to receive?
- are your teaching methods compatible with your intentions?

Obviously courses will be very different depending on whom they are organised for. The details and content of a course organised for experienced remedial reading teachers who will be paid to teach a class in a College of Further Education will be entirely different from the content and details of a course organised for volunteer tutors with little formal education who will be teaching in an individual situation. The first will have the task of helping them transfer their knowledge, decide which elements of it are relevant to the different demands of the new job, and introduce them to approaches and methods suitable for adults. The second will have to take very seriously its own proposition that a tutor with no previous training *can* teach an adult, and will have to be devised in such a way that the issues are raised and information imparted without overwhelming the volunteers with the magnitude of the task and scaring them with their unfamiliarity with our concepts and procedures. We talk a lot about the nervousness of the student, but perhaps not enough about the nervousness of the tutor. If the tutor is as close as we might wish to the student's own social experience, he or she may also have left school with relief, and may need a careful demonstration of how his or her ability to read, human sensitivity, and practical experience, can become adequate resources for the job in hand. Tutor training needs to be as good an educational job as teaching itself, if we are to make the lay tutor confident and competent, and not drive away the working class tutor who may find it less natural to be on the giving side in education. And yet the basic aims may be the same: to help the prospective tutor to understand what is involved in teaching an adult to read, write and spell; to see the social and political implications of this process; and to give him the tools with which to work.

One of the products of the Adult Literacy Resource Agency will be training packs, which would be a great help for anyone unsure how to start.

Here are two training programmes, on the following page, that have been used in ongoing adult literacy projects. Remember whatever the project means the training course to be like, the first impression will be received by the tutor from reading the programme.

Look at each training programme. Can you answer these questions? Do the programmes give you enough information to answer them?

Can you form an idea of the objectives of the project for which it was organised?

What is the aim of each training programme?

Is the programme designed for any one particular group of tutors?

What teaching methods are used on the course?

Is the course designed to encourage any particular attitudes towards the students?

Is the course designed to give any particular skills to the tutors?

If you are a tutor think of your own needs; if you are an organiser think of the needs of a specific group of tutors in your project:

Plan a training programme; identify the aims of your training programme and the people for whom it is designed.

Tutor training course syllabus – an example

SYLLABUS

Lecture 1   *Reading*
Reading tests
Reading levels
Discussion of levels of course members' pupils
Causes of reading failure

Lecture 2   *Reading method*
a. Sentence, whole word, i.e. Look-say
b. Breakthrough to Literacy
c. Use of appropriate reading materials –
newspapers, magazines, recipes, and
self-created books

Lecture 3   *Reading method*
Teaching of phonics
When to read
Levels of phonic difficulty

Lecture 4   *Vocabulary*

Reading for understanding

Key words to literacy

Lecture 5   *Writing and spelling*

Lecture 6   *Record keeping*

General discussion

Please bring notebook and pen to each session.

Two training programmes above and right

Tutor Training

Week 1:   Film: *A well kept secret.*
2 Hours   Talk: the political and social implications of Adult
Illiteracy.
Discussion.
Introduction to project: aims, organisation etc.,
initial interview and diagnosis.
Week 2:   Discussion: Small groups – what do adults bring to the
learning situation?
– what do adults need from a
learning situation?
Chinese Exercise: designed to enable course members to
understand how it feels to be unable to
read. (People are presented items in
Chinese and 'taught to read').
Literacy Log: designed to bring home to course
members how much they use their
Literacy, and by deduction the range of
needs the student has to satisfy.
Week 3:   *Working with a non-reader.*
Language experience approach (using practical experience,
students own language and experience).
Social sight words.
Basic writing.
Useful materials.
Week 4:   *Working with a partial reader.*
Word attack skills.
Introducing phonics.
Context cueing.
Writing development
How these are made interesting to the Adult.
Useful materials.
Week 5:   Developing reading and writing fluency.
Spelling methods.
Creative/practical writing of forms.
Punctuation/grammar.
How these are made interesting to the Adult.
Useful materials.
Week 6:   Planning a programme with your student.
Materials Workshop.
Week 7:   Responsibilities of tutor.
Aims of tutor.
Responsibility of project.
Course evaluation.

One point that is worth mentioning here is that one project, which has tried to look at students' development over a certain period, has found, as might be expected, that students who are working with trained tutors are making better progress than those whose tutors who have not been trained. This may or may not reflect on the quality of any particular training programme, but at the least it does seem to indicate that six or seven evenings spent by tutors in thinking about what they are doing cannot be but helpful to both tutors and students.

Group contact workers

As a project expands, particularly in the area of individual tuition, it is impossible for the central organisation to maintain the availability and personal contact that is necessary to ensure good efficient teaching. One possible solution to the isolation of part-time tutors spread over a large geographical area is to organise small group coordination. Most schemes involved in individual tuition work with group contact workers. The best way to illustrate the organisation of this system is to reproduce the following letter:

Dear
As you know for every 10 tutors there is a group advisor who is responsible for knowing how the tutors in her group are working and assisting their development.
Group Advisor
1. Should be responsible for contacting each tutor in her group at least once every month to see how everything is going.
2. Should be available for any help needed with teaching methods and in day to day difficulties encountered by the tutors and students.
3. Should hold group meetings of all tutors at least once every 3 months.
Tutors
1. Should realise the importance of letting the group advisor know of any problems *before* they get too serious to deal with.
2. Should realise the importance of keeping in touch with the group advisor and of sending in regular report forms.
3. Should realise that group advisors are available to discuss programme of work.

If this system is to work it is essential that both the group advisor and the tutors know exactly what is expected of them. Since the organisation is delegating a crucial area of its responsibility, group advisors need to be very carefully selected and there must be frequent and regular contact between them and the central administration of the project. If a group contact worker is to fulfil her brief she will need to contact tutors and students by phone, post and travel, and call regular meetings. This costs money. Ideally group contact workers should be paid; if this is not a possibility at least they must not be out of pocket. One small point that must be emphasised is the nature of the meetings that are called. Vague meetings to discuss 'how you are getting on' are unsatisfactory. What is needed are opportunities for regular discussion of progress and problems combined with specific talks, lectures and workshops. It is also important that students working in individual teaching situations be provided with the opportunity to meet together regularly to discuss progress, problems and specific issues. One of the disadvantages of individual tuition is that it can reinforce the sense of shame and isolation that many illiterate adults feel. This must be avoided at all costs if it is central to your perception of illiteracy that it is not an individual failing but a product of social and economic deprivation. One way of overcoming the isolation is to ensure that groups of students meet to discuss problems and develop forms of mutual help.

It is interesting to look back to the days before organised adult education, when people who knew very clearly why they needed literacy came together and gave each other the help, encouragement and solidarity needed to tackle their learning. It is an aspect of basic literacy tuition which it is important to remember today; but it won't do to try to reproduce the forms if we haven't the motivating content.

5. Objectives and organisation

The difficulty of writing our contribution to this book has been that some of the themes we have wanted to include are not yet generally considered to be part of the subject of adult literacy at all. We venture to predict that this will not always be so. It is only quite recently that it has been brought to public attention that there are many adults who are not able to make free with reading and writing, and that we have started to teach them. At this stage it is the practical and technical questions which have dominated our minds, and it is to those that a handbook such as this one addresses itself most properly. But it is a truism that, for those in charge of an organisation, it is not always practical to confine oneself to the practical; and so we have tried from time to time to lead your attention to broader questions, in particular to questions of the assumptions that underline your practice.

At the moment these questions can perhaps only be raised and not answered. But they must be raised, if only because it is a common experience that patterns of work, once set, are hard to break, especially if you are working under pressure. The more you clarify the objectives of your work, the more likely you are to make effective decisions on specific points.

Let us look at statements, which we have gathered from various sources, about the way in which five different literacy projects have formulated the problem or defined their aims:

In very general terms a backward child is educationally inadequate and a problem in the school. A backward adult is socially inadequate and a problem in the community.

An illiterate adult is a person who has been wronged and deprived by the social, political and educational system. Literacy is a right which he can only gain by understanding the causes of his deprivation.

The club seeks to improve the social skills of its members, literacy is one of them, so is playing ping-pong, so is chatting over a cup of tea and if no one learns to read the club will still be doing a great job.

This project seeks to further the greatest possible growth in reading ability.

This project aims to provide a situation which will result in the most fruitful application of the students' general intelligence to the specific problems of reading and writing.

The assumptions reflected in these statements must surely affect every aspect of literacy provision. And yet, at the moment, we might find that these five projects work in remarkably similar ways. We have all borrowed each other's practice – handbills, interview sheets, divisions of labour – often because we have begun the job before we have had time to consider what we thought was involved. Surely the next development is likely to be an increasing difference between project and project as, with more experience behind us, we reconsider and bring our particular talents and emphases to bear on the work. This seems to us a sound development, not one that in any way puts the students at risk. We cannot afford to settle into an unchangeable pattern of provision too soon, while we are still learning.

Let us summarize the points on which the organiser will have to make decisions:

- advertising for tutors and students;
- contact with other organisations, educational and otherwise;
- accepting students/enrolment procedure;
- selection of tutors;
- training tutors, teaching methods;
- allocation of students and tutors;
- individual teaching;
- class teaching;
- fees;
- terms;
- class size;
- class closure;
- rooms;
- frequency of lessons;
- progress;
- materials and resources;
- finance;
- local structures and alliances;
- propaganda.

What your practice is on all these points, and whether you consider them to be elements of organising literacy provision at all, will depend on your aims and values; or if you haven't formulated any, it will depend on the assumptions that silently underlie the dominant practice. It is worth defining *your* objectives – in agreement, if you can, with those who work with you and for whom you work – and trying to run the job in conformity with definite purposes, rather than simply following current norms.

Look at the statements above made by the five literacy projects. Using the check list, write down:

how would each project act on each point?
how does your project act on each point?
how would you like your project to act?

One important area that we have not yet fully covered is the question of which body is ultimately responsible for making adult literacy provision. We do not want to enter into debate on the relative merits of statutory and non-statutory provision. Both exist and it is crucial that we work towards co-operation and co-ordination of both.

However the question cannot be totally skirted. We strongly believe that literacy is a right and that in the final analysis it is only statutory bodies that have the resources to ensure that it is a right available to all. We feel that independent projects must build this realisation into their aims and objectives. In the present situation it is unlikely that statutory bodies will make sufficient resources available to do more than nip at the problem. This either means good teaching for a very few, or teaching for more that is not good enough. It is a choice that faces us urgently when we consider the increased demand for tuition that is likely to be produced by the very initiative by the BBC which has brought about the publication of this book. Will we be able to take everyone who comes and offer effective teaching? Will we be forced to erode standards that are hardly established, and to fall back on 'whatever gets them going' instead of taking the care with methods and materials that is being urged upon us? Will we be forced into the absurdity of a selective system of literacy teaching, rejecting those we think we will make least progress with, or those who are too good for us (though not competent in their own eyes), or those whose situation at work or at home is less than critical? We are caught between the recognition that we are working in poverty, which means that no resource can be refused, and the knowledge that to act without care and forethought is in the end not to help at all. There is no room for either an independent or a statutory scheme to settle for maintaining its own existence; all providers of literacy teaching must surely try to get this work established as a real priority, not just as a temporary enthusiasm.

But if we sometimes feel alarmed by the prospect of more demand than we can meet, there is a more hopeful prospect, perhaps, in thinking that the problem of adult literacy may soon drop back out of the false isolation which has recently overtaken it, and be seen in essential relation to other issues and debates. (This is not to undermine anything we have said so far about the need for separate conditions of work.) The isolation is the more curious in that most of us who work in this field have done so for so little time and have acquired our main experience elsewhere. To return to the subject of a project's objectives: these need to be of two kinds. There are objectives which are those of your organisation as a working unit, and these need to be specific and realistic. To quote from Haviland again, we too would like to improve our students' prospects of 'obtaining and holding a job', but we have to face the fact that while the Department of Employment and government grants fail to attract enough jobs in certain areas, and where large numbers of literate adults are employed, we are unlikely to have much success. It might, however, be reasonable for us to have it as an objective to *lobby* for changes in the apprenticeship structure or for improving specific economic circumstances. Similarly, it is outside our powers to improve remedial teaching in schools, but it is within our powers and might well be among our objectives to collect information and press a case for such improvements.

There are also objectives which it will not be sensible to think of as circumscribed, but which will call on all your understanding of the relation of this subject to areas of experience that lie around and beyond it. In this kind of thought we are hardly even at a beginning. The subject of literacy has become isolated even from the debates that take place about other kinds of adult education for the working class, from other educational debates in general, and from debates about the kinds of social and economic change that are likely or possible in this country, although with the other side of our mouths we acknowledge that all of these things, and many more, have a close relationship to the situation of our students and the teaching approaches that are likely to be successful. A clear example of our temporary paralysis seems to us to be the British reading of the work of Paolo Freire. We read and quote his work and go to hear him speak, and try to apply concepts drawn from his writings which we transmute into a more familiar language of 'student-centredness'. But what we apparently cannot cope with is his fundamental position that there is no such thing as an educational programme in isolation, but that what can be taught and what should be taught depend intimately on the condition of, and the movements facing, those who engage in education in any capacity, as tutor, student, or both. What follows for us in this country, of course, is that we need to understand our own and our students' condition before we can think of applying Freire's insights; we cannot borrow them out of context especially if we are not willing to consider what our context is. While we begin this process we can hold on to some of the fundamental notions as best we can understand them, and, as we work, let this understanding deepen and grow. However provisionally we say it, we can try to work with our students to enable them to find their full human autonomy, and to embark on the 'difficult apprenticeship in naming the world'. The phrase is Freire's. For us, it names the adventure.

Imagine you are planning a literacy programme from scratch:
write down your objectives;
would you show them to your boss?

Bibliography

1 Association of Teachers in Technical Institutions *The education of the 16–19 age group – part-time* ATTI, 1973.
2 BEN-TOVIM, M. and KEDNEY, R. J. eds. *Aspects of adult illiteracy* Merseyside and District Institute of Adult Education, 1974.
3 British Association of Settlements *How to start a literacy scheme* 1973. do. *The right to read* 1974.
4 Department of Education and science *Adult education: a plan for development* (Chairman, Sir Lionel Russell) HMSO, 1973.
5 FREIRE, P. *Cultural action for freedom* Penguin Books, 1972.
  FREIRE, P. *Pedagogy of the oppressed* Sheed and Ward, 1972; Penguin Books, 1972.
6 KOHL, H. *Reading – how to* Penguin Books, 1974.
7 School of Barbiana *Letter to a teacher* Penguin Books, 1971.
8 THOMPSON, E. P. *The making of the English working class* Penguin Books, n.e. 1968.
9 HAVILAND, M. *Provision for adult literacy in England* University of Reading, Centre for the Teaching of Reading, 1973.

We would also like to acknowledge and thank all the colleagues who have supplied material, ideas, criticism and funny stories.

Useful addresses

Adult Literacy Resource Agency,
33 Queen Anne Street, London W1

Association of Tutors in Adult Education/ASTMS Group,
Trevor Cave, National Secretary,
7 Elvin Way, New Tupton, Chesterfield, Derbyshire

Association of Teachers in Technical Institutions,
Hamilton House, Mabledon Place, London, WC1H 9BH

The British Association of Settlements,
7 Exton Street, London, SE1

The Centre for the Teaching of Reading,
University of Reading, School of Education,
29 Eastern Avenue, Reading RG1 5RU

National Association of Remedial Education,
Central Office, 4 Oldcroft Road, Walton-on-the-Hill, Stafford

National Fountation for Educational Research,
2 Jennings Buildings, Thames Avenue, Windsor, Berkshire

United Kingdom Reading Association,
Honorary General Secretary, 63 Laurel Grove, Sunderland

The Adult Literacy Resource Agency

The director of the Adult Literacy Resource Agency, W. A. Devereux, describes the role of the agency in this way, 'The agency has been set up under the aegis of the National Institute of Adult Education to allocate £1 million provided by the Department of Education and Science and the Scottish Education Department, for the development of adult literacy provision LEAS and other organisations have been invited to claim the re-imbursement of costs for extra provision (not recurrent expenditure) of training courses for paid and volunteer tutors, special teaching materials and equipment, including audio-visual and technological aids. It can help voluntary organisations with the minor improvement of premises for literacy tuition schemes, and may also generally assist other approved adult literacy projects.

The £1 million is available for one year only – until 31st March 1976. The Agency wishes to encourage LEAS to be responsible for the co-ordination of literacy provision, both statutory and voluntary, in its area. Its main effort will be: helping to establish, and supporting, area or regional courses for training the trainers, centre or organising tutors, and volunteer tutors. It hopes also to collect information about adult literacy provision throughout the country, relay it by means of regular newsletters, help link the various agencies with each other, and, by means of expert advisory panels, produce a training model and a basic guide pack for volunteer tutors.'

Index

Acknowledgment is due to the following:
THE BODLEY HEAD for extract from *Autumn of Terror* (Jack the Ripper) by Tom Cullen; CONTROLLER, HER MAJESTY'S STATIONERY OFFICE for extracts from *Adult Education – A Plan for Development* (The Russell Report) 1973 and extract from *Driving*; EDUCATORS PUBLISHING SERVICE for lists of Phonic Initial and Final Blend compiled by Sally and Ralph Childs contained in *Sound Phonics*; GARRARD PUBLISHING COMPANY, 1607 North Market Street, Champaign, Illinois 61820 for Dolch 220 Basic Sight Word List from *A Manual for Remedial Reading* by E. W. Dolch; INNER LONDON EDUCATION AUTHORITY for reading assessment test; PENGUIN BOOKS LTD. for extracts from *Reading: How to* by Herbert Kohl. (Penguin Education, 1974). Copyright © Herbert Kohl, 1973, and extract from *School of Barbiana – Letter to a Teacher* translated by Nora Rossi and Tom Cole; UNIVERSITY OF READING for extracts from *Survey of Provision for Adult Illiteracy in England.*
CITY AND GUILDS OF LONDON INSTITUTE for extract from examination form on page 3; CONTROLLER, HER MAJESTY'S STATIONERY OFFICE for Census form on page 3 Crown copyright; ROBERT GIBSON, PUBLISHERS, for test on page 12 from *Get Reading Right*, Handbook, by S. Jackson; GRANADA PUBLISHING LTD. for extract on page 28 from *The Standard Reading Tests* by Daniels and Diack; GEORGE G. HARRAP & CO. LTD. for the Holborn Reading Scale on pages 7 and 53; LEARNING DEVELOPMENT AIDS for Check Lists of Basic Sounds and Harder Sounds and Rules on page 56 associated with Remedial Phonic Reference Cards by Gill Cotterell; NFER PUBLISHING CO. LTD. for diagram on page 15 based on one from *The Trend of Reading Standards* by K. B. Start and B. K. Wells; THE EMPLOYMENT SERVICE AGENCY for Job Centre Card on page 3; THE ROYAL BRITISH LEGION for membership application form on page 3.
The photographs on pages 21 and 76 were specially taken by Nick Hedges, by permission of the Holloway Adult Education Institute. Illustrations on cover and pages 5, 7, 8, 10, 23, 31, 36, 44 by Jenny Thorne, pages 4, 14, 15, 28, 34, 35, 39, 45, 58, 59, 60, 69 by David Ashby, pages 1, 48, 76, 77, 78, 82 by Wendy Smith.

BBC Adult Literacy Project
We should be grateful if you could complete and return this letter to us. In doing so, you will help us in the planning and evaluation of the BBC Adult Literacy Project.

Fold down along the dotted line

Fold here

Postage will be paid by the Licensee

Do not affix Postage Stamps if posted in Gt. Britain, Channel Islands or N. Ireland

Business Reply Service
Licence No. WD 25

Adult Literacy Project
BBC Television
London W12 8QT

Fold here and tuck in

Publisher's addresses

Arnold, E. J. and Sons Ltd, Airebank Mills, South Accommodation Road, Leeds LS10 1AX.
BBC Publications, 35 Marylebone High Street, London W1M 4AA.
Benn, Ernest Ltd., Sovereign Way, Tonbridge, Kent.
Black, A. and C., Ltd., 4 Soho Square, London W1V 6AD.
Blackie and Son Ltd., Book Centre Ltd., Rufford Road, Crossens, Southport, Lancs.
Blackwell, Basil and Mott, Ltd., 108 Cowley Road, Oxford OX4 1JH.
Blond Educational see Granada Publishing Ltd.
Brockhampton Press Ltd., see Hodder Publications
Cambridge Institute of Education, Shaftesbury Road, Cambridge CB2 2BX.
Cape, Jonathan, Ltd., 30 Bedford Square, London WC1B 3EL.
Cassell and Co. Ltd., 35 Red Lion Square, London WC1.
Centre for the Teaching of Reading, School of Education, The University, 29 Eastern Avenue, Reading RG1 5RU, Berks.
Centerprise, 136 Kingsland High Street, London E8.
Chambers, W. and R. Ltd., 11 Thistle Street, Edinburgh 2.
Chatto and Windus Ltd., 40–42 William IV Street, London WC2N 4DF.
Chatto and Windus Educational Ltd., see Granada Publishing Ltd.
Collins, Wm., Sons and Co. Ltd., 42–50 York Way, King's Cross, London N1.
Collins Educational, 144 Cathedral Street, Glasgow, G4 0NB.
Dent, J. M. and Sons Ltd., Dunhams Lane, Letchworth, SG6 1LF.
Evans, Bros. Ltd., Book Centre Ltd., Neasden.
Galt, James and Co. Ltd., 30 Great Marlborough Street, London W1.
Gibson, Robert and Sons Ltd., 17 Fitzroy Place, Glasgow G3 7FF.
Ginn and Co. Ltd., Elsinore House, Buckingham Street, Aylesbury, Bucks.

Golden Press see Western Publishing Co. Inc.
Granada Publishing Ltd., Park Street, St. Albans, Herts.
Hart-Davis, Rupert, Ltd., see Granada Publishing Ltd.
Heinemann Educational Books, 11a Gower Mews, London WC1.
Holmes McDougall Ltd., 30 Royal Terrace, Edinburgh EH7 5AL.
Hope Educational Suppliers
Hulton Educational Publications Ltd., Raans Road, Amersham, Bucks.
Hutchinson Publishing Group, Tiptree Book Services Ltd., Tiptree CO5 0SR.
ILEA Media Resources Centre, Highbury Station Road, London N1.
Invicta Plastics, Harborough Road, Oadby, Leics.
Jarvis-Porter Ltd., Parkside Printers, Dewsbury Road, Leeds LS11 5TF.
Ladybird Books Ltd., Beeches Road, Loughborough, Leics. LE11 0BR.
Longman Group Ltd., Pinnacles, Harlow, Essex.
Macdonald and Co. Ltd., BPC Publisher's Service Centre, Paulton, Bristol BS18 51Q.
Macmillan International Ltd., Houndmills Estate, Basingstoke, Hants. RG2 2BR.
Manchester University Press, 316–324 Oxford Road, Manchester M13 9PL.
Merril, Charles E. Publishing Co. distributed by Prentice-Hall International, 66 Wood Lane End, Hemel Hempstead, Herts HP2 4RG.
Methuen Children's Books Ltd., 11 New Fetter Lane, London EC4P 4EE.
Mills and Boon Ltd., Book Centre Ltd., Neasden.
NARE, 4 Old Croft Road, Walton-on-the-Mill, Stafford S217 0LF.
NFER, 2 Jennings Buildings, Thames Avenue, Windsor, Berks.
NSMHC, Pembridge Hall, 17 Pembridge Square, London W2 4EP.
Nelson, Thomas, and Sons Ltd., Lincoln Way, Windmill Road, Sunbury-on-Thames, Surrey.
Nisbet, James and Co. Ltd., Digswell Place, Welwyn, Herts.
Osmiroid Educational E. S. Perry Ltd., Osmiroid Works, Fareham Road, Gosport, Hants.
Oliver and Boyd see Longman Group Ltd.
Oxford University Press, Ely House, 37 Dover Street, London W1X 4AH.
Pan Books Ltd., Brunel Road, Basingstoke, Hants.
Parker Bros., 15 Grosvenor Gardens, London SW1.
Penguin Books Ltd., 21 John Street, London WC1.
Pepys, Castell Bros., 15 Cross Street, London EC1.
Pergamon Press Ltd., Headington Hill Hall, Oxford OX3 0BW.
Philip and Tacey Ltd., North Way, Andover, Hants SP10 5BA.
Pitman, Book Centre Ltd., Neasden.
Programmed Learning Centre, St. Albans. CFE., St. Albans, Herts.
Purnell and Sons Ltd., see Macdonald and Co. Ltd.
Reader's Digest Association Ltd., 25 Berkeley Square, London W1X 6AB.
Remedial Supply Co., Dixon Street, Wolverhampton, Staffs.
Routledge and Kegan Paul Ltd., Broadway House, Reading Road, Henley-on-Thames RG9 1EN.
Schofield and Sims Ltd., 35 St. Johns's Road, Huddersfield, HD1 5DT.
Schoolmaster Publishing Co. Ltd., Derbyshire House, St. Chad's Street, London WC1H 8AJ.
SEFA see National Society for Mentally Handicapped Children.
Sidgwick and Jackson Ltd., Book Centre Ltd., Neasden.
Spear, J. W. and Sons Ltd., Green Street, Enfield Highway.
Special Education Publications
UKRA, 2 Taviton Street, London WC1.
University of London Press Ltd., see Hodder Publications Ltd.
Waddington, John Ltd., Games and Jigsaw Division, Castle Gate, Oulton, Leeds.
Ward Lock Ltd., Pretoria Road, London N18.
Western Publishing Co. Inc., 850 Third Avenue, New York, NY10022.
Wheaton, A. and Co., Headington Hill Hall, Oxford OX3 0BW.

Publishers of selected reading and spelling tests

Holborn reading scale, George C. Harrap & Co, PO Box 70, 182–184 High Holborn, London, WC1V 7AX.
JC DANIELS AND HUNTER DIACK *The standard reading tests,* Chatto and Windus Educational, Frogmore, St. Albans
Neale analysis of reading ability, Macmillan & Co., 4 Little Essex Street, London, WC2.
S. JACKSON *Get reading right (tests and handbook)* Robert Gibson, 17 Fitzroy Place, Glasgow, G3 7BR.
RNID Meaning test cards, Royal National Institute for the Deaf 105 Gower Street, London WC1E 6AM.
Schonell essential spelling lists, MacMillan & Co. 4 Little Essex Street, London, WC2.
Gill Cotterell's check list of basic sounds, 52 Birmingham Road, Walsall, Staffs.
JOHN TURNER *The assessment of reading skills* compiled by United Kingdom Reading Association, 63 Laurel Grove, Sunderland
Assessment of reading ability, West Sussex Psychological Service c/o Educational Department, County Hall, Chichester

---

Name _________________________________ Mr/Mrs/Miss

Address _________________________________

____

____

1. Present occupation _________________________________

2. What was the most important reason for you in obtaining this book? (Please tick)

  a Currently organising adult literacy groups/classes ☐

  b Intending to organise adult literacy groups/classes ☐

  c Currently a tutor (paid) of adult illiterates ☐

  d Currently a volunteer tutor of adult illiterates ☐

  e Intending to be a tutor of adult illiterates ☐

  f General interest ☐

  g Other (please state)

3. Would you like to be placed on our mailing list and receive information about the BBC Adult Literacy Project and to feed-back your opinion to us? **yes/no**

4. If you would like to become a tutor, would you like your name to be forwarded to the appropriate agency in your area? **yes/no**